THE ART OF
NATURAL
HISTORY

Babirussa Pig. Wood engraving by G. Mutzel
from A. E Brehm's *Tierleben (Saugetiere)*,
1891.

HISTORIÆ NATVRA-
lis de Insectis. Libri. III .
de Serpentibus et Draconib, Libri II
Cum æneis Figuris
IOHANNES IONSTO
nus Med. Doctor
Concinnavit
FRANCOFVRTI
ad Mœnum
Impensis
Hæredum Merianorū
MDC LIII .

M. Merian Jun. Inventor

THE ART OF
NATURAL
HISTORY

S. Peter Dance

ARCH CAPE PRESS
NEW YORK

The Art of Natural History
first published in 1978 by The Overlook Press, New York

This 1990 edition published by Arch Cape Press,
a division of dilithium Press Ltd.
distributed by Crown Publishers, Inc., 225 Park Avenue South,
New York, New York 10003.

This edition produced by arrangement with
Cameron Books, 2A Roman Way, London N7 8XG

Printed and bound in Malaysia

ISBN 0-571-69629-0

h g f e d c b a

Edited and designed by Ian Cameron
Additional photography by Rodney Todd-White Limited,
Ray Gardner and Derek Balmer

The two major sources of illustration for this book were the Linnean Society
of London and the National Museum of Wales in Cardiff which houses the
invaluable Willoughby Gardner collection of early natural history books.
We are particularly indebted to these two institutions and above all to Gavin
Bridson, the Librarian of the Linnean Society, for his assistance.

Others who have provided us with illustrations or access to zoological
books which they hold include Bernard Quaritch, the antiquarian
booksellers, the British Library, the British Museum (Natural History), the
Victoria & Albert Museum, the Museum of English Rural Life at Reading
University, the American Museum in Britain at Claverton Manor near
Bath, the Mansell Collection and Mr Malcolm Lindsay.

NOTE ON THE ILLUSTRATIONS
In virtually every case, except where otherwise stated, the illustrations in
this book are reproduced to their original size or smaller. The captions
usually give the title, artist, author or editor, date and printing process for
the plates of the books from which pictures are taken.

Many of the animals depicted are not identifiable down to species or even
to genera. Except where the animal is easily identifiable, we have avoided
giving modern scientific names, opting instead for more general
descriptions. The problems and controversies of modern nomenclature
which we would otherwise have had to confront would have extended across
most of the Animal Kingdom. For the benefit of those with a detailed
knowledge of particular groups, we have, where practicable, included in
quotes the biological and/or vernacular names as given in the original titles
or captions.

Frontispiece: Frontispiece to a seventeenth-
century book on insects. Copper engraving designed by Matthaeus Merian the Younger from
Johann Jonston's *Historiae Naturalis, De Insectis*, 1653.

Contents

Preface

The significance of animals in our lives and in the development of art can hardly be overstated. Dramatic and powerful representations of them on the walls of caves and in various parts of the world attest their importance to our earliest forbears and suggest, although they do not prove, that animals were the fertilising agents of their latent creative impulses. As the early history of zoological art has been investigated fully in recent years, it occupies a relatively small part of this book. My main theme is the development, application and significance of zoological illustration since the Renaissance, with special emphasis on work which has been duplicated by various means.

In Part I, zoological art is surveyed chronologically from its prehistoric origins through the age of the early printed book. The historical discussion deals successively and in greater detail with the curious and often fanciful representations of animals which were characteristic of the seventeenth century; the increasingly sophisticated and frequently amusing productions of the more enlightened eighteenth century; and finally the extraordinarily varied and abundant treasury of animal illustrations, ranging from the diminutive woodcuts of the Bewick school to the magnificent aquatints of Audubon's bird paintings and the exquisite lithographs of Joseph Wolf's perceptive animal studies, which are among the more delightful legacies of the nineteenth century.

Part II discusses several aspects which could not be incorporated in the chronological framework of Part I. A study of anthropomorphism is followed by some observations on the representation of movement in animal pictures, a slight sketch of the artistic achievements of those who studied life through the microscope and a review of the illustrations in books intended for popular consumption (with special reference to the art and influence of P. H. Gosse). Appendices describe some of the graphic reproduction processes mentioned in the course of the book and give biographical details for many authors and illustrators.

While I hope that I have not ignored any important aspect of zoological art, I have not attempted to mention every important book in which that art is represented. This is not an annotated list of fine illustrated books which deal with animals, and I have not tried to assess the relative merits of such books, as has been done elsewhere—even to the extent of awarding star ratings—with illustrated books on birds. Rather, I have tried to link the art of zoological illustration to the illustrators, their subjects and their circumstances. Instead of reeling off title after title, artist after artist, I have preferred to dwell on certain key figures and events. This, I believe, will make the book more readable. If my somewhat personal interpretation of zoological art antagonises some readers, they will surely find solace in looking at the illustrations, which are, after all, what this book is really about.

S. Peter Dance
Priory Wood,
Hereford.

Interior of a splendid 'cabinet of curiosities'. Copper engraving from Levin Vincent's *Wondertoonel der Nature*, 1706. It is hard to believe that this is anything more than an imaginary view of an early private museum. The arrangement of the specimens is credible enough, but the great hall containing them seems altogether too magnificent.

To GAVIN BRIDSON,
who tells all he knows
and knows all he tells.

PART ONE

CHAPTER I
The Prehistory of Animal Art

The beginning of all art was animal art. When someone first tried to depict a beast whose body supplied some of the necessities of life, art, as modern man comprehends that abstract term, was born. It was to be many thousands of years, however, before anyone would see prehistoric animal paintings as works of art. Although the primary subject of this book is animal art as represented in books published since the Renaissance, it would be absurd to ignore the first, longest and most remarkable phase of that art. This initial phase, conservatively estimated to have lasted about three times as long as the whole of written history, witnessed some astonishing artistic achievements. The most remarkable that have survived to the present day embellish the walls and ceilings of deep. dark caves in various parts of Europe, Asia and Africa.

The best cave paintings have never been surpassed for vitality, economy of line and beauty. Equally, they have no obvious connections with the later development of western art as they were not rediscovered until the late nineteenth century. The paintings found in certain caves in Andalusia exhibit such an ability to express animal form and movement within the limits of their crude materials that it is small wonder that the experts were reluctant at first to accept their prehistoric origins. The subsequent discovery of similar paintings in other European caves confirmed their great age—those adorning the Lascaux caves in the Dordogne have been in existence for an estimated thirty thousand years.

The animals in these ancient art galleries are shown in broadside view, often in headlong flight or springing in the air or contorted in the agonies of a death ordained and implemented by men. One of the striking things about them is the absence of irrelevant detail. Only the hunter and the hunted were important; no space was given over to trees, flowers, hills, rivers or any of the ancillary features which would help make a picture

Red-Breasted and, probably, Greylag Geese in a meadow. Painting on stucco from a tomb near Medum, Egypt, Fourth Dynasty, *c* 2900 BC, Cairo Museum.

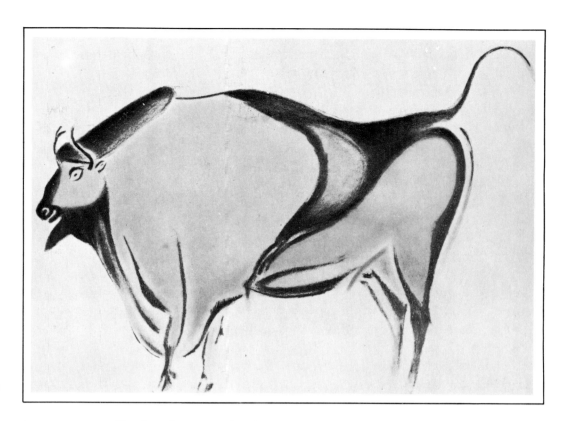

Bison. Copy of a cave painting at Altamira, northern Spain.

into a scene. Curiously enough, this bareness, this isolation of essentials, is characteristic of some very early animal pictures from the Far East. Early Chinese drawings often show animals resting or moving, but in complete isolation. In European cave art and the later animal art of primitive Asian cultures, no useful purpose would have been achieved by filling up empty spaces with anything but pictures of animals.

There is a great difference between the artistic remains of Paleolithic (hunting) man and those of Neolithic (farming) man. During Neolithic times, an essentially peasant culture developed. There was a preoccupation with order, seasons and diurnal rhythms, with weaving and pottery—things which had meaning for people in a pastoral society. In the place of the vivacious animal paintings were geometrical designs, precise and often abstract, the productions of people able to give artistic expression to ideas originating as much from their own imagination as from the visible external world.

In a purely European context, this is a reasonably true picture of events as far as our researches allow us to reconstruct them. But the contrast between Paleolithic and Neolithic art forms is less clear cut in early Egypt and its neighbouring lands in the Middle East. In the 'Fertile Crescent', from Egypt to Mesopotamia, the world's first great civilisations developed their remarkable technologies and art forms. Animals abound in their art, particularly in ancient Egypt where they were inextricably mixed up with religious or totemic beliefs. The gods and goddesses all had appropriate animal manifestations: Bastet was the cat-goddess of Bubastis, Buto the cobra-goddess of Lower Egypt, and the reigning pharaoh was identified with Horus the falcon-god.

Among the many rock engravings and tomb paintings showing animals—as opposed to gods in animal forms—are some very life-like and beautiful studies. Egyptian artisans were keenly aware of the abundant animal life around them and recorded it graphically, just as they recorded everything else. For the Egyptians, as for the European cave painters, there was no such thing as art for art's sake. Egyptian art was nothing more than an expression of Egyptian life, in which animals played a significant part.

A fragment of a clay-floor painting from Tel el-Amarna (now in the Egyptian Museum in Berlin) depicts three wild ducks flying above papyrus and cyperus grass. The painting on the clay dates from about 1370 BC and is obviously the work of a painter who had watched flying ducks. There is nothing stilted or conventional about the bird portrayals, unlike those shown on many Egyptian limestone carvings. Essentially, the scene depicted is close in style to pictures of similar subjects by artists such as Archibald Thorburn, Peter Scott and J. C. Harrison which were painted well over three millenia later.

Another bird group is painted on a wall of Chnemhotep's tomb near Beni Hassan. Painted about 1900 BC, it shows several different kinds of bird in a bush. The composition is balanced, the colours pleasing, and a competent ornithologist could identify most of the species. The only distracting element is a bird shown in the conventional broadside view, but with a pair of outstretched wings apparently sprouting from its breast and back. The artisan who painted it could not escape entirely from the limitations of his inherited tradition. These paintings of bird groups show an important feature that is absent from Paleolithic art: the plant life which forms an integral part of each scene. In striking contrast to these bird groups is the statuesque perfection of the walking crane depicted on a wall of the funerary temple of Queen Hatshepsut at Deir el-Bahri. Dating from 1450 BC, this is a graphic record of the appearance of a bird in the full vigour of life.

Well over three thousand years ago, then, painters were portraying animals in naturalistic poses and settings. The Egyptians and other peoples of the Fertile Crescent had reached an enviable maturity in this branch of representational art. But accomplished though many of them are, these ancient portrayals do not display any real delight in animal form and movement. Whatever else they were, the artisans who produced these pictures were not nature lovers. In one way or another, their art glorifies the power and supremacy of man. A depressingly large number of the animals depicted on cave walls, tombs and limestone edifices have arrows or spears sticking into them.

Mycenaean art, particularly that of Minoan Crete in the second and third millenia BC, is refreshingly different. Scenes of war and the hunt are largely replaced by vital and engaging scenes evoking peace and carefree pleasures. Graceful youths and girls play or dance together, and even the animals seem to be enjoying themselves. On stucco reliefs, frescoes, clay pots and figured bronzes, we see cats stalking, gazelles leaping and cows suckling their young. The essence of this art is movement. It implies that life is more important than death. Nowhere is this principle of movement better expressed than in the enchanting octopus motifs which decorate many of the vases and floors unearthed by students of Mycenaean archaeology. For the first time in the history of art, there were representations of marine organisms, swirling, swimming and gliding, as though through limpid water. It was all new, exciting, alive— but it did not lead anywhere. The life-affirming art of Mycenae and

Detail from hunting scene. Painting from the tomb of Nakht, Egypt, 18th Dynasty. Note the stylised wings of the flying birds.

Fresco showing stylised dolphins and fishes, from the east wing of the Palace of Minos at Knossos, Middle Minoan III, *c* 1600 BC.

Minoan Crete came to an abrupt end and was buried under the earth. It had little influence on later Greek art, which was interested above all in perfection.

Before we look at the work of the Greeks, there are some general points to be made about the way animals were represented in earlier cultures. In any random selection of animal portrayals from pre-classical cultures, most will show a degree of similarity. Certain conventions of style and content seem to have been followed, of which the most noticeable is the way animals are shown in broadside view. One reason for this could be that the mental image we form of any three-dimensional object takes the viewpoint which presents the maximum amount of information. To recall any other view requires a special and conscious effort. Birds, quadrupeds and fishes reveal most of their salient characteristics from the side. Insects and other arthropods reveal most of theirs when seen from above. Molluscs or their shells may be viewed in various ways because they have such varied and often asymmetrical shapes. The most evocative image of any species is the one which provides the most information.

Most animal representations from the earliest phase of art are displayed in isolation; an animal is treated as having a definite edge, while the area circumscribed within the contour is shown indistinctly with little recognition of colour and no variations of tone caused by light and shade. The first paintings appear almost as direct translations of Paleolithic man's mental images of animals.

Also noticeable in primitive pictures is the lack of overlap: objects which in nature would be behind one another are separated out. The Egyptians and Assyrians, it is true, often showed objects overlapping, but each object revealed enough of itself to make identification easy. The Egyptians, as we have seen, introduced ancillary features such as trees and crops into their animal scenes, but never the hills, streams and other elements of the more recent traditions of landscape art.

Ancient Greece was the first civilisation in which works of art were consciously created as such. In several respects, the Greeks produced animal art which was not very different to that of the Egyptians, Assyrians and other Middle Eastern peoples. On occasion, indeed, it could be just as primitive. This is especially true of the figures on vases decorated in the 'Dipylon style'. Animals and human beings are shown strung out, as it were, around the vases so that, in the attempt to display each animal and human being in its broadest view, reality is sacrificed to to simplicity. Bodies are twisted, heads are squint-eyed, and often the subjects seem to be suspended in mid-air. These are clearly pictures painted from memory and not from nature. There is no foreshortening, no emotion displayed, no suggestion of movement or life. In later Greek art, animals are represented, as are humans, with near-perfect proportions, their poses and juxtapositions suggesting total harmony. It is all very imposing and heroic but not very natural. Few animals and humans have physiques approaching perfection, fewer live in harmony and none is naturally heroic.

Of course, the attainment of naturalness is not the only objective of animal art but it is the one towards which more recent artists, beginning with the Romans, have largely directed their talents. Romans delighted in ordinary things and liked animals for their own sake, just as we do today. Wall paintings and mosaic floors at Pompeii and elsewhere are evidence of great interest in natural objects; they show the Romans to have been good observers—as opposed to memorisers—of animals. There is a welcome emphasis on naturalism in their portrayal of even the humblest creatures; many of the accurate representations of marine life would have been difficult to achieve without close observation of the animals in their natural element.

Opportunities for close observation were afforded by the frequent displays of animals in the arena and in the menagerie, but there was also a genuine interest in natural history, as the compendious writings of Pliny the Elder amply demonstrate. This, and a widespread enthusiasm for hunting, fishing and animal husbandry, ensured that artisans were kept busy making pictures of a multitude of different animals. Naturalistic scenes incorporating various kinds of animal persisted in one form or another right up to the Middle Ages, appearing with great beauty in Byzantine art. The exquisite animal motifs displayed in the thirteenth-century Creation Mosaic at St Mark's Cathedral in Venice merely restate the elements of an art which had been appreciated by Romans before the advent of Christianity.

In the Far East, the first highly sophisticated animal art was produced under the Shang Dynasty of China, which spanned a 500-year period from about 1523 to about 1028 BC. Most surviving Shang art, like that of the ensuing Chou period which ended about 200 BC, is carved in jade or cast in bronze, and a large part of it is in stylised animal form. Among the most popular animal motifs in Shang and Chou art were the cicada, owl, bear, rabbit, deer, tiger and, unlikely though it seems, the tapir and the Indian rhinoceros. Often, two or more animals are combined in a single jade or bronze piece; this feature, representing the metamorphosis of one animal into another, is an important motif in early Chinese art. Shang and Chou animal art gives the impression that the animals it commemorates were not of interest primarily as living creatures but as three-dimensional shapes which could be appropriated for aesthetic and decorative purposes.

Mosaic showing animals from the Nile delta. Pompeii, 1st century BC. National Museum, Naples.

Mosaic showing domestic animals. Pompeii, 1st century BC. National Museum, Naples.

Mosaic showing marine fishes, an octopus, a squid and crustaceans. Pompeii, 1st century BC. National Museum, Naples.

During the Han Dynasty, which flourished for two centuries before and two after the birth of Christ, Chinese artists began to show greater sensitivity in their interpretation of animals. Among the most distinctive of Han art forms are stone reliefs, some of which portray stylised horses, birds and other animals. Han pottery tiles have also been found which show various animal images picked out in relief. Like most Han animal art, these tile pictures are more realistic, more natural, more intimate than those of Shang and Chou origin. It is interesting to note, too, the presence of landscape features in some Han reliefs. Probably for the first time in the history of art, birds are seen to be flying in space over trees that are rooted in the ground.

In AD 105, an event of momentous importance to the development of the graphic arts occurred in China: paper was invented. Although no paintings on paper survive from the Han period, some lively animal pictures preserved on damask and other textiles suggest that Han artists could have produced very pleasing pictures of animals on paper. After all, paper is the most suitable surface for that most pliant of all graphic tools, the Chinese brush.

In post-Han Chinese art, the horse figured very prominently, achieving its finest artistic expression in the standing figures modelled in glazed pottery during the T'ang Dynasty, a most august period of Chinese culture which lasted from about AD 600 to 900. T'ang graphic work was also highly accomplished; some lovely animal studies, spirited horses especially, are known from this period.

A painting on silk from the Five Dynasties period of the tenth century shows a herd of deer in a grove. For truth of detail and movement combined with beauty of form, the animal figures in this delightful painting have seldom been surpassed. In the overall balance of the composition and the subtle blending of rich foliage colours, this is really a great landscape painting, one of the earliest true landscapes with animals.

Sensitive studies, especially of birds, also typify the animal art of the Sung Dynasty (tenth to thirteenth centuries). Many of them are drawn in ink on hanging silk scrolls and show animals in natural and often lively poses against attractive landscape backgrounds. The animals were obviously drawn from living subjects by artists in whom a love of animals was combined with a reverence for accuracy and naturalism. T'ang and Sung artists could have taught their European contemporaries a great deal about animal art. No European artist working at that time could have shown anything like the sensitivity, delicacy of touch and accuracy of observation which characterise the art of Mu Ch'i, one of the greatest of Sung artists. His scroll drawing of a crane walking in a bamboo grove is just one of several fine animal studies made by him in the thirteenth century which have survived to the present day.

The continued excellence of Chinese portrayals of animals is well illustrated by a leaf from an album of sketches painted by the Ming artist Liu Ts'ai between 1300 and 1400. Three exquisitely painted fishes are shown swimming, with their streamlined bodies describing graceful curves and a suggestion of spiralling movement linking them. But, with notable exceptions, the style of Chinese animal art after Ming times became hackneyed. From the fifteenth century onwards it was adulterated by contact with the work of European artists.

Japanese art was initially very similar to Chinese art and, to Western eyes at least, gives the false impression of having few outstanding features of its own. The Nara Period (about AD 600 to 800) produced some delightful animal motifs including ivory carvings, paintings on wood and mother-of-pearl inlay work. These purely decorative motifs are sometimes very well observed and frequently take the form of hunted animals. The most popular subject is the horse, which is usually portrayed in a lively attitude and involved in a blood sport.

In the fifteenth and sixteenth centuries, during the Ashikaga Period, a school of monochrome painting flourished and has left behind some paintings which show horses and other animals depicted with equal concern for accuracy and animation. A screen painting by Sesshu, one of the founding fathers of the Ashikaga school, shows several birds, mostly cranes, standing or flying. A section of a hanging scroll, painted a few years later by Kano Motonobu, shows a single crane standing on one leg. In both these scenes, tree branches and other landscape details look contrived and false by comparison with the birds, which are painted sympathetically and accurately, although they are in no way superior to the paintings of Sung Dynasty China. Although some fine nature studies were produced during the Tokugawa Period (sixteenth to seventeenth centuries), Japanese art was then already under Western influence.

In India, under the umbrella of Buddhism and Hinduism, the arts tended to glorify the human body rather than animals. Most of the animal representations, usually sculpted in stone, are of elephants, cattle and other creatures closely associated with the human economy. Beasts of the chase, such as lions and tigers, occur frequently, and birds of various kinds are fairly common.

Mughal miniature painting of a zebra by Mansur, Jahangir period, *c* 1621. Victoria & Albert Museum, London.

From the sixteenth century, when the Mughal school of painting came into being, Indian artists produced detailed and realistic paintings which owed much to the influence of Persia. The best of them date from the reign of Akbar the Great, an enlightened monarch who was brought up a Moslem and married a Hindu princess. His son Jahangir had similar artistic tastes and was passionately fond of flowers and animals. He insisted that paintings executed for him by the artists who accompanied him on his numerous travels should not just be stylised records of everything interesting he saw. A picture of a zebra painted by Mansur in 1621 shows how carefully Jahangir's artists worked. Noticeable in this small painting—Mughal pictures are like miniatures—is the way Mansur has shown the hair of the tail and mane, the docility of the eye, the correct angle between the ears and the almost dainty appearance of the hooves. Evidently Mansur wished to record more than the most distinctive and obvious feature of a zebra: its stripes. Akbar, who admired Western art and owned Dutch and Flemish paintings, had not only ensured that Mughal artists were aware of European ideals of perspective, atmospheric effects and landscape vistas, but had helped to ensure that those ideals had a lasting effect on native Indian art forms. Here, as elsewhere, European artistic influence had come to stay.

Europe during the period from the collapse of the Roman Empire to the Renaissance was surprisingly rich in forms of artistic accomplishment, with much of the inspiration for them coming from the animal kingdom. Many of the illuminated manuscripts compiled during medieval times are decorated with pictures of the Creation, Jonah and the Whale, Noah and the Ark, the fearsome beasts mentioned in the Book of Revelation and many other subjects contained in that inexhaustible treasury of animal stories, the Bible.

In many illustrated manuscripts, animal pictures were put in purely as ornament, but it is among these decorative subjects that some of the liveliest medieval representations of animals are to be found. Evidently they were put in by the illuminators to satisfy themselves rather than to illustrate scriptural themes. A leaf showing the crucifixion will occasionally have naturalistic vignettes of rabbits, foxes, lions, insects or other animals disporting themselves around the margins. Thus did medieval artists temper the gruesome with the frolicsome, the accepted myths with the observed realities. So liberally did they scatter animal motifs around

Before the Hours of the Cross. From a Flemish Book of Hours decorated with naturalistic motifs. Ghent-Bruges School, 15th century.

their gilded leaves that it seems as if they constantly welcomed the opportunity to turn to the animal kingdom for light relief.

A feature of many illuminated scriptural texts is the way that real and imaginary animals are placed together. Well observed birds, quadrupeds, insects and other creatures mingle unconcernedly with dragons, griffins, harpies, hydras, unicorns and other monstrous figments of the imagination as though they were all equally real or equally fictitious. Sometimes it is possible to recognise in the picture of an apparently fictitious creature some salient characteristics of a real one which was infrequently seen in medieval Europe. The elephant usually appears as something more like a long-nosed, tusked pig, while the camel, which was frequently mis-represented about the head and neck region, is identifiable by its humped back. Horses, naturally enough, are usually recognisable for what they are, and so, as a rule, are lions, tigers and monkeys—animals which were found in medieval menageries or even in households.

The mixture of the real and the imaginary is also apparent in the illustrations which accompany the texts of bestiaries. These allegorical accounts of animals and their ways had their origins in the ancient anonymous compilation known as the *Physiologus*. Until the later Middle Ages, naturalism in animal art was of little importance because animals were used primarily to point morals, to adorn tales intended to promote the contemplation of universal truths. By the thirteenth century, however, scholars such as Albertus Magnus were unable to shut their eyes to more particular truths and began describing some of the real but previously ignored things, including animals, they observed around them. But science, as distinct from philosophical speculation, had a long and painful birth. It was to be many years before the accurate observation of nature became accepted as a worthwhile goal in its own right. Hence, fabulous animals continued to feature in many books published during the fifteenth, sixteenth and seventeenth centuries.

We rightly criticise our medieval ancestors for their credulous attitude to unnatural marvels, but we tend to overlook their more solid achievements and their ability to see many things objectively and well. Some of the illuminations in psalters, bestiaries, books of hours, bibles and other manuscripts show that they deserve our respect as well as our criticism. In their animal art, they might have been expected to pay exclusive attention to the more conspicuous animals but, surprisingly perhaps, they were at their best when dealing with humbler creatures. Moths, butterflies, ladybirds, bees and many other kinds of insect occur frequently in their work and most are very well drawn. Undoubtedly, many of them were observed closely, at first hand. Insects and other invertebrates decorate several leaves of the Cocharelli Book of Hours, a fourteenth-century manuscript in the British Museum. On the lower margin of one leaf, for example, there is a row of insects comprising two moths, a butterfly and an ichneumon fly, each of them probably identifiable by an entomologist. The side view of the ichneumon fly is particularly realistic and must surely have been drawn from the living insect. A vignette of a

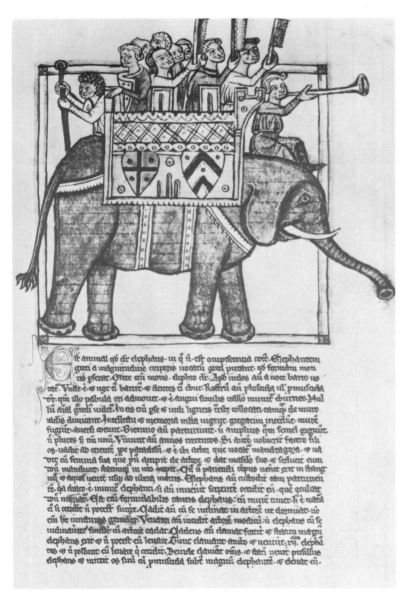

Above: Elephant. *Right:* The Naming of the Beasts. From early 13th century Latin bestiaries in, respectively, the British Museum, London, and the Bodleian Library, Oxford.

dragonfly in the fourteenth-century Luttrell Psalter, also in the British Museum, is as accurate as many illustrations of dragonflies published more than three centuries later.

The small size and brilliant colours of many insects made them admirable subjects for the medieval illuminator. Just possibly they were also of some interest to other members of the community. The *Romance of Alexander*, an early fifteenth-century manuscript in the Bodleian Library at Oxford, has one of its leaves decorated with a scene showing several women using their peculiar headgear to catch butterflies.

The butterflies and bees depicted in the illuminated manuscripts seem to have been individually painted and differ from one to another manuscript. The same cannot be said for many other animal vignettes. Most of them were also to be found in pattern books, some of which, evidently, were in use over a long period. Some of the earliest animal pictures ever published may also have originated in artists' pattern books. But by the middle of the fifteenth century, the triumph of realism over tradition was visible in the animal art of several painters, such as the Italian master Pisanello (*c*1395–*c*1455). Many surviving Pisanello drawings are spirited animal studies executed with such fidelity that they were once thought to be by Leonardo da Vinci, who was not even born until 1459. Occasionally, Pisanello turned to early pattern books for guidance, but most of the models for the animal subjects in his finished pictures were his own sketches done from the life. To a considerable extent, the animal art of men like Pisanello formed an artistic bridge between old ideals and new practices. The next important development was to be a mechanical one: the invention of printing with movable type.

Pair of horses. Print, from a drawing attributed to Pisanello.

CHAPTER II
The Early
Illustrated Book

The ancient Egyptians had within their grasp the means to duplicate pictures. So, to some extent, did one or two other early civilisations, but it did not occur to any of them to print from their engravings on wood, clay or stone. The fundamental idea of printing was not exploited until about the eighth century AD, when the first books and prints were produced from woodblocks in the Far East.

The first Chinese and Japanese wood engravers mostly reproduced paintings. Although movable type had been used earlier in China and Korea, it was not until the fifteenth century that the printing press, using type and designed primarily to reproduce words, was first used in Europe. This, more than any other technical innovation, catapulted mankind into the modern world. All at once, the knowledge which had circulated only among scholars and wealthy collectors of illuminated manuscripts began to become available to a wider public.

Much that was printed on the early presses was new but just as much was old. The favourite books of the Middle Ages were also the money spinners of Renaissance printers and publishers. Among these favourites were several rich in animal imagery, such as the ancient *Fables of Aesop* and a compendium of natural and unnatural history called *The Properties of Things*, which had originally been brought together in the thirteenth century by Bartholomew the Englishman. Many of these early printed books contained errors of fact, and the illustrations were fanciful, but it was more important then for the contents to be available than for them to be right.

Conrad von Megenberg's *Buch der Natur*, the first illustrated book which attempted to inform its readers about animals, was published in folio in 1475. Its twelve plates contain a hundred or so pictures of animals and plants. There is nothing novel in the text, but the illustrations amount to a significant event in the history of zoological iconography. In the middle of the thirteenth century, Thomas of Cantimpré had studied the theories of nature put forward by classical authors and written them up as a book, with additions supplied by his own fertile imagination. A century later, Conrad von Megenberg translated the book from Latin into German but did not revise it. After another hundred and twenty-five years had elapsed, Conrad's manuscript was published, again unchanged. The *Buch der Natur*, therefore, was more than two and a half centuries old when it was first published, and almost everything written in it that was not extracted from classical Greek, Roman and Persian authors was probably a product of Thomas's inventive mind.

The illustrations in the *Buch der Natur* could have come from various sources, but almost certainly Thomas was not one of them. They possibly originated in medieval pattern books, but some, such as those of the dog, the horse and other domestic animals, are superior to those of such exotica as the elephant and the camel and may have been based on sketches from nature.

Before the *Buch der Natur* was published, the only ways in which the appearance of an unusual animal could have been communicated from person to person or place to place were by word of mouth, by original sketches and perhaps by printed woodcuts. The advantages of having a portable and relatively inexpensive book to convey such information are obvious. Furthermore, erroneous information recorded in a mass-produced book was likely to be detected and corrected quicker than it would have been if recorded in an illuminated manuscript intended for the delight and instruction of a select few.

As the elephant had been known in Europe for many centuries before the *Buch der Natur* was published, it is not surprising that an illustration of one is included. Whoever drew the original picture, however, had either never seen an elephant or had decided that it looked better with cloven hoofs, diminutive head and tusks, abbreviated trunk and out-size eyes. Anyone who had seen a real elephant would have known that this illustration was wildly inaccurate. The conception which it represents of this largest of all land quadrupeds had probably been accepted as truthful by generations of artists, illuminators and owners of precious manuscripts. It compares strangely with the excellent figure, easily recognisable as that of an African elephant, which was published ten years later, in 1486, in the Dutch edition of *The Properties of Things*. After 1486, published illustrations of the elephant were much closer to the creature they supposedly portrayed. By contrast, Albrecht Dürer's erroneous impression of a rhinoceros haunted European graphic art for over two hundred and fifty years.

It is worth noticing here that illustrations of flowers and other botanical subjects had attained a high standard of artistic and scientific excellence in Renaissance Europe at a time when illustrations of birds, mammals and other zoological subjects often left much to be desired. To some

Stag Beetle. Watercolour drawing by Albrecht Dürer.

extent, the different standards attained are attributable to the relatively more advanced condition of botany in those times. More importantly, the study of plants was not complicated by so many emotionally charged errors, and to a considerable extent it was the handmaiden of gardening, agriculture and pharmacy, branches of human enquiry with practical rather than philosophical ends.

Describing and drawing a plant, most biologists would admit, is easier than describing and drawing an animal. Given a description of a rose bush and a drawing of part of it, you should be able to describe and draw a complete one. But no matter how competent and imaginative you may be, you will not be able to describe and draw a complete fox without seeing the whole animal—the appearance of a fox's tail gives no clue to the appearance of its head. To draw an animal well, an artist needs to get close to it and study it carefully in its living state. Pisanello, Leonardo and Dürer—especially Dürer—were among the first artists to realise this fully and thus were able to produce representations of animals which rivalled or excelled the best from earlier, non-European cultures. Pisanello's cheetah, Leonardo's horses and Dürer's minutely observed stag beetle are all examples of animal art at its most naturalistic. But in addition to naturalism and artistic excellence, there is something else in these pictures: in a word, science.

Defined as the pursuit of knowledge by observation and experiment, systematically classified and organised under general principles, science is in any picture that has been executed with attention to truth and naturalism. To some extent, even pictures from remote antiquity had a scientific content. Not until the fifteenth century AD, however, were pictures created in an intellectually scientific atmosphere. At that point, animal artists began to look to the Book of Nature rather than the Book of God for inspiration and models. Only then did beasts of the Apocalypse move over to make way for beasts of forest, plain, mountain, river and sea. Thereafter, art became more and more aware of science.

As scientific progress gathered momentum, a need arose for presenting facts in pictorial form. The systematic cataloguing of natural and artificial curiosities acquired by potentates, dilettante collectors and philosophers sometimes gave rise to publications. Such books were clearly more informative if they were illustrated, and from about the middle of the sixteenth century a good number of them became available. They are the ancestors of today's illustrated books. The impact of science on art was timely and beneficial. At last, all kinds of natural objects could be represented accurately, free from the pattern book tradition and largely free of the dictates of changing artistic fashion.

Science has undoubtedly been advanced by the dispassionate use of pictures, but passionless pictures are presumably the work of passionless artists, and such artists are perilously close to not being artists at all. Perhaps the ideal for natural history pictures is compounded of scientific truth and artistic feeling in about equal porportions. The felicitous blending of science and art has been achieved most in the work of botanical illustrators because plant forms, broadly speaking, are more decorative than animal forms. A living plant is also easier to observe and draw, as it does not move about and the artist has ample leisure to compose his picture. We should not be surprised, then, if the animal pictures in some early books of a predominantly scientific or didactic nature are not aesthetically pleasing. Science and art often make agreeable bedfellows, but it is just as likely that one will push the other out of bed. During the adolescence of the illustrated natural history book, science too often had the bed to itself.

It was the Swiss scholar Conrad Gessner whose labours during the first half of the sixteenth century resulted in the first large-scale illustrated works on zoology. Between 1551 and 1558, his folio-sized *Historia Animalium* was published in Zürich, its four volumes liberally embellished with bold woodcuts (a fifth volume was published posthumously in 1587).

Ostrich. Woodcut, a page from Conrad Gessner's *Icones Animalium,* 1560.

Porcupine and Crabs. Woodcuts from Conrad Gessner's *Icones Animalium*, 1560.

R VRSVS Galli mar. uulgò dicti, (quem Cancrum Heracleoticum Bellonius facit,) qualem olim ex Italia Corn. Sittardus nobis attulit, alia eicon.
GERMAN. Aeben der selbig Meerkrabb/auff ein andere weyß gecontrafeet.

Eiusdem Cancri icones alias duas aliter expres-
sas, proximè retrò posuimus.

VRSVS (uel Vrsa, Ἄρκτ⊙ *n*.) Rondeletij: idem qui Cancer Heracleoticus Bellonij (& Scaligeri: Vide superius) proximè exhibitus: quo cum plura leges. Vr si nomen (inquit) non à forma impositum est, ut Locu- stis: sed ab actionib. moribusq, ut Lupo, Cinædo. ¶ Bel lonius Vrsum seu Vrsam facit, quã Rondeletius Squil- larum generis esse ostendit, & latam cognominat: quam nos etiam ex Italia olim Vrsi nomine à uiro quodam e- rudito missam accepimus. Crediderunt nimirum hunc esse Vrsum aliqui à corporis forma: quæ crassa ei & re- curta est, sicut terrestri. & quia genus alterum per omnia huic simile, Ligures uulgo Vrsetam appellant: quæ an eadem sit Squillæ cælatæ Rondeletij, quærendum. Vi de infra inter Squillas.
GERMAN. dici poterit ein Bärenkrabb: uel alijs nominibus in Cãcro Heracleotico Bellonij iam positis. [Bellonij uerò Vrsa, ein Bärenkrebs. hic enim longus & caudatus est, ille rotundus.] Ein andere contrafeetung deß nächstgemelten Seekrabben.

Icon Paguri ueluti in dorso iacentis, expressa Venetijs: similis à Bellonio exhibitæ.

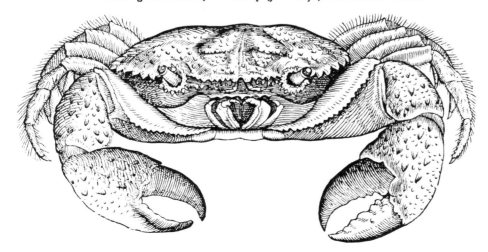

Nautæ in dorſa Cetorum,quæ inſulas putant,anchoras figentes,ſæpe periclitantur. Hos cetos **Trolual** *ſua lingua appellant,Germanicè* **Teüfelwal.**

Similis eſt & illorum icon apud eundem,capite,roſtro,dentibus,fiſtulis: quos montium inſtar grandes eſſe ſcribit,& naues euertere,niſi ſono tubarum aut miſſis in mare rotundis & uacuis uaſis abſterreantur. Idem in Balthico mari circa Balænam fieri aiunt.

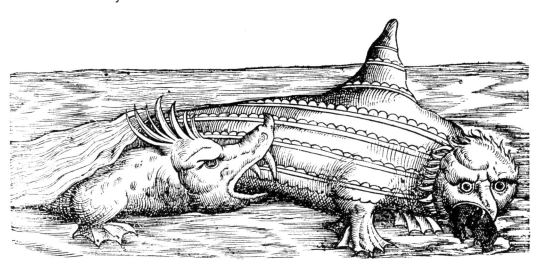

Sea Monsters. Woodcuts from Conrad Gessner's *Icones Animalium,* 1560.

A glance at the woodcuts is enough to show that they instruct rather than bewitch. That is what Gessner wanted and why they proved to be his most original and lasting contributions to science. He employed eminent artists to try to ensure that the woodcuts were as accurate—and as unemotional—as they could be. In view of the state of zoology at the time, he succeeded remarkably well. His illustrations are coarse and intensely black because his engravers could not cut their woodblocks finely enough to show fine detail. Many years were to elapse before engravers on wood could attain results comparable to those achieved by engravers on copper and steel.

Gessner's apparent omniscience, the extent of his writings and the multiplicity of bold illustrations accompanying them led to a considerable amount of plagiarism by contemporary and later scholars. One in particular, Ulisse Aldrovandi of Bologna, modelled his work on Gessner's.

Vlyſsis Aldrouandi

Tawny Owl. Woodcut from Ulisse Aldrovandi's *Ornithologiae*, 1599.

His published volumes—and their illustrations in particular—look remarkably similar to those of Gessner, his one-time tutor. Both men were immensely industrious and had a very wide knowledge of animals, but both were over-credulous, Aldrovandi especially so, and many of the illustrations they reproduced are fanciful or largely inaccurate. Aldrovandi, who was less critical than Gessner, wrote a lot of nonsense about animals, but his illustrations were marginally better. In many ways, the woodcuts of Gessner and Aldrovandi may be fairly described as wooden, but they exercised a considerable influence on succeeding illustrators of zoological texts and were not eclipsed until Buffon published his magnificent *Histoire Naturelle*.

They were two of the five giants of sixteenth-century systematic zoology. The others were Pierre Belon, Guillaume Rondelet and Hippolyte

Left: Bat. Woodcut from Ulisse Aldrovandi's *Ornithologiae*, 1599.

Below: Spiny Ray. Woodcut from Guillaume Rondelet's *De Piscibus Marinis*, 1554.

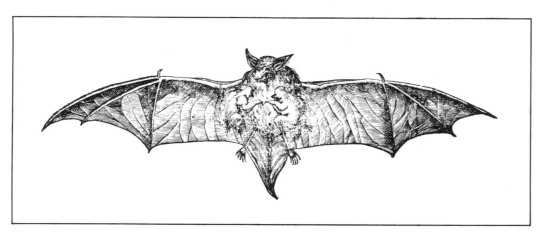

De Stella arborefcente.

CAPVT XIIII.

Gorgon-Head Starfish. Woodcut from Guillaume Rondelet's *De Piscibus Marinis*, 1554.

Below : Killer Whale. Woodcut from Guillaume Rondelet's *De Piscibus Marinis*, 1554.

Right : Chamois. Woodcut from Pierre Belon's *Les Observations de Plusieurs Singularités et Choses, trouvées en Grèce, Asie, Indée, Egypte, Arabie, etc.*, 1555.

Salviani, all of whom were in the medical profession and made important contributions to the study of fishes. Almost simultaneously, these three published substantial illustrated books on marine life. Rondelet was perhaps the most remarkable. His *De Piscibus Marinis*, a fine folio publication issued in 1554 and 1555, contains illustrations which are good enough for many of the fishes depicted to be identified with certainty. Whoever drew them was not trying to create works of art but works of reference. Even so, the book includes descriptions and pictures of some very strange and evidently apocryphal creatures (some of which are also depicted by Gessner, Belon and Aldrovandi). Among these was the 'Bishop Fish', one of the best known fabrications in the annals of zoological iconography, the genuineness of which Rondelet refused to affirm or deny. Similarly, he said of his 'Monk Fish' (which differed only in minor details from one published in 1553 by Belon) that, in his opinion, 'certain details beyond the truth of the matter have been added by the painter to make the thing seem more marvellous.' Despite Rondelet's reservations about these monsters, the fact that they were illustrated in his book was enough to validate the stories which gave them birth, and many later books reproduced them unaltered.

Salviani's carefully executed copper engravings have a more scientific look about them than those of his famous contemporaries because of their greater detail and their arrangement on the page—one above the other and with the plates occupying a whole page at a time. Only the scales of some of the fishes, represented by formal cross hatching, have an unnatural appearance. Published between 1554 and 1557 in his *Aquatilium Animalium*, these are possibly the earliest engravings of fishes which may be said to have a totally scientific purpose. Rondelet's and Belon's woodcuts are not artistically in the same class, but in some respects theirs score over Salviani's. They are bolder, clearer and integrated into their texts whereas Salviani's are brought together on separate plates. The virtue of situating illustrations close to the relevant text rather than lumping them together is apparent to anyone who uses a book as a reference tool (although the practical difficulties of integration are such, especially when colour is used, that most illustrated books bring the plates together in one place, usually but not always at the end of the book).

æquoris fiftula.Pinguitudinis, carnis eadem natura , idem vfus qui fuperioris, denique eadem pifcandi ratio.

De Orca.

CAPVT XIII.

ORCA ex beluarum marinarũ eft genere, cui nomen pofitũ eft à vafis olearij fiue vinarij fimilitudine quod tereti eft,& vniformi fpecie, eo hodie in prouincia & Gallia Narbonéfi ad hauriédam & feruandã aquam vtimur,& parũ mutato nomine *dorgos* vocamus,quafi orchos,id eft,orcas.Talis eft huius beluæ figura: nam toto corpore eft valde craffo & rotũdo, extremis nõ valde prominentibus & tenuioribus.Santones *efpaulars* vocant,ab humerorum feu potiùs fcapularum latitudine & crafsitudine.Eft igitur orca roftro & fiftula pinnis & cauda delphino fimilis,corpore vigefies crafsiore, potifsimum cir

Le portraiĉt du Chamois,ou Yfard.

Si les cornes de ceft Yfard,ou Chamois eftoyent ramées, lon pourroit dire que c'eft de luy que Pline à entendu, parlant de Caprea, quand il difoit: Nec fecit vt Ceruis decidua. Car ils ne laiffent point leurs cornes l'hyuer non plus que les Boucs eftains: mais ne les ayant point ramées, aufsi ne peut eftre Caprea. Il à bien l'habitude du Cheureul & le pelage de femblable fa-

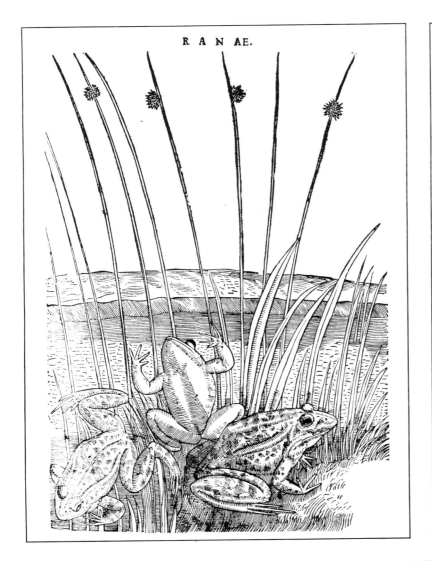

RANAE.

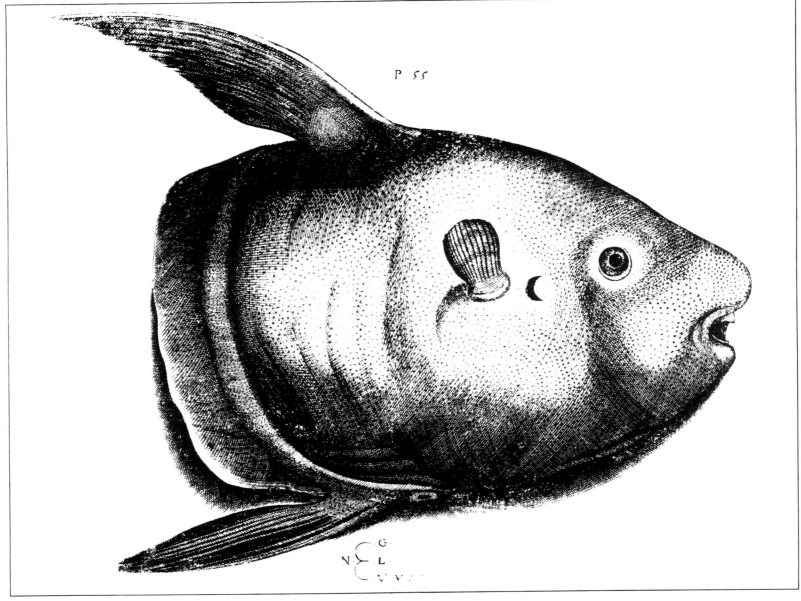

P 55

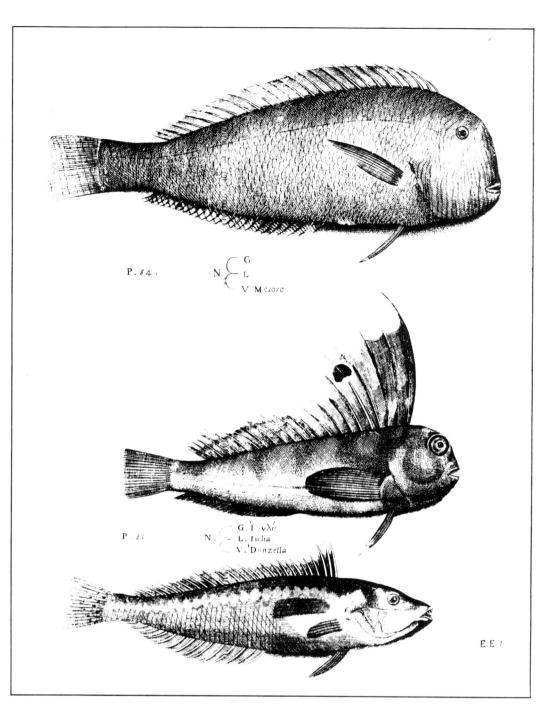

Far left: Frogs by a pond. Woodcut from Pierandrea Matthioli's *Commentarii sex libros Pedacii Dioscoridis*, 1565. This remarkably spirited and well composed woodcut, like Matthioli's other animal illustrations, is all the more remarkable for being tucked away in a massive herbal.

Left: Groups of hogs and deer. Woodcuts from Matthioli's *Commentarii*.

Right: Cuckoo Wrasse, Butterfly Blenny, etc. Copper engraving from Hippolyte Salviani's *Aquatilium Animalium*, 1554–57.

Below: Bed-Bugs. Woodcut from Matthioli's *Commentarii*.

Left: Sunfish. Copper engraving from Hippolyte Salviani's *Aquatilium Animalium*, 1554–57.

We should notice, in passing, the animal illustrations in Pierandrea Mattioli's *Commentarii in sex Libros Pedacii Dioscoridis*. As Mattioli was a botanist whose book is renowned as one of the largest and best herbals ever published, it is surprising that he wrote about animals and illustrated them in this commentary on the plants of Dioscorides. The earlier editions contain only small woodcuts, but between 1562 and 1585 four large-sized editions with larger and better pictures were published.

Many of these woodcuts are excellent and at their best are superior to those in most sixteenth-century zoological treatises. The figure of a common lobster is outstanding: it bears comparison in all essential points with the best illustrations of this creature published before the nineteenth century. A group of three frogs set against a pond-side landscape exhibits charm and balance in the composition at the same time as it adheres closely to an accurate and naturalistic portrayal of the animals. Only in the portrayal of some living molluscs—notoriously difficult subjects at all times—does the artist indicate that he can transgress the boundary separating the land of the real from the swamp of the imagined. Even in the next century, few books dealing with animals had better illustrations. None had as anomalous a setting as a herbal.

Remarkably few books published during the sixteenth century dealt at length with zoological subjects and illustrated them. It is as if those five remarkable naturalists, with Gessner at their head, had said enough about animals and illustrated enough of them to supply the needs of that century (although it should be mentioned that Aldrovandi's work was

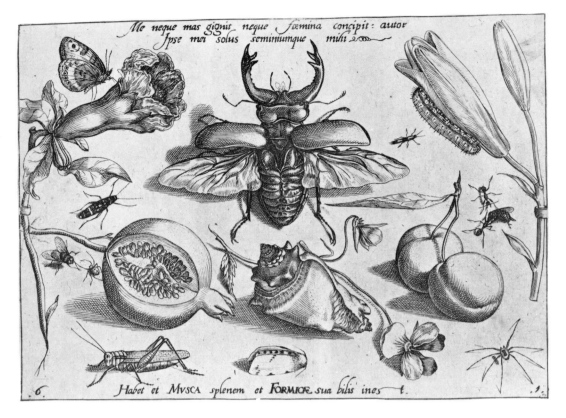

Insects, a shell, plants and fruit. Copper engraving by Jacob Hoefnagel from the first edition of George Hoefnagel's *Archetypa*, 1592. The overall design of the plates in this edition is more satisfying and the engraving is better than in the 1630 edition.

nearly all published after 1600 and a fair amount of it did not appear until he was dead). One of the last animal books to be published in the sixteenth century, and one of the most charming, was the *Archetypa* of George Hoefnagel (1592). The illustrations, by Jacob Hoefnagel, comprise figures of plants and animals attractively but meaninglessly assembled on each page. One of the pages, for instance, shows a butterfly squatting on the carapace of a lobster surrounded by flowers, fruit and insects. The illustrations are very well engraved, and Jacob evidently studied his subjects very closely, but the style of the book suggests that zoological iconography at the end of the sixteenth century had lost its impetus and purpose.

These apparent losses were made good during the following century. Science and the scientific method became more and more acceptable, particularly in Britain; the Royal Society came to exercise a healthy influence; the natural classification of animals and plants received the attention of highly intelligent men; the nature of fossils became a vital issue; and the invention of the microscope helped men to look much closer at natural objects and to watch the operation of previously hidden life processes.

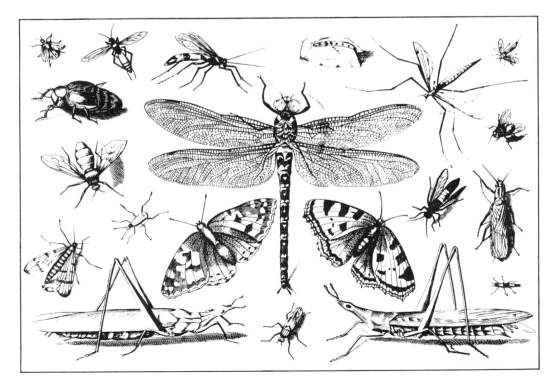

Insects. Copper engraving by Jacob Hoefnagel from the 1630 edition of George Hoefnagel's *Archetypa*.

CHAPTER III
Into the Light

To progress from the sixteenth to the seventeenth century is to move, albeit gradually, out of the age of bestiaries and fabulous creatures into the more rational and organised world of zoological science. The seventeenth century was the first in the history of European thought that could truly be called scientific in its outlook, but it was not a very zoological century. The invention of the telescope, for instance, had a far more profound impact than the contemporary invention of the microscope. Galileo got into serious trouble for the conclusions he drew from looking at the boundlessly great but he annoyed no-one when he examined the infinitesimally small through the 'optic tube' he had made.

Even the human body was looked upon as a kind of mechanical model. Human internal organs were intensely interesting to seventeenth-century scientists, who also, because human bodies were still somewhat sacred, found it necessary to examine in detail the internal organs of the higher animals—a study known as comparative anatomy. Living animals, except those important in husbandry, were still not considered very interesting. Not until the Age of Exploration was under way did men begin to appreciate fully the wonderful variety of form and colour of living animals. Only then did they produce sumptuously illustrated volumes celebrating the marvels of animate nature. The difference between a late seventeenth-century book on animals and a late eighteenth-century one is the difference between the dead and the living. During the seventeenth century, circumstances were not yet right for a large output of fine illustrated books on animal subjects.

It is apposite to mention at the outset Thomas Moffet's *Insectorum Theatrum*, which was not published until 1634 although based largely on unpublished material gathered up by Gessner for his *Historia Animalium*. Moffet's neighbour and friend Thomas Penny, had custody of Gessner's notes on insects and spent fifteen years bringing together additional material. Moffet acquired the much expanded manuscript after Penny's death and added a great deal to it (the additions being mostly literary rather than scientific). When Moffet died in 1606, the manuscript was ready for the press, but not until it was purchased by Sir Theodore Mayerne was it finally published. Gessner's projected book on insects had had to wait for about three-quarters of a century before any of it reached the public. Such are the caprices of publishing.

As a pioneering entomological work, the *Insectorum Theatrum* is now appreciated for its many illustrations, mostly thumb-nail size, which embellish the text throughout. Because of their small size and the coarseness of the engraving, most of the woodcuts are useless for identification purposes. Moffet (or should it be Mayerne?) was one of the first to consider that small creatures, such as insects, merited only small pictures in descriptive books. Nevertheless, the illustrations do at least seem to portray real insects. The same cannot be said of the cuts which appeared in 1622 in a book by Jean Bonoeil '*commanding the present setting up of Silke Works, and planting of Vines in Virginia . . . also a Treatise of the Art of Making Silke*'. One of the cuts shows the silkworms flying about, pairing, laying eggs and issuing from the cocoon. But no silkworms ever

By this figure is shewed the portraits of the cods, and the Butterflies comne forth of them, to engender and lay their egs vpon blacke Serge, Chamblet, Tammey or such like stuffes as hath been said.

Silkworms. Woodcut from Jean Bonoeil's *Treatise of the Art of Making Silke*, 1622.

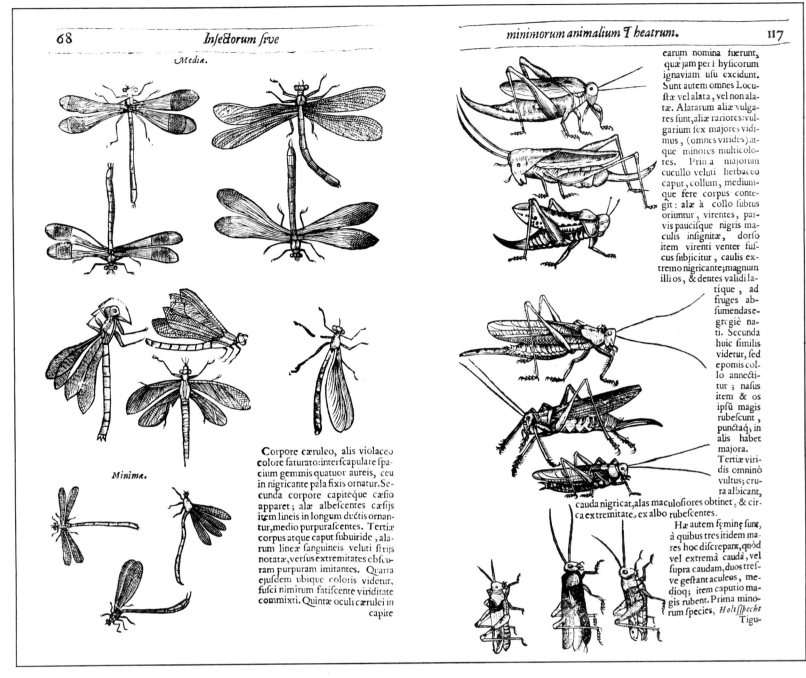

looked like these, the artist having given them deer-like horns, bird-like faces and near-human eyes. Moffet would never have sanctioned that kind of artistic licence.

The published engravings of the *Insectorum Theatrum* are among the few produced at an early date in the history of zoological iconography which may be compared with the original drawings from which the engraver worked. The originals, integrated with Moffet's manuscript text, are preserved in the British Library, tangible links with that great

Dragonflies and Damsel Flies, Grasshoppers and Crickets. Two pages from Thomas Moffet's *Insectorum Theatrum*, 1634, illustrated with woodcuts.

Leopard and mythical beasts, the Su and Horned Hares. Copper engravings from Gaspar Schott's *Physica Curiosa sive Mirabilia Naturae et Artis,* 3rd edition, Herbipoli (i.e. Würzburg), 1697. According to Topsell, the Su, so called because it 'liveth for the most part neere the waters', is found in Patagonia. He describes it as 'of a very deformed shape, and monstrous presence, a great ravener, and an untamable wilde beast'. Belief in the existence of horned hares and rabbits seems to have had ancient origins. The myth has been exploited more recently for playful purposes in the form of the 'Jackalope', described as 'a nearly extinct antlered species of rabbit' and said to be found 'almost exclusively on the high plains of Wyoming', according to a picture postcard sold to visitors at Yellowstone National Park. It seems unlikely that the perpetrators of this modern joke knew about the obscure and rare book by Gaspar Schott, a Jesuit, which was first published in 1662.

sixteenth-century encyclopedist Conrad Gessner, and surprisingly close in appearance to the published engravings.

Moffet was also linked, though less tenuously, with Edward Topsell, an English divine whose lively imagination amply compensated for his abysmal ignorance of natural history. In 1607, Topsell published his *Historie of Foure-footed Beasties,* following this up in 1608 with his *Historie of Serpents.* These two books were reissued in 1658, together with an English translation of Moffet's book (entitled *The Theater of Insects*), under the title *The History of Four-footed Beasts and Serpents,* one of the most notorious, most popular, most scientifically worthless, most plagiarised and most fascinating of all books purporting to deal with members of the animal kingdom. A good nine-tenths, maybe more, of its contents are pure fiction. This is at once apparent from the illustrations which show many curious and fearsome creatures such as the dreaded Su, a 'cruell, untamable, impatient, violent, ravening, and bloody beast', and the cattle-eating Boas, 'which Serpent was an hundred and twenty

Three versions of the same curious image of a hyena. *Left to right:* woodcuts from Conrad Gessner's *Icones Animalium,* 1560, and Edward Topsell's *History of Four-Footed Beasts and Serpents,* 1658; copper engraving from Gaspar Schott's *Physica Curiosa,* 3rd edition, 1693. Topsell's re-engraved copy of Gessner's woodcut shows how faithfully engravers could copy each other's work. Schott's rather crude copper engraving still obviously uses the same source.

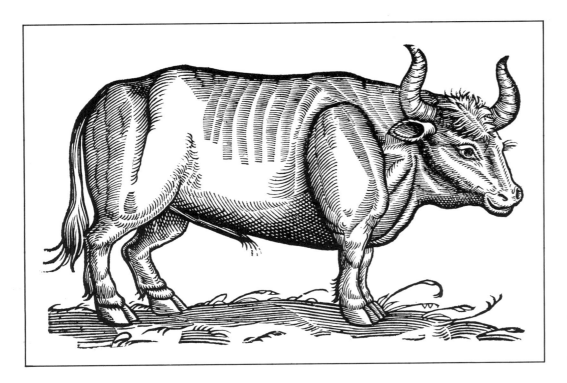

foote in length.' It is the combination in one book of a delightfully un-scientific and quaintly worded text with bold woodcuts of wildly im-probable creatures which has ensured Topsell's *History* a permanent place in the annals of pseudo-zoology. The reissue of such illustrations in the middle of the 'enlightened' seventeenth century suggests that the bestiary tradition was not yet moribund, and their constant reappearance in modern books and magazine articles indicates that they have yet to lose their appeal.

From Topsell's *History* to the *Historia Naturalis Brasiliae* of Piso and Marcgrave is not a long journey in time, but in spirit the two books are far apart. Topsell's materials for illustrating his book were the pictures which had appeared in other mens' books and a fertile, unchecked imagination. Piso and Marcgrave did not have such easily tapped sources at their command. During a seven-year period as Governor-General of north-eastern Brazil from 1637 to 1644, Count Moritz of Nassau-Siegen assembled a very rich portfolio on the country, including a great deal about its botany and zoology. Several good artists were employed to compile pictorial records, which they did in a variety of ways, from sketches in monochrome and watercolour to oil paintings and tapestries. An inspection of these records could provide vital clues to the identity of many animals illustrated in Piso and Marcgrave's book. But the illustrations published in the book in 1648 do not provide those clues: a great deal of the truth and most of the appeal of the original drawings

Ram. Probably because it represents an accessible creature, this is one of the more accurate woodcuts in Edward Topsell's *History of Four-Footed Beasts and Serpents,* 1658.

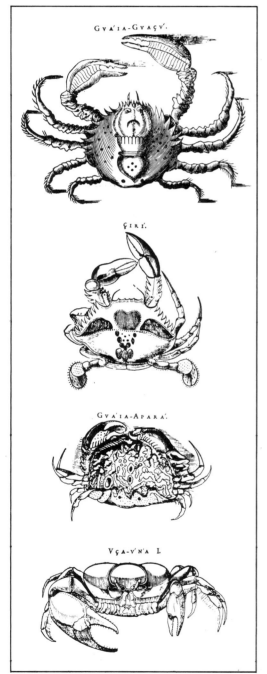

Crabs, Dodo and Humming Bird. Copper engravings from W. Piso and G. Marcgrave's *Historia Naturalis Brasiliae,* 2nd edition, 1658. The Dodo, a native of Madagascar seems oddly out of place in a book on the natural history of Brazil.

seems to have been lost in the engraving process. The book's crabs and lobsters, for instance, are sometimes no better than caricatures.

As with so many of these early books, the best picture is the frontispiece. That of the second edition of 1658 is especially interesting, as it shows, among other things, a Dodo, an Indian rhinoceros and a Babirusa pig. Piso and Marcgrave's book is one of the earliest to deal with the natural history of a tropical region; most of its illustrations are refreshingly new and are founded on facts rather than myths. The book-buying public, however, have often supported the perpetuation in graphic form of well-loved fables while overlooking natural history books in which the illustrations do not hit them between the eyes. For these, if for no other reasons, the illustrations in Topsell's *History,* unlike those in the *Historia Naturalis Brasiliae,* have been almost constantly in print in one form or another ever since they were first published. The scientific importance of the Piso and Marcgrave illustrations has been fully realised only in recent years, and attempts to locate the original drawings—so far unsuccessful—have involved painstaking research by scholars and delicate political manoeuvring in several countries on each side of the Iron Curtain.

Topsell was perhaps the only seventeenth-century writer on natural history whose ignorance of the subject is conspicuously evident in almost every line he wrote, but there were other men who were so fond of tall stories about fabulous animals that they could not resist the temptation to repeat them, often with literary and graphic embellishments. One such

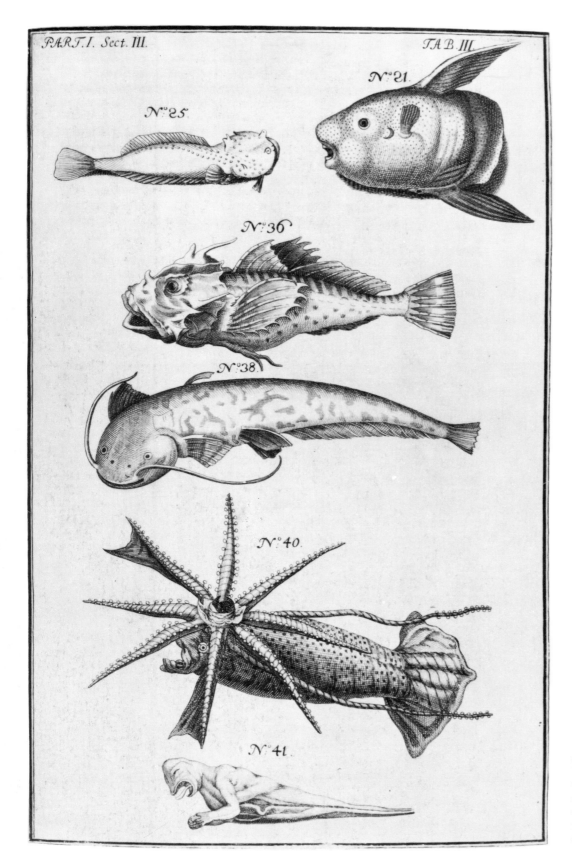

Fishes, a Squid and a 'Mermaid'. Copper engraving from Oliger Jacobaeus and Johannes Laurentzen's *Museum Regium*, 1710. The sunfish at the top right could have been copied from Salviani's figure (see p. 26). The 'mermaid' was a fish of the skate or ray tribe artificially mutilated and distorted. Such a monstrosity, which was sometimes called a 'jenny haniver' was offered to gullible collectors such as the owner of the collection containing the specimens illustrated in this plate; it was sometimes passed off as a mermaid.

man in the mid-seventeenth century was Johann Jonston, a well-travelled and prolific writer on natural history who has been described as a weak successor to Aldrovandi (the weakness being in his lack of stature as an encyclopedist).

Jonston's compilations are usually full of pictures, though their quality varies from good to execrable. Most of those which grace—or disgrace—his *De Quadrupedibus*, for example, display such a stony impassivity as to suggest that the artist and engraver had worked from statues rather than live animals. In any case, some of the illustrations probably never had living counterparts. A tuskless hippopotamus with paws and another one with a dog's head and bovine hooves look more improbable, but rather less lively, than a griffin which shares Jonston's Plate 49 with them.

Apparently Jonston could not or would not distinguish between the creatures haunting the misty but always accessible regions of human imagination and those roaming in sunlit but uncharted regions of the real

Tab. XLIX

Griffin and two versions of the Hippopotamus. Copper engraving from Johann Jonston's *Historia Naturalis, De Quadrupedibus,* 1650–53. An eloquent reminder that the Age of Reason was still some years away.

world. That he may have preferred the former is indicated by the frontispiece to his book which is nearly filled by a couple of heavyweight centaurs holding a lion's skin between them. Through their legs may be seen the distant and inconsequential forms of an elephant, a giraffe and two lions. In fairness to Jonston, it should be pointed out that the frontispiece designs in his day, and well into the eighteenth century, often incorporated motifs which were outlandish in relation to the texts that followed them. In many ways, too, Jonston's writings were ahead of those of his predecessors and some of his contemporaries, and his work on fishes was exceptionally good for its time.

Jonston's approach to zoology was not typical of those commentators who published treatises on animals in the second half of the seventeenth century. Thus, the folio-sized plates of Claude Perrault's *Mémoires pour servir à l'Histoire des Animaux* (1671–76), though primarily devoted to portraying anatomical features, also contain well-engraved illustrations

TAB. VIII

Falco peregrinus.
The Peregrine or
haggard Falcon

Gyrfalco.
The Gerfalcon.

Peregrine Falcon and Gyrfalcon. Brass engraving from Francis Willughby and John Ray's *Ornithology*, 1678. In his preface to this book, Ray implies that the engravings were made in brass and not in copper.

Moths, Caterpillars and Pupae. Copper engravings making up four of the small pages of Johannes Goedart's *Metamorphosis et Historia Naturalis Insectorum*, 1663. Note the human faces that Goedart has given to two of the pupae.

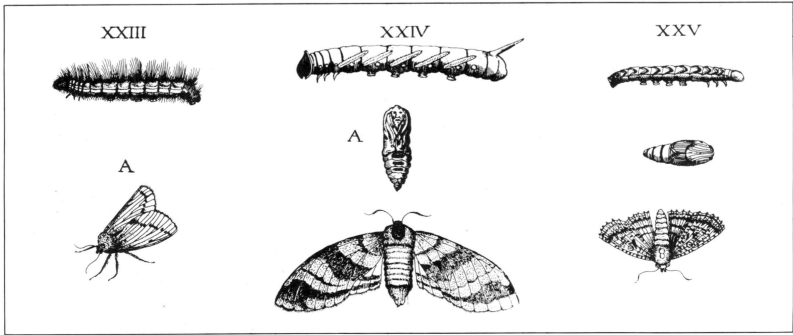

XXIII   XXIV   XXV

A

A

Porcupine and Hedgehog. Part of a copper engraving from Alexander Pitfield's *Natural History of Animals,* 1702. The upper part of the plate displays the animals' internal organs. Pitfield's book, which went into several editions, was adapted from Claude Perrault's *Mémoires pour servir à l'Histoire des Animaux,* 1671–76. The engraving of the porcupine is distinctly superior in conception to that of the hedgehog.

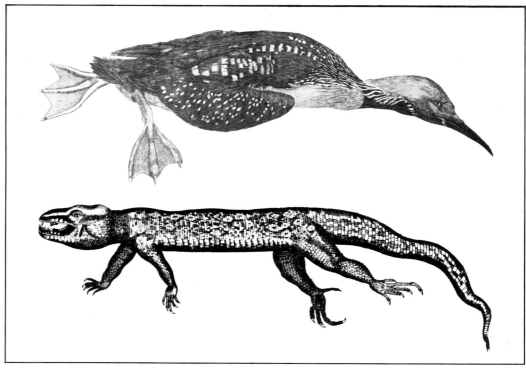

Right : Black-Throated Diver and Lizard, both very clearly not drawn from living animals. Copper engravings from Ole Worm's *Museum Wormianum,* 1655.

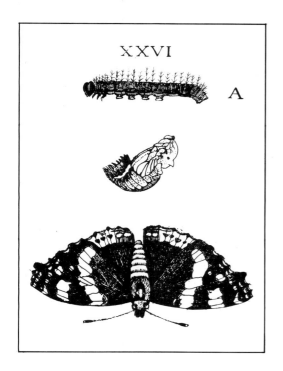

of the animals whose guts are so artistically displayed. Perrault's porcupine, in a delicately-engraved landscape setting, is particularly striking. The visual excellence of this book must have contributed substantially to its popularity; the illustrations were reproduced many times in the works of other writers.

While Perrault's *Mémoires* were being issued, John Ray, the great botanical systematiser, was steering a book on birds through the press. This was the *Ornithology* of Francis Willughby, which first appeared in a Latin edition in 1676. The manuscript of this well-illustrated folio volume had been left incomplete by Willughby who died, still a young man, in 1672. The illustrations, paid for by Willughby's widow, Emma, are well engraved if occasionally rather lifeless. Though some are copied from illustrations in other books, many are new. Some of the birds are shown perched on isolated branches or on the ground, or as corpses. Evidently the engraver worked from various sources, and we have a very good idea of their nature because Ray tells us, in his preface to the book, that Willughby bought a volume of pictures showing waterfowl of the Rhine from a Strasbourg fisherman and another volume of coloured

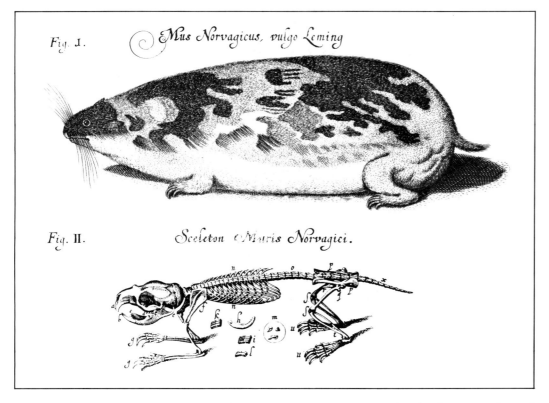

Fig. I.   *Mus Norvagicus, vulgo Leming*

Fig. II.   *Sceleton Muris Norvagici.*

Lemming and its skeleton. Copper engraving from Ole Worm's *Museum Wormianum*, 1655.

Right: Armadillo, Fishes and other curiosities. Two copper-engraved plates from Nehemiah Grew's *Musaeum Regalis Societatis,* 1681.

Right: Sinistral species of *Busycon* and other marine gastropod shells. Drawn and engraved by Susanna or Anna Lister, copper engravings from the 1770 edition of Martin Lister's *Historia Conchyliorum.*

'Eme'—Cassowary. Woodcut from Cornelius Geraldson's *Additions to the Sea Iurnall of Navigation of the Hollanders,* 1598.

drawings from someone in Nuremberg. Willughby had also employed good artists to draw some species. Many of the original drawings are still in existence, and the accompanying manuscript notes make it clear that some at least were drawn from preserved specimens. With this Willughby material (now held in the University of Nottingham Library), there are two sets of published engravings of birds. The person who engraved the illustrations for Willughby's book would have had the opportunity to copy some of these earlier engravings. The pictures in many early natural history books may have been brought together in just such a haphazard manner.

The *Ornithology* was the most important of several books researched by Willughby and edited by Ray. In the *Historia Piscium* (1686), the figures of fish are well engraved and again there is tangible evidence of the sources of many of them in the form of drawings, paintings and engravings preserved at Nottingham. The excellence of these Willughby and Ray compilations is best appreciated by comparing them with other natural history books produced in seventeenth-century England. Nehemiah Grew's *Musaeum Regalis Societatis* (1681), an exposition of the contents of the Royal Society's collection of natural and artificial curiosities, has engravings of shells, fishes and other animals, but they are dull, lifeless and lacking in the boldness of execution that characterises the *Ornithology.* In contrast, the *Historia Conchyliorum* of Martin Lister, a good friend of Ray's, has many fine engravings of shells, but their arrangement on the plates gives this otherwise commendable book an unprofessional appearance compared with those which Ray edited for Francis Willughby.

Cornelius Geraldson's *Additions to the Sea Iurnall of Navigation of the Hollanders* (1598), dealing with the first Dutch expedition to the East Indies, includes what may be the earliest published illustration of a cassowary (there called an 'Eme bird'). Because of the great rarity of this book, its one animal engraving was overlooked by later compilers of natural history encyclopedias. Travellers were expected to meet the unusual, the rare and the frightening, and their books usually continued to satisfy the public's predilection for strange and fearsome creatures on land and in the sea. At one time, as readers of *Sir John Mandeville's Travels* will know, travellers filled their accounts with tales of apocryphal creatures. Thus, in later years, readers of books such as Geraldson's were rightly suspicious of things like the 'Eme bird' and were disinclined to accept them as authentic. As early cartographers frequently adorned their atlases and charts with fanciful and unfriendly creatures, it is hardly

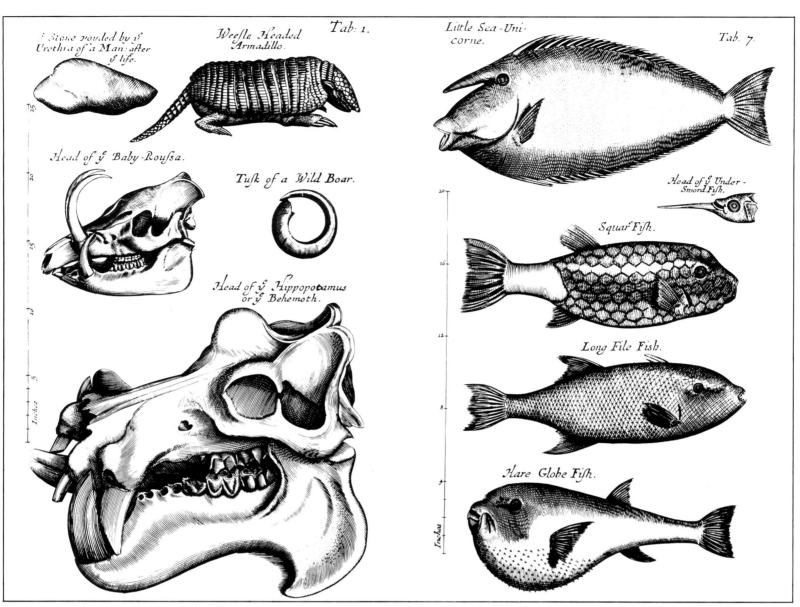

Tab: 1.

ɣ Stone voyded by ɣ
Urethra of a Man: after
ɣ life.

Weesle Headed
Armadillo.

Head of ɣ Baby-Roussa.

Tusk of a Wild Boar.

Head of ɣ Hippopotamus
or ɣ Behemoth.

Little Sea-Uni-
corne.

Tab. 7.

Head of ɣ Under-
Sword Fish.

Squar Fish.

Long File Fish.

Hare Globe Fish.

Inches

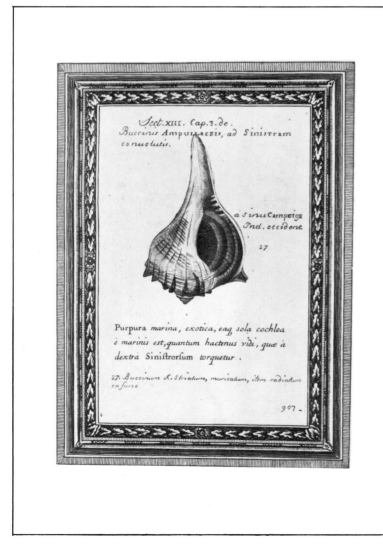

Sect. XIII. Cap. 3. de
Buccinis Ampullaceis, ad Sinistram
convolutis.

a Sinu Campeige
Ind. occident.

27

Purpura marina, exotica, eaq, sola cochlea
è marinis est, quantum hactenus vidi, quæ a
dextra Sinistrorsum torquetur.

27. Buccinum R. Striatum, muricatum, item radiatum
ex fusco

907.

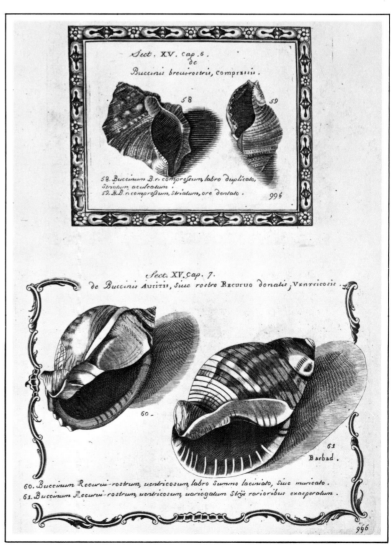

Sect. XV. cap. 6.
de
Buccinis brevirostris, compressis.

58

59

58. Buccinum B. r. compressum, labro duplicato,
Striatum aculeatum.
59. B. B. r. compressum, Striatum, ore dentato.

995

Sect. XV. cap. 7.
de Buccinis Auritis, Sive rostro Recurvo donatis; Ventricosis.

60

61
Barbad.

60. Buccinum Recurvi-rostrum, ventricosum, labro summo laciniato, sive muricato.
61. Buccinum Recurvi-rostrum, ventricosum, variegatum Strijs rarioribus exasperatum.

996

Hippopotamus. Copper engraving from Job Ludolphus's *New History of Ethiopia* (English translation by J. P. Gent), 1682.

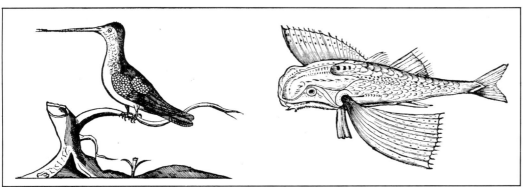

Left: Humming Bird and Flying Fish. Copper engraving from Ole Worm's *Museum Wormianum*, 1655.

Flying Fish. Copper engraving from Sir Thomas Herbert's *Relation of some Yeares Travaille . . . into Afrique and the greater Asia*, 1634.

Herd of Elephants. Copper engraving from Job Ludolphus's *New History of Ethiopia*, English translation, 1682.

surprising if travellers using them were predisposed to see and subsequently to report sightings of the non-existent. More often than not, the monsters they reported had a real foundation, but after the artist or engraver had finished work, there was often little resemblance between what the traveller saw and what the picture in his book implied he had seen.

Even familiar animals could be transformed into monsters like those in medieval manuscripts. Sir Thomas Herbert's *Relation of Some Yeares Travaille . . . into Afrique and the greater Asia*, first published in 1634, has a picture of a so-called 'Sharke fish' devouring a man. Although the man is real enough, the 'Sharke fish' is less like a shark than a crocodile-headed, scaly-backed monster with the flukes of a whale.

'A Sharke Fish' devouring a man. Copper engraving from Sir Thomas Herbert's *Relation of some Yeares Travaille . . . into Afrique and the greater Asia*, 1634.

'African' scene. Copper engraving from Olfert Dapper's *Description de l'Afrique*, 1686. Heraldic lions, bestiary-inspired snake's head and accurately observed tulip do not make a convincing combination.

Artists and engravers commissioned to illustrate books describing distant lands did not always treat animals in so cavalier a fashion. In 1667, Athanasius Kircher published his *China Monumentis*, in which some of the natural phenomena of China are described and illustrated. One charming picture shows several turtles ambling along contentedly while the sun's rays play on a clutch of turtle eggs half buried in the sand. The artist/engraver has attempted to reconstruct a scene he could never have witnessed. But for the shape of the eggs, which are like those of a bird instead of being more spherical, he has succeeded well.

Olfert Dapper was another author who wrote a book about a far-off land without ever setting foot in it. His bulky book on Africa proved to be a very successful compilation and was translated into several languages out of the original Dutch. In their attempts to reconstruct scenes in African settings, Dapper's artists, predictably, did not always succeed. One of their less authentic reconstructions shows several lions of a distinctly heraldic nature sharing a forest glade with a large snake which looks as though it has just escaped from an early painting of the Garden of Eden; in the foreground is an unlikely tulip. Such illustrations, it must be assumed, fulfilled a primarily decorative function and helped to sell the book. But as the eighteenth century approached, the intellectual climate of Europe began to undergo a radical change. The Age of Reason, in which Natural History would dethrone Geometry as the supreme science, was dawning.

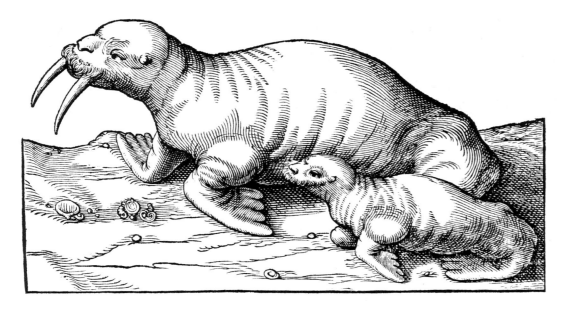

Seals. Copper engraving from Ole Worm's *Museum Wormianum*, 1655.

42

CHAPTER IV
A Comedy of Animals

From 1680 to 1720, Newtonian science and the massive intellects of Descartes, Leibnitz, Spinoza, Locke and other philosophers pushed forward a revolution in human thought which effectively buried the ancient, medieval and Renaissance worlds and laid the foundations of the one we now inhabit. Although Nature and Reason were placed on pedestals and universally worshipped, eighteenth-century Europe became a battleground for conflicting and variant philosophies. At the same time, it became a proving ground for freedom of thought and speech and, above all, for freedom to differ. This ultimate freedom allowed two very different personalities to influence the pattern of natural history studies in that century: Buffon and Linnaeus. Directly or indirectly, both had a considerable effect on the course of zoological iconography.

Early eighteenth-century animal art, with some exceptions, is neither very lively nor very colourful. The published illustrations of animals were usually based on dead, often poorly-preserved, specimens and the attitudes portrayed are thus often unnatural. Invertebrates, or rather their remains, were sometimes portrayed very well, as long as no attempt was made to place them in natural settings. In the *Museum Gottwaldianum* (1714), the shells are particularly well engraved, at least as well as those in Lister's *Historia Conchyliorum*, and there is an excellent figure of a

Coconut Crab. Copper engraving from Georg Eberhard Rumpf's *Amboinsche Rariteitkamer*, 1705.

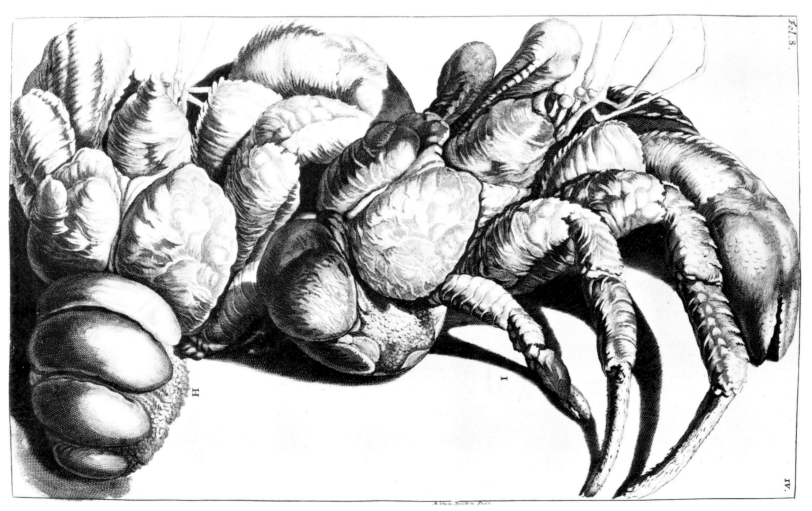

Turtle. Copper engraving from Christophorus Gottwald's *Museum Gottwaldianum*, 1714.

King Crab. Copper engraving from Georg Eberhard Rumpf's *Amboinsche Rariteitkamer*, 1705.

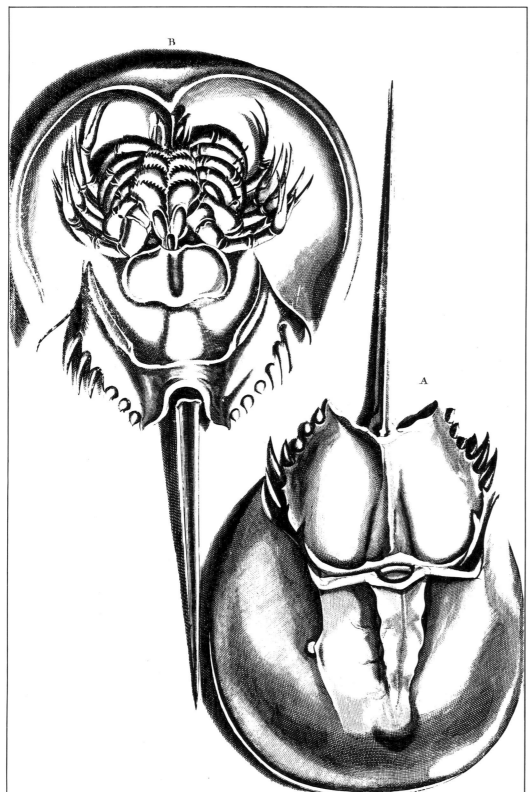

Right: Tuscan animals and various crustaceans and shells. Copper engravings from James Petiver's *Opera*, 1767.

Right: Part of a collection of natural curiosities. Copper engravings from Levin Vincent's *Wondertoonel der Nature*, 1706. Note the reversed coiling of the seashells. Engravers frequently failed to appreciate that a shell's direction of coiling should be engraved in reverse to ensure that it is reproduced correctly on the printed plate.

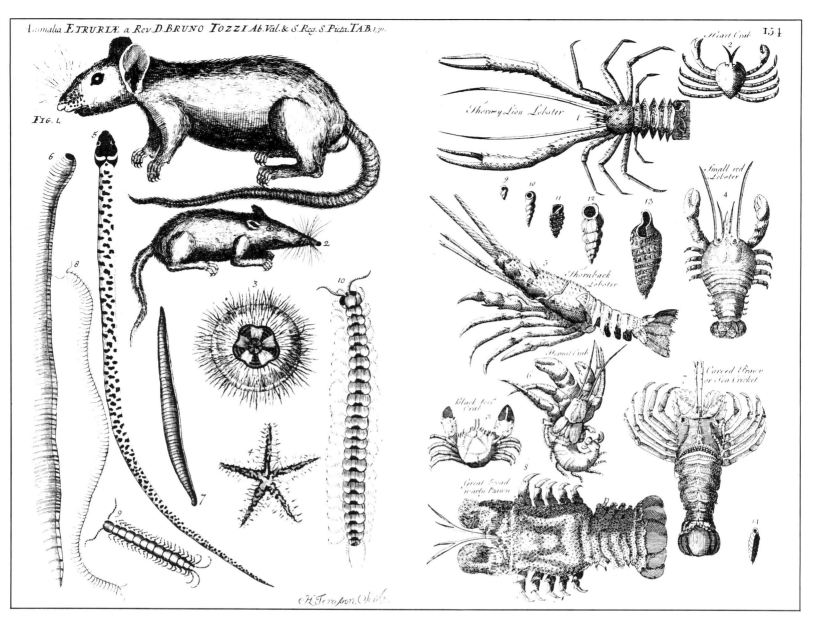

TAB. XXXVIII.

turtle. Similarly, in the *Wondertoonel der Nature* of Levin Vincent (1706), the shells and corals are well engraved although the artist has crowded them together in, on and under the cabinets which housed the actual specimens in Vincent's museum.

Many of the natural objects amassed by the Dutch apothecary Albert Seba were described and illustrated in the four folio volumes of his *Locupletissimi Rerum Naturalium* (1734–65). The engravings make it clear that the artist had seen his subjects only in Seba's museum, although he

Two plates and two details from Albert Seba's *Locupletissimi Rerum Naturalium*, vol. 3, 1758. Note the unsystematic gathering of Opossum, Armadillo and various exotic birds in a single plate and the attempts to instil some life into the subjects, with the exception of the artistically coiled but incontrovertibly dead snake.

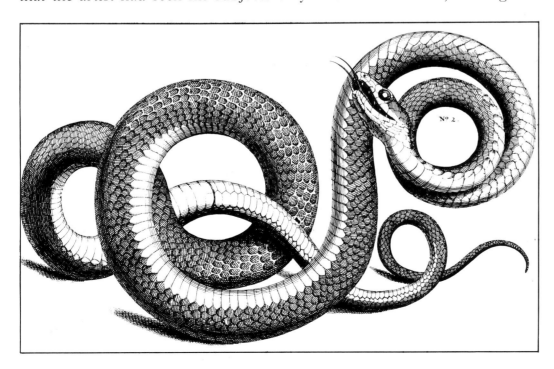

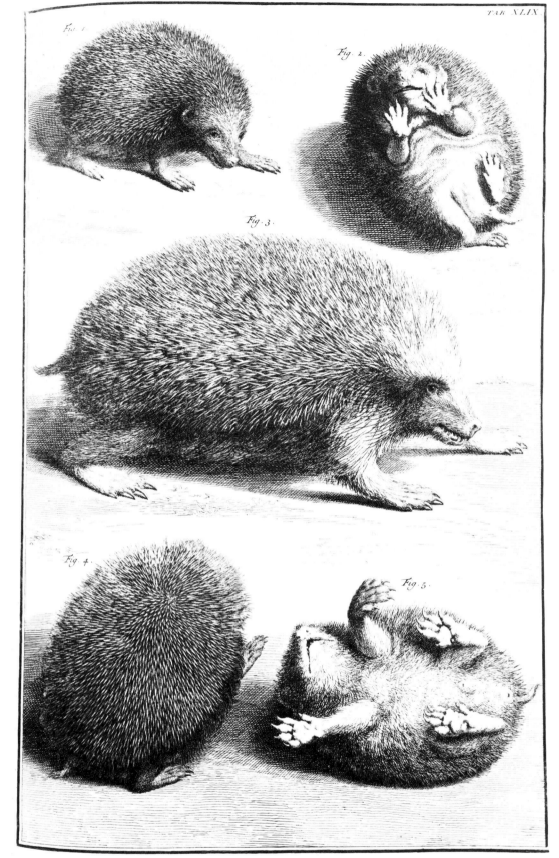

made some brave attempts at giving life-like attitudes to some of the higher animals, in which category Seba's notorious hydra presumably falls. The book is noteworthy more for the artistry of the illustrative work than for its value as a contribution to natural history.

European artists still had to rely a great deal on their imaginations when depicting creatures from far-off lands and oceans. At best, they may have had a glimpse of an exotic animal brought home alive in a ship's hold but more often than not they had to work from a badly preserved specimen or from inadequate sketches. For some artists, the mangled carcase or untutored scrawl was enough material from which to work up a finished drawing. For others, probably for most, the indispensable ingredients of a drawing came out of their own heads.

There is abundant evidence that artistic licence sometimes ran riot. A perfect example is the *Poissons, Ecrevisses et Crabes* of the Amsterdam author and publisher Louis Renard. Improbably swimming and crawling over the hundred plates of this folio book which Renard presented to an incredulous public in 1718 and 1719 are weirdly formed and riotously coloured fishes, crabs and lobsters, all inhabitants of Pacific waters. These fantastic hand-coloured figures would not look out of place among the wilder creations of mid twentieth-century art. The only comparable images in the whole of zoological literature were derived from Renard's originals.

Renard's phantasmagoria were apparently irresistible to the Dutch writer Valentijn whose *Oud en Nieuw Oost-Indien*, an encyclopedic survey published between 1724 and 1726 of what were then the Dutch East Indies, contains many engravings of fish conspicuously modelled on Renard's. Valentijn's fishes are beached in untidy assemblages, incongruous against the well-drawn seascapes which usually form an integral part of his engravings. Valentijn could not resist the temptation to improve upon Renard's grotesque, double-plate picture of a mermaid

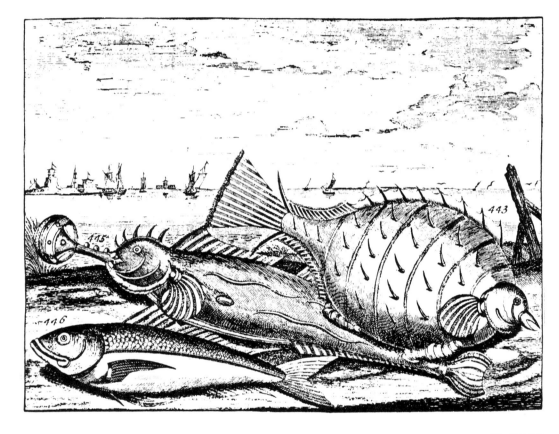

Exotic fishes supposedly found in Indonesian waters. Copper engravings from François Valentijn's *Oud en Nieuw Oost-Indien*, vol. 3, 1726.

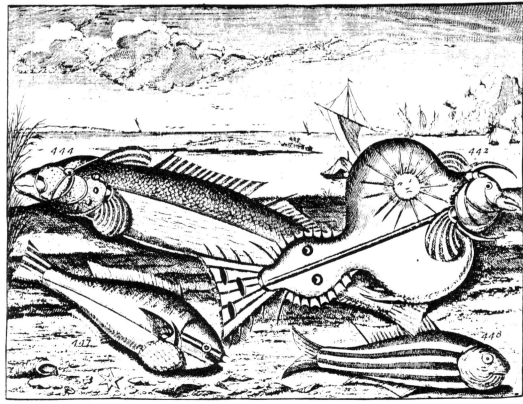

Right : Moth. Hand-coloured copper engraving from Maria Sibylle Merian's *Metamorphosis Insectorum Surinamensium*, 1714. As in all her compositions, Merian pays equal attention to the insects and the plants.

49

'taken off the coast of the island of Borneo'. His version still has the inordinately long fish tail and webbed fingers of Renard's mermaid (both engravings being based on the same original drawing), but Valentijn glamourises everything above the discreet, leafy skirt.

Maria Sibylle Merian was less gullible than Valentijn. In 1698, this extraordinary woman, born 51 years earlier of a German father and a Swiss mother, set sail with her daughter for the Dutch colony of Surinam in South America and remained there two years, collecting and painting insects and other animals and flowers. Already the authoress of several exquisitely illustrated books on insects and flowers, she spent the next three years working on the book which was to represent the culmination of her career as a zoological and botanical artist. Her *Metamorphosis Insectorum Surinamensium*, published in 1705, was easily the most magnificent work on insects so far produced. It combines science and art in unequal proportions, meeting the demands of art at the expense, when necessary, of science—Maria came from a very artistic family and for a time had been married to a painter of flowers. Sometimes an insect is incorrectly portrayed, sometimes a flower or a fruit, but in spite of the incongruities Merian's engraved plates are usually accurate and always visually pleasing; when hand coloured, they are enchanting.

Merian and Renard are at the opposite poles of zoological art in early eighteenth-century Europe. Merian, who showed future generations of zoological and botanical artists just what was possible if they combined artistic talent with close observation of nature, may be forgiven her few deviations from the path of scientific rectitude. Renard, who showed how far it is possible to stray from that path, may also be forgiven, even though he utterly fails to instruct, for it is a rare gift to be able to amuse.

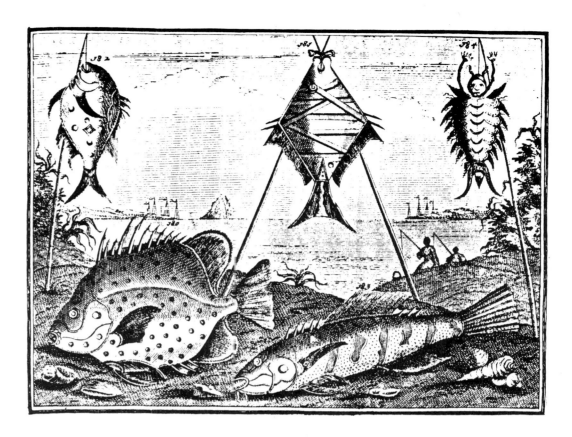

Mermaid and fishes. Copper engravings from François Valentijn's *Oud en Nieuw Oost-Indien*, 1724–26. The mermaid is a glamorised version of an engraving in Louis Renard's *Poissons, Ecrevisses et Crabes*, 1718–19.

If the most celebrated zoological artists of all time, the Audubons, Goulds, Haeckels and Swainsons, may be said to have a spiritual ancestor then it is difficult to think of a more worthy claimant to the title than Maria Sibylle Merian. Certainly she was a highly original artist, and her portrayals of living insects and other animals were imbued with a charm, a minuteness of observation and an artistic sensibility that had not previously been seen in a natural history book. Directly or indirectly, she may have exerted a long-term influence on the work of subsequent zoological artists and the authors of books in which animal illustrations appear.

Merian's work contrasts strangely with that of another traveller/artist, Mark Catesby, whose *Natural History of Carolina* was published between 1731 and 1743. Like Merian, he sought and found his inspiration in a region far from home. Unlike her, he possessed only a limited, if natural, artistic talent. He spent several years in Virginia and the Carolinas collecting and studying animals and plants; then after a sojourn in the Bahamas, he returned to England in 1726. The rest of his life was spent raising plants, drawing and painting natural objects, and writing and illustrating books.

Catesby's *Natural History of Carolina* is a monument to patience, endurance and persistence. Too poor to pay for the services of professional engravers, he learned the engraving process himself and transferred his own drawings to the copper plates. Then he coloured all the engraved plates himself. Apart from the typesetting, this was very much a one-man venture.

As well as providing us with an invaluable record of the flora and fauna of a part of North America in the eighteenth century, Catesby gives some fascinating details of his working methods. 'In designing the Plants,' he writes, 'I always did them while fresh and just gather'd: And the Animals, particularly the Birds, I painted them while alive (except a very few) and gave them their gestures peculiar to every kind of Bird, and where it would admit of, I have adapted the Birds to those Plants on which they fed. Fish, which do not retain their Colours when out of their Element, I painted at different times, having a succession of them procur'd while the former lost their colours'. Above all, he devoted his energies to recording the appearance of the birds, there being 'a greater Variety of the feather'd kind than of any other Animals (at least to come at) and excelling in the Beauty of their Colours, besides having oftenest relation to the Plants on which they feed and frequent.'

Sciurus   Cornus

Catesby has peculiar ideas about bird and plant relationships. He often superimposes a bird on a plant whether or not there is any natural connection, as though the arrangement were obligatory. This curious feature is nowhere displayed with more charming absurdity than in his portrayal of a flamingo. It is shown standing on a strip of beach in front of what looks like a leafless tree approximately the same height as

Chipmunk and Flamingo. Two hand-coloured copper engravings from Mark Catesby's *Natural History of Carolina, Florida, and the Bahama Islands*, 1731–43. The combination of species on Catesby's plates was partly dictated by economy and sometimes produced incongruous results—see also illustration on p. 105.

T.73

Phænicopterus.

Keratophiton &c.

53

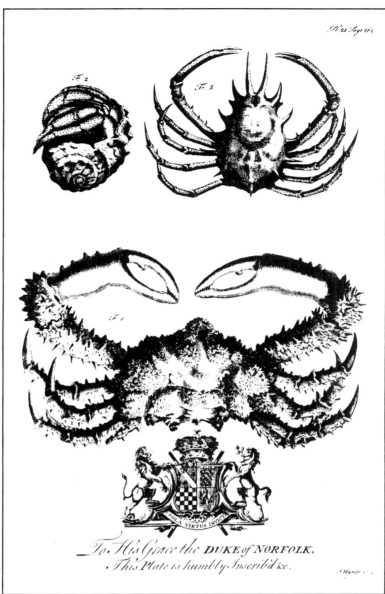

the bird. The accompanying text, however, reveals that this 'tree' (which is actually a gorgonian coral and thus of animal origin) grows to a height of about two feet, and is found 'in great Plenty at the bottom of the shallow Seas and Channels of the *Bahama* Islands, the water there being exceedingly clear.' Catesby adds, 'I have plainly seen them growing to the white Rocks in above ten Fathom Water.' Perhaps he had in mind occasional artistic and scientific incongruities like this when he wrote, 'As I was not bred a Painter, I hope some faults in Perspective, and other Niceties, may more readily be excused.'

Compared with Catesby's book, a colourful enterprise in every way, the nearly contempoarary *Natural History of Barbados* (1750) by Griffith Hughes is rather dull. It shows a very different approach to the illustration of New World natural history. Each plate is 'humbly inscribed' to a nobleman and bears an appropriate crest above which natural objects are distributed symmetrically, or as symmetrically as their diverse shapes allow. The keynote is elegance; it was not the author's intention to make naturalists of his wealthy patrons but rather to help satisfy their taste for fine libraries. On the other hand, his crabs, sea urchins and the rest are faithfully copied from the real things and well engraved. But they lack the sparkle, the originality, the innocence, the individuality and the exuberance of the animals which enliven *The Natural History of Carolina*.

After the elegant dullness of Hughes, it is easy to forgive Catesby his pictures of fish besporting themselves in front of the branches of trees and his coral shooting up from dry land. The most memorable pictures in zoological art are not always the most accurate and are frequently those in which the artist has allowed his or her imagination free rein.

Hughes was not the only author to dedicate individual plates to members of the nobility or to other wealthy and influential figures. Until well into the nineteenth century, it was a common practice for an author to curry favour in this way in order to gain financial or other support. Without this support, many fine illustrated books could not have been published. Before the era of photo-mechanical reproductions, the publication of a high-quality book was usually a very costly business. Early book catalogues and advertising brochures put out by publishing firms show that only the wealthy could afford to buy a sumptuously illustrated book before the nineteenth century. Usually, the only way such a book could be produced was by securing a list of subscribers whose advance commitment lessened the financial risk. Naturally anyone who supported an expensive literary venture was flattered to be named in the book; hence the flattering dedications, inscriptions, crests and lists of subscribers.

The scientific study of animals progressed steadily throughout the eighteenth century, helped by improvements in the microscope and microscopical techniques and underwritten by wealthy or influential people who were eager to be associated with the discovery of previously unknown forms of life and gave their patronage to travelling naturalists. More and more, the nature of life itself came to occupy the attentions of the more philosophically inclined. This was not a century of great innovators, as the previous century had been and the succeeding one was

Corals. Copper engraving from J. S. Schröter's *Musei Gottwaldiani Testaceorum, Stellarum Marinarum*, 1782.

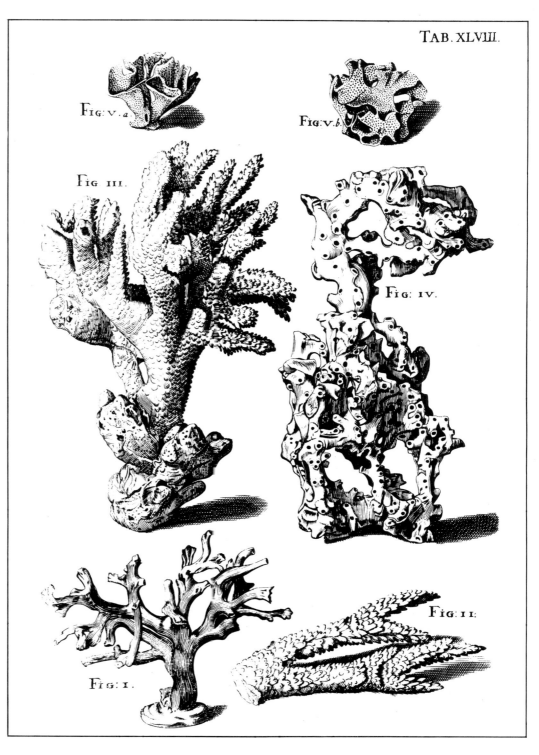

TAB. XLVIII.

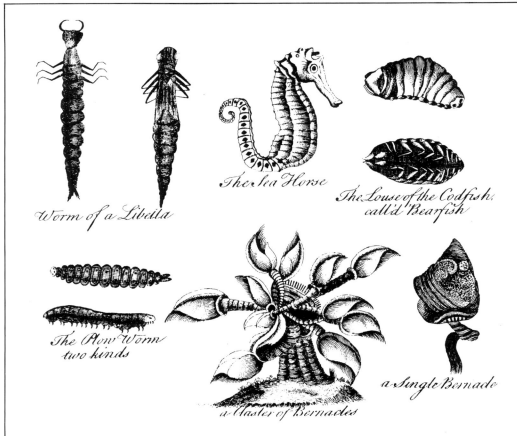

Worm of a Libella

The Sea Horse

The Louse of the Codfish, call'd Bearfish

The Plow Worm two kinds

a Master of Bernacles

a Single Bernade

Gestochen auf Kosten des

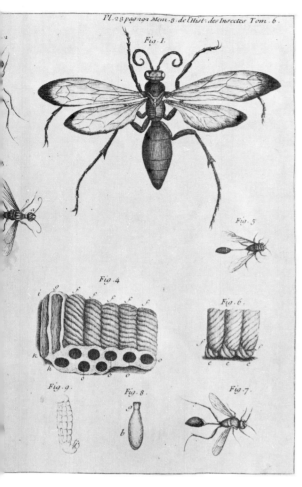

Digger Wasps. Copper engraving from R.A.F. de Réaumur's *Mémoires pour servir à l'Histoire des Insectes*, 1734–42.

to be, but it spawned a host of competent, often brilliant investigators and observers who built on the epochal discoveries which had been made by Harvey, Malpighi and Borelli about the working of the human body, and by Swammerdam and Leeuwenhoek in microscopy. The eighteenth-century biologists produced many impressive and well-illustrated books which their successors, in turn, could utilise in their own researches.

In addition to the wide-ranging activities of such men of mark as Haller, Camper, Spallanzani, Pallas and Hunter, there were the more specialised researches of such careful observers as Réaumur and Trembley. René-Antoine Ferchault de Réaumur's six-volume *Mémoires pour servir à l'Histoire des Insectes*, which continued and refined the work of Swammerdam, is filled with illustrations of insects and their anatomy. Abraham Trembley's *Polypes*, a detailed study of the freshwater *Hydra*, started research into regeneration in animals. Then there was Charles de Geer who continued Réaumur's investigations, concentrating on previously neglected insect forms and publishing a sequel to Réaumur's great work which was in every way its equal. And we should not forget Pieter Lyonet, entomologist, shell collector and one-time diplomat, whose wonderful monograph on the larva of the goat-moth caterpillar is without equal even today. All of them were observers—not a theoriser among them—and fine artists, too. They may have pulled everything to pieces, but the pieces were beautifully drawn.

There was, however, one theoriser: Georges-Louis Leclerc, Comte de Buffon, the philosopher *par excellence* for whom style was everything, the significance of well-observed facts nothing.

Disenchanted with mathematics, which until then had been queen of the sciences, Buffon set about the task of acquainting mankind with the marvels of the natural world. On the pretext of producing a sumptuous catalogue of Louis XV's 'cabinet of curiosities', he launched the first

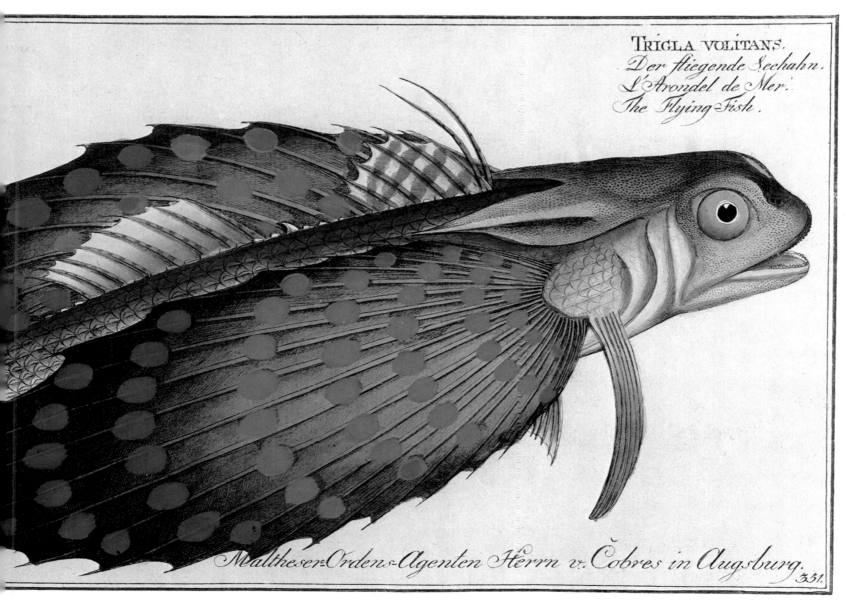

Fishes. Copper engraving from Laurentius Theodore Gronovius's *Zoophylacium Gronovianum*, 1781.

Hornbill, Giant Anteater, Female Panther, Hedgehog with and without spines. Four copper engravings after original drawings by de Sève from Buffon's *Histoire Naturelle, Generale et Particuliere avec la Description du Cabinet du Roi*, 1749–1804. The ruins form an incongruous background for the Anteater and help to deprive it of any semblance of life.

volume of his monumental *Histoire Naturelle, Générale et Particulière avec la Description du Cabinet du Roi* in 1749, when he was in his early and brilliant forties. Publication continued throughout the rest of his dazzling life and the enterprise built up such impetus that volumes went on appearing for some years after his death in 1788. These, in turn, were followed by extensive *Suites à Buffon* and innumerable editions of 'Buffon' in various languages

The illustrations to his original edition are exquisitely engraved and exude aristocratic elegance and charm. Whether the animal depicted is a lion or a pig, it is shown as if in a tableau revealed to our curious gaze by the drawing aside of a curtain—this was probably just the effect intended because some of the scenes actually include a curtain drawn to one side. The animals do not seem like wild beasts roaming free in their native woods, deserts and mountains, but like actors performing among stage props and painted scenery for the benefit of the lords of creation.

Buffon's animal engravings—most of the ones he lived to see were by de Sève—had a considerable effect on zoological art, and pastiches of his elegant set pieces proliferated in such diverse publications as Alessandri and Scattaglia's *Descrizioni degli Animali* (1773–75) and Church's *Cabinet of Quadrupeds* (1805). On balance, their influence was beneficial rather than harmful, but they are still just elegant set pieces which tell us more about Buffon and his circle than about the animals themselves.

Strangely enough, this is as good a place as any to introduce the subject of sporting art. Buffon and his tame artists must surely have seen many portrayals of hunting and domestic scenes in which the animals were truly animated. Cattle, horses, sheep and other domestic animals had been realistically portrayed by artists for many years, and paintings by such seventeenth-century artists as Cuyp, Potter and Berchem were probably very familiar to Buffon and his circle, who may also have seen the wildfowl pictures of Hondecoeter, Bernaerts and other Flemish painters, or the less gentle hunting scenes by Rubens and Snyders. But none of these influences reached the pages of the *Histoire Naturelle*.

As well as paintings and drawings, numerous publications, usually in the form of sets of prints, had provided evocative portrayals of hunting and domestic scenes. Some of the earliest of these were produced by Dürer, Lucas van Leyden and Hans Baldung. In 1578, an extensive series of plates depicting, among other subjects, aspects of the hunt in sixteenth-century Europe was published under the title of *Venationes* by the Flemish artist Giovanni della Strada (or Stradanus). The same series contains some exotic items such as elephant hunting and ostrich hunting. Della Strada's pupil, Antonio de Tempesta, published many prints in the same manner. Hans Bol's *Venationis, Piscationis et Aucupii Typii*, published in 1582, contains a mixture of European and exotic hunting scenes. But none of these galleries of living animals seems to have had any influence on the *Histoire Naturelle*.

Among the finest published illustrations of wildlife which could have been available to Buffon and his minions were those in the *Betrachtung der Wilden Thiere (Contemplation of Wild Animals)* by Barthold Heinrich Brockes, which was published in 1736. The folio-sized engravings by J. E. Ridinger show animals in natural settings, more often than not being hunted by men with firearms or by mounted men armed with pikes and other weapons of the chase. The most spirited and best composed pictures are those with human figures in them, although one or two of those without humans in view, such as the group of chamois in their mountain retreat and the deer foraging by a stream in a forest clearing, are also very fine. The minuteness of observation in these lovely studies is astonishing and shows intense understanding of the habits and postures of wild animals. In these exquisite engravings, Ridinger has captured the natural elegance of his subjects rather than using his artistry to present them in an artificially elegant manner. But again, they seem to have made no impression on the artists whose works adorn the *Histoire Naturelle*.

An illustrious contemporary of Buffon was Jean-Baptiste Oudry, one of the finest and most prolific painters of birds and beasts, particularly those associated with blood sports, that France has ever produced. Many animal subjects by Oudry, who died only six years after publication

Left: Small Tortoiseshell Butterfly. Hand-coloured copper engraving from Jacob L'Admiral's *Nauwkeurige Waarnemingen omtrent de Veranderingen van Veele Insekten*, 1774. Though not without charm, L'Admiral's plates lack the draughtsmanship and delicate colouring of those by Moses Harris in *The Aurelian* (see illustration on p. 104) which evidently inspired them.

Below: Garden Tiger Moth. Hand-coloured copper engraving from J. C. Sepp's *Beschouwing der Wonderen Gods*, 1762–1860.

'The Eared or Horned Dob-Chick', i.e. Slavonian or Horned Grebe. Hand-coloured copper engraving from George Edwards's *Natural History of Uncommon Birds*, 1743–51. Edwards was taught by Mark Catesby how to engrave his own plates.

of Buffon's first volume of the *Histoire*, may be seen worked into magnificent tapestries, for he became director of the Beauvais tapestry factory and was later also inspector of the Gobelins factory, designing for it the hunting scenes of Louis XV. In much of his work, which Buffon must have seen time and again in the fashionable salons he frequented, Oudry shows animals doing the things *living* animals do: fighting, strutting, flapping, pecking, galloping. Oudry's animals must

have been all over Paris, but they had no effect on the *Histoire Naturelle*.

Buffon's artists had their own ways of showing animals off to best advantage and always endeavoured to make them look clean, neat and innocent. Usually, they gave them only a few stage props for company. Martinet, the artist responsible for the bird illustrations, removed even these comforts and scarcely gave his subjects room enough to flap their wings, so tightly are their gaudy bodies squeezed into the allotted spaces. They are made to fit the book and not the book to fit them. These bird pictures are not significantly better than many of those in Willughby's *Ornithology* of 1676, but the hand colouring increases their appeal. They are still closer in spirit to the seventeenth century than to the nineteenth.

Buffon covered many aspects of nature in his *magnum opus,* but did not delve deeply into all of them. In a pictorial sense, anyway, the *Histoire Naturelle* is top-heavy in some subjects and undernourished in others. The larger, gaudier and more impressive the subject, the more attention it received from his artists. He was supposed to be very interested in discoveries made by the microscope, and some important, though misleading, observations are attributed to him. Unfortunately, he did not train his artists to peer through the magic tube. They could have made something dramatic of the wonderful variety of infusorians whirling around in his rainbutts or his flower vases, of the mites and fleas creeping their way through the fur forests of his pets, or of the lice luxuriating in that dirtier forest under his own wig.

Carl Linnaeus, like Buffon, was a man of immense industry and great personal charm. He was destined to bring order into the chaos of animal and plant names and thereby to give biologists an intelligible, if artificial, system of classification. His *Systema Naturae* was a comprehensive catalogue of all living things then known. Not perfected by its author until it had gone through a dozen editions, every one of which was totally unillustrated, it proved ultimately to be of more lasting value and significance

Above: Chamois in a mountain setting. *Right:* Deer foraging by a stream in a forest clearing. Two copper engravings by Johan Elias Ridinger from Barthold Heinrich Brockes's *Betrachtung der Wilden Thiere* (1736).

than the many eloquently reasoned and lavishly illustrated volumes of the *Histoire Naturelle*. Ironically, the value of the *Systema Naturae* was largely dependent on the thousands of bald references in its pages to pre-existing illustrations of animals and plants. Without these illustrations for reference, very few of the animals named and described by Linnaeus could be identified with any certainty—an essential operation as the tenth edition of the *Systema Naturae*, which was published in 1758, is

Bearded Sheep. Copper engraving after Jean-Baptiste Oudry, from Thomas Pennant's *History of Quadrupeds*, 3rd edition, 1793.

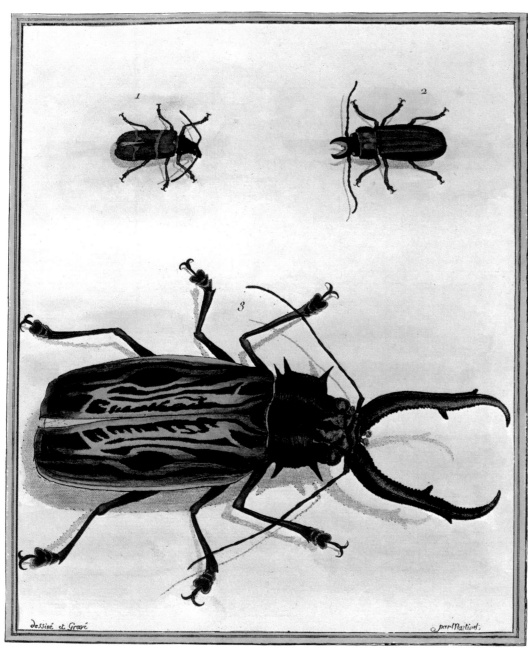

Beetles. Hand-coloured copper engraving by François-Nicolas Martinet from Louis-Jean-Marie Daubenton's *Miscellanea,* an album of unpublished plates from the library of Carl Linnaeus.

the starting point for modern zoological nomenclature. Thus, while many early woodcuts and copper engravings of animals have little more than an artistic and historical interest, many others are of permanent scientific importance. Indeed some of them are so important, or have been deemed so, that specialists seeking more precise information on the animals depicted have spent many hours trying to track down the original drawings from which the published engravings were made, as has been done with the Piso and Marcgrave drawings. It has often been necessary to track down the specimens from which the original drawings were made to identify the species.

This goes some way towards explaining why a zoological library is not considered well appointed unless it contains the works of Gessner, Aldrovandi, Salviani, Merian, Lister and many other early authors. They may be woefully out of date in most respects, but their pictures can still be of vital importance. Thus, a student of tropical marine fishes and their classification may spend many hours trying to decide which species long-forgotten artists had in front of them when they produced drawings for early fish books.

From the personality and outlook of Linnaeus, we should not look for (and with the exception of one fine botanical volume we do not get) any grand literary productions. Destined for scientific immortality though he was, this busy cataloguer of the world's fauna and flora was far too humble and certainly too poor to contemplate publishing a large-scale, beautifully illustrated book on natural history in the manner of Buffon. Instead, he inspired others by his example and high ideals to go out and meet Nature face to face, to gather up specimens of her handiwork, to

Mole Cricket, Grasshopper and Bush Cricket. Hand-coloured copper engraving from Johann Heinrich Sulzer's *Die Kennzeichen der Insekten,* 1761. In spite of the heading, these insects are now all included in the order Orthoptera.

64

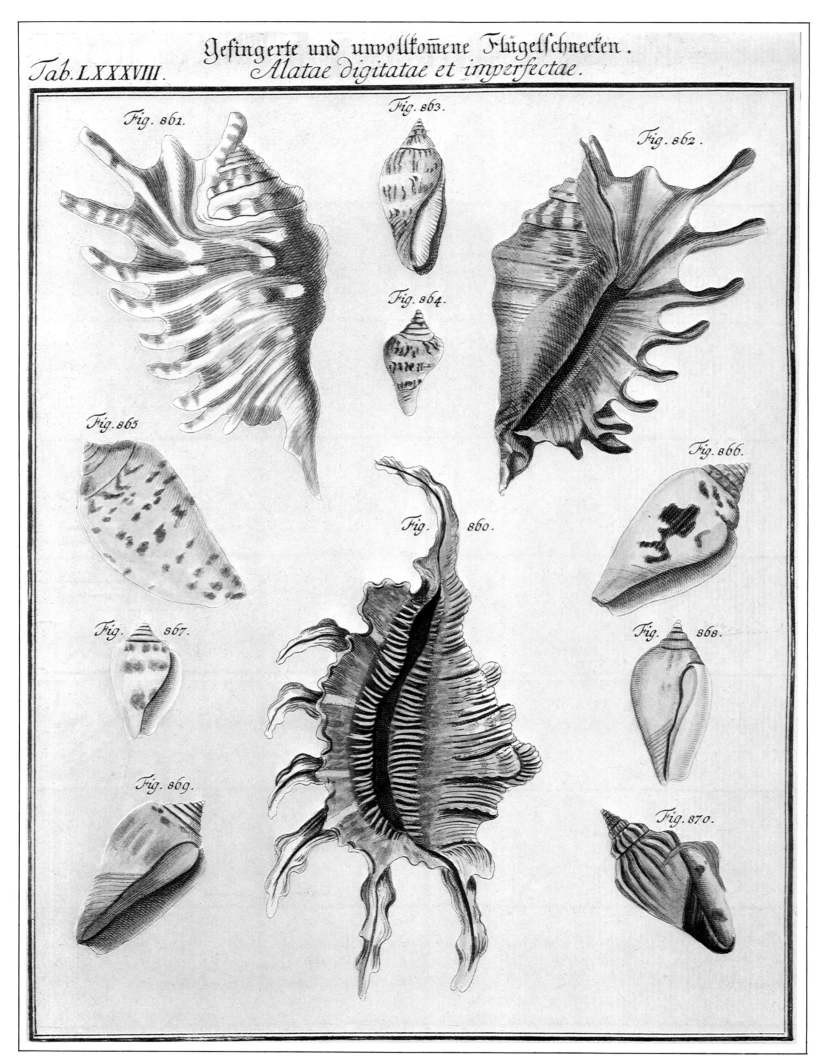

Fig. 861.

Fig. 863.

Fig. 862.

Fig. 864.

Fig. 865

Fig. 866.

Fig. 860.

Fig. 867.

Fig. 868.

Fig. 869.

Fig. 870.

Specimens of Scorpion Shells (*Lambis*) and Strombs (*Strombus*). Hand-coloured copper engraving from F. H. W. Martini and J. H. Chemnitz's *Neues Systematisches Conchylien-Cabinet*, 1769–95.

study them and eventually—if they lived long enough, which many of his disciples failed to do—to publish their findings for the benefit of posterity. Nothing could have been more foreign to his nature than to commission drawings of animals to embellish any of his multifarious publications. Those which were prepared for him in connection with a book on the

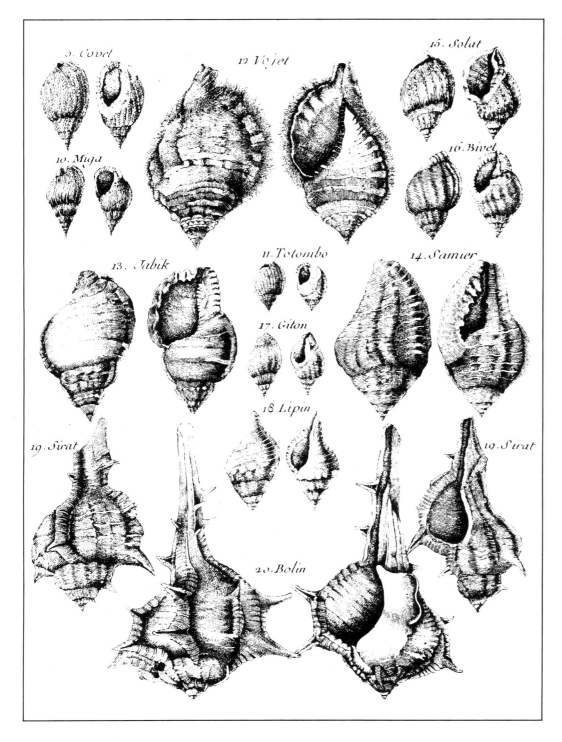

Gastropod Shells from Senegal. Copper engraving from Michel Adanson's *Histoire Naturelle du Sénégal, Coquillages*, 1757. Until fairly recently, it was customary for French conchological illustrations to show gastropod shells upside down (although the convention of showing them the other way up is no more correct biologically), and some modern French publications still show shells upside down.

Queen of Sweden's collection remain unpublished to this day. And yet, indirectly, he did more to advance the standards of zoological iconography than did Buffon.

He did so, of course, by providing a sound systematic basis for the study of natural history. Having named and described all known animals according to his own system, he made it possible for others to recognise new organisms when they came across them. These novelties, in turn, had to be named, described—and illustrated. The importance of illustrating newly discovered animals and plants was obvious to the young Joseph Banks when he was preparing to accompany Captain Cook on his first voyage to the South Seas. As well as taking with him Daniel Solander, a favourite pupil of the aging Linnaeus, Banks brought along his own artists, whose job it was to draw and paint the novelties as they were acquired or seen. The idea was to publish illustrated accounts of the natural history of the voyage. Similarly, artists were engaged for the other two circumnavigations undertaken by Cook and a large number of pictorial records were amassed. Only a series of unforseen circumstances—Solander's early death, Banks's involvement with too many conflicting interests, the sheer magnitude of the task—prevented the planned publications from coming to fruition. Later exploratory voyages paid great attention to the natural history of the countries visited and some fine illustrated accounts were published. These works belong to the

Right: Copper engravings from the 3rd edition, 1793, of Thomas Pennant's *History of* Quadrupeds. 'Ursiform Sloth' (i.e. Sloth Bear), Bactrian Camel, Kangaroo (from an original oil painting by George Stubbs), Llama, Elephant Shrews, 'Bay Lynx' or Bobcat.

nineteenth century, but the inspiration for them had an eighteenth-century origin.

The advancement of science was not the only impulse behind the publication of natural history books in the second half of the eighteenth century; for some enterprises, it was most important to nurture the self esteem of their clientele. Natural history was all very well in its place, but in the mansion or the castle its place was in the library, and the library was a show-place for displaying books which were splendidly bound, spaciously printed and lavishly illustrated. It did little for the owner's self esteem to have on his shelves books that were small in stature, thinly illustrated and skimpily covered, the kind of book Linnaeus wrote. The *Systema Naturae* was a clever piece of work, no doubt about that, but it did not make a fine show in the library, unlike Buffon's endless *Histoire* which looked as if it would need a new shelf every ten years.

Some of the more resplendent natural history books of the eighteenth century were undoubtedly intended to amuse or bedazzle rather than to impart useful information, and various ruses were adopted to distract the reader's attention from their inadequacies. A book could be made impressive merely by making it impressively large. Franz Michael Regenfuss, a German painter and engraver, used an extravagant page size and large print to compensate for a thinly informative text and a mere dozen hand-coloured plates in his *Choix de Coquillages et de Crustacés* of 1758. Even the figures on each plate are spaciously arranged and mostly give front and back views of sea shells which were well known

Grasshoppers. Hand-coloured copper engraving from Dru Drury's *Illustrations of Natural History, wherein are exhibited Figures of Exotic Insects*, 1770–82.

Right : Exotic seashells. Hand-coloured copper engraving from F. M. Regenfuss's *Choix de Coquillages et de Crustacés*, 1758. The plates in this book are larger in area than those in any other shell book. Despite their opulent setting, however, most of the shells portrayed were not rare even in 1758, and the appearance of some species twice on a plate suggests that Regenfuss was more interested in attractive presentation than in scientific content.

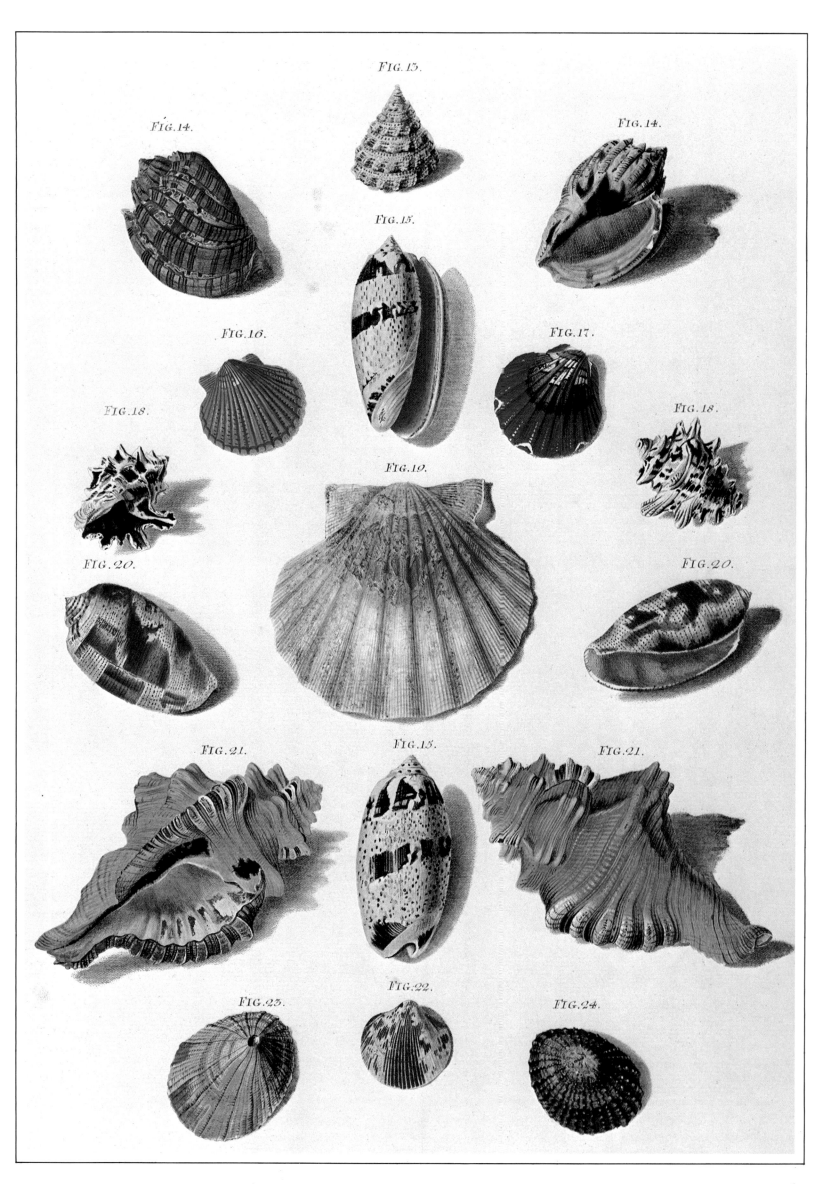

FIG.13.

FIG.14.

FIG.14.

FIG.15.

FIG.16.

FIG.17.

FIG.18.

FIG.18.

FIG.19.

FIG.20.

FIG.20.

FIG.21.

FIG.15.

FIG.21.

FIG.22.

FIG.23.

FIG.24.

Echelle de 6. pouces.

and fairly easily obtained, even in 1758. But Regenfuss was engraver to Frederick V of Denmark at the time and dedicated the book to his royal patron. At least the king could take comfort in the knowledge that the most grandiose book on shells ever published—it would make a very generous fire screen—had been dedicated to him.

Impressive, too, was Xaverio Manetti's *Ornithologia Methodice Digesta*, the flamboyant forerunner of the splendid ornithological folios which were to appear in the nineteenth century. The production of its five massive folio volumes must have been one of the most remarkable publishing ventures ever undertaken in Florence. Begun in 1767 and completed ten years later, it was larger, better engraved and more vividly coloured than any previous book on birds, but these are not its only claims to fame. The attitudes of the birds themselves give this book its unique character. Strutting, parading, posturing and occasionally flying over its 600 hand-coloured plates are birds whose real-life counterparts would surely disown them, and not without reason, for Manetti seems in these pictures to be depicting the human comedy, the habits and mannerisms of contemporary Italian society. Nonetheless his book may still be rated among the very greatest bird books, if only for its magnificent comicality.

One person who was certainly inspired by Manetti's book was Madame Maddalena Bouchard, although she does not say so anywhere in her *Recueil de Cent-Trente-Trois Oiseaux des plus belles Espèces*, which she had the nerve to publish in 1775, a year before Manetti completed his own work. This unscrupulous lady, not content with copying Manetti's figures, added little irreverent touches of her own, an extra bird here, a grasshopper there, and generally tried to make her pictures even more comical and more improbable than Manetti's.

Above: Gyrfalcon. Engraving by François-Nicolas Martinet from Mathurin-Jacques Brisson's *Ornithologie*, 1760.

Opposite page.
Top left: Harrier. Copper engraving from Giovanni Antonio Scopoli's *Deliciae Florae et Faunae Insubricae . . . in Insubria Austriaca*, 1786.

Top right: Blue-Tits and their nest. Hand-coloured copper engraving from Cornelius Noseman's *Nederlandsche Vogelen*, 1770–79.

Bottom left: Coral. Engraving from John Ellis's *History of Zoophytes*, 1786.

Bottom right: Polychaete Worms. Copper engraving from John Ellis's *Essay towards a Natural History of the Corallines*, 1755.

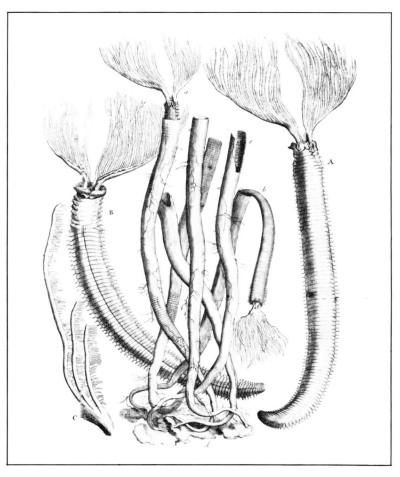

Birds had already been singled out for special and lengthy treatment a
century and more earlier in such books as Willughby's *Ornithology*,
while fishes had been the subject of some large illustrated treatises even
further back, in the middle years of the sixteenth century. Moffet,
Goedart and others had published illustrated accounts of insects at

Le Grand Duc de Virginie. La Hulotte.   Strix maior, sive Strix Aluco.   Strige maggiore, o Strige Allocco.

Maddalena Bouchard sculp.

various times in the seventeenth century, towards the end of which Buonanni and Lister brought out their well-illustrated shell books. By the late eighteenth century, illustrated books dealing with specialised branches of zoology had become fairly common; even some of the more obscure animal groups had been dealt with at length in such books as the *Essay towards a Natural History of the Corallines* (1755) and the *Natural History of Zoophytes* (1786), both written by John Ellis, with whom Linnaeus maintained a lengthy correspondence.

Some of the illustrated books from this period on particular animal

Tawny Owl. Hand-coloured copper engraving from Maddalena Bouchard's *Receuil de Cente-Trente-Trois Oiseaux des plus belles Espèces*, 1775. Bouchard's plates are even more fantastic than those in Xaverio Manetti's *Ornithologia Methodice Digesta*, 1767–76, on which they are unashamedly based.

Right: Frontispiece (hand-coloured copper engraving) from Roesel von Rosenhof's *Historia Naturalis Ranarum*, 1758, which is both accurate and decorative.

ADMIRANDA T
LEVIVM SPECTACVLA
RERVM

73

groups are exceptionally fine and stand comparison with anything produced in the nineteenth century. For instance, Roesel von Rosenhof's illustrations of frogs and other batrachians have never been surpassed in their beauty, accuracy and vitality. The frontispiece to his *Historia Naturalis Ranarum* (1758), showing frogs in a pond surrounded by wild roses, is beyond praise. No early zoological treatise can show more brilliant and more carefully applied hand colouring than this one, unless it be the same author's *Insecten-Belustigung* (1740–49). In draughtsmanship and colouring, Roesel von Rosenhof's work excels even the much-vaunted productions of Thomas Martyn and his little Academy.

Martyn, who had been impressed by the beautiful and rare shells collected during Captain Cook's voyages to the Pacific Ocean, purchased many of them from the ship's crews. Wishing to immortalise their beauty in an appropriate manner, he thought it probable 'that in the productions of boys, all of whom had received their first rudiments of good taste from the same common preceptor, and who should execute whatever they did under his immediate inspection and control, there would generally be found that uniformity and equality of style, conception, and execution which it would be in vain to require from a variety of independent artists.' This was the origin of his Academy, a small group of God-fearing, artistically precocious and utterly brainwashed youngsters, which was based in London.

With a life of spartan simplicity their only reward, Martyn's lads were put to work on the great shell book—not so great in the event as the supply of conchological novelties dried up embarrassingly soon—and eventually *The Universal Conchologist* was presented to the public. Although copies containing 80 plates are not uncommon, it is very rare for a copy to be seen with the full complement of 160 plates, usually bound up in four volumes and signed by Martyn. The quality of the work varies from

Left: Sea Urchins. Copper engraving from Antoine-Joseph Dezallier d'Argenville's *L'Histoire Naturelle . . . Le Lithologie et la Conchyliologie*, 1742.

Below: Various species of Scorpion Shell (*Lambis*). Copper engraving from Niccolo Gualtieri's *Index Testarum Conchyliorum*, 1742.

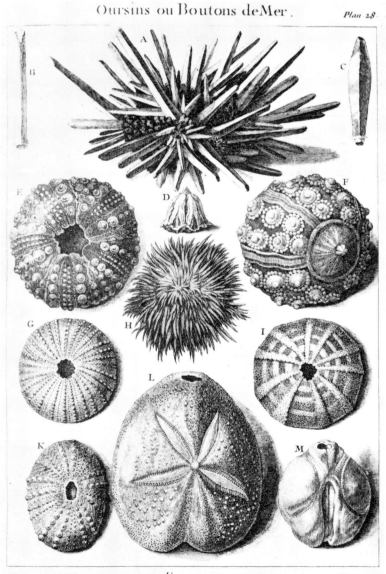

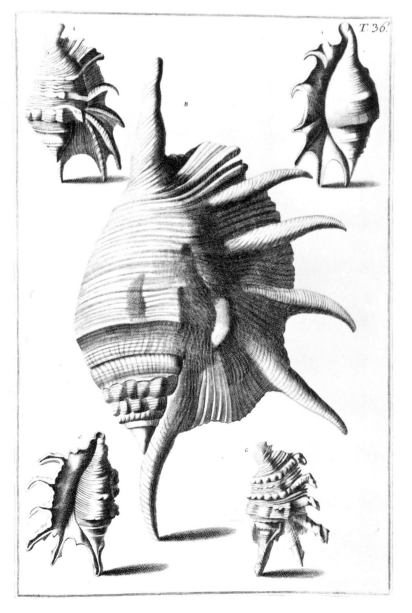

Butterflies. Hand-coloured stipple engraving from Thomas Martyn's *Psyche*, 1797. One of the great rarities of entomological literature, *Psyche* has a complicated history. It appears that the author distributed about a dozen sets of plates to friends and patrons as examples of the work he intended to publish. In the event, only two printed parts were published containing a few leaves of text and four plates.

Right: Keyhole Limpet. Hand-coloured stipple engraving from Thomas Martyn's *Universal Conchologist*, 1743–78.

copy to copy, but at its sparkling best the colouring very closely approaches that of the original subjects. Martyn considered that the undertaking was as 'worthy of himself, of his country, and of the learned world as art and his utmost abilities could effect.'

He went on to produce several more well-illustrated books on natural history including *The English Entomologist* (1792), *Aranei, or a Natural History of Spiders* (1793) and *Psyche, Figures of Non-descript Lepidopterous Insects* (1797). This last item, consisting of 32 engraved plates and no text, is among the rarest of all entomological books as only about a dozen sets of the plates were prepared by the author for distribution to friends and prospective patrons. Its fame among collectors and bibliophiles, which is out of all proportion to its importance, must be attributed more to its great rarity than to its undoubted beauty and charm.

Vignette showing a Bubble Shell. Copper engraving from Ignaz Born's *Testacea Musei Caesarei Vindobonensis*, 1780.

Tab III

A.J.Röfel fecit et exc.

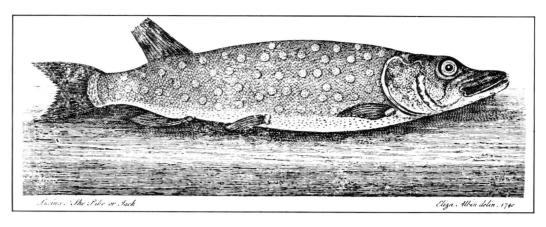

Left: Common Frogs. Hand-coloured copper engraving from Roesel von Rosenhof's *Historia Naturalis Ranarum*, 1758.

Right: 'The Pike or Jack'. Copper engraving from Eleazar Albin's *History of Esculent Fish*, 1794.

It should not be assumed that all or even a majority of illustrated books on animals published in the eighteenth century were impressive in format and content. It was pointless to present information destined for the less wealthy strata of society in an expensive, outsized and lavishly illustrated book. There was, as there had always been, ample scope for modest but informative illustrated texts. Occasionally these took the form of encyclopedias, but more often they were presented in one or two unpretentious volumes.

In 1737, for example, Eleazar Albin published his *Natural History of English Song Birds* than which nothing could be more modest. A pocket-sized guide illustrated with plain plates showing song birds and their eggs, it proved to be a very popular little book and was republished several times. Owners of the book would often colour up the illustrations for their own amusement. Albin's other books on various animal groups are larger, more ambitious affairs, which went through only one or two

Goliath Beetle. Hand-coloured copper engraving from Dru Drury's *Illustrations of Natural History, wherein are Exhibited Figures of Exotic Insects*, 1770–82.

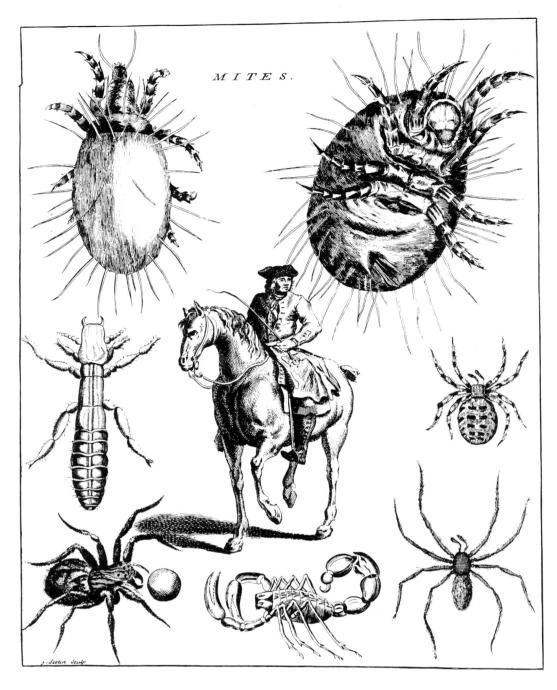

MITES.

Mites, Spiders, Scorpion. Copper engraved frontispiece from Eleazar Albin's *Natural History of Spiders, and other Curious Insects,* 1736. The horseman is reputed to be Albin himself.

Right: Spiders from the same book.

Far right: Bactrian Camel and Tapir. Two hand-coloured copper engravings from Georg Wolfgang Knorr's *Délices Physiques Choisies,* 1766–67. The pyramid in the background of the Tapir suggests that the animal occurs in Egypt, but it is not found anywhere on the African continent.

Bottom right: Lynx and Moose. Engravings from Oliver Goldsmith's *A History of the Earth and Animated Nature,* 1774. Written towards the end of Goldmith's life, this was one of his most successful books and was kept in print throughout the following century. Goldsmith does not attempt to hide his debt to Buffon's *Histoire Naturelle* for his pictures. Most of them, including these, were modelled on de Sève's illustrations for Buffon.

Elephant, Rhinoceros and 'Sea Horse' (Hippopotamus—see illustration on p. 40). Copper engraving from Richard Brookes's *New and Accurate System of Natural History,* 1763.

editions each. But the hey-day of the cheaply produced popular book was still a long way off. Even Albin's little book on song birds must have been too expensive for most would-be purchasers when it was published. In those days, books were luxuries that few people could afford.

The demand for illustrated encyclopaedias of natural history was sparked off by Buffon's *Histoire*, which also provided much of the basic information which went into them. Oliver Goldsmith's *History of the Earth and Animated Nature*, itself an adaptation of Buffon's book, was first published in an illustrated edition in 1774, and its engraved plates are mainly reduced copies of those in the first edition of the *Histoire*. Goldsmith, a playwright and poet rather than a biologist, knew very little about animals and their ways, but he was a good writer and commanded a wide readership. Consequently, until illustrated editions of Cuvier's *Animal Kingdom* came on the market in the early part of the following century, Buffon and Goldsmith, via countless editors, ruled almost unchallenged.

One of the few challengers was the little known *New and Accurate System of Natural History* of Richard Brookes, a small-format, six-volume compendium published in 1763. As Buffon had issued only a few volumes of his *magnum opus* by that date, and as Goldsmith did not sign the contract for his until 1768, it is obvious that Brookes had to depend on other sources for most of his information and illustrations. Although the book is popular in character, the illustrations are of considerable interest because they include some American animals which had never before been represented in a book.

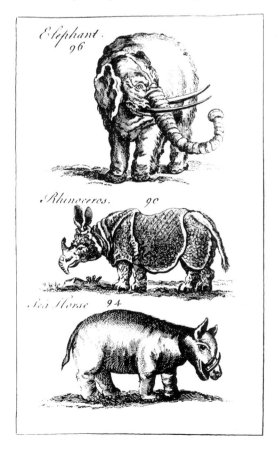

Elephant
96

Rhinoceros.
90

Sea Horse
94

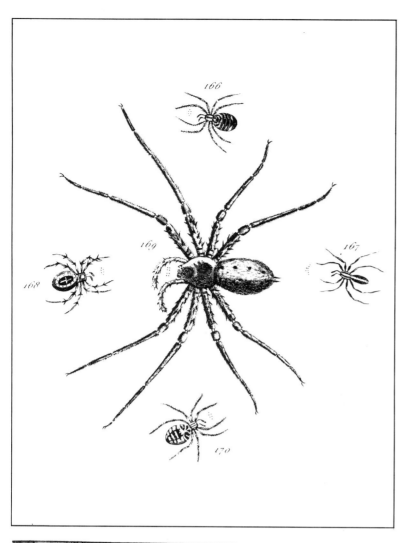

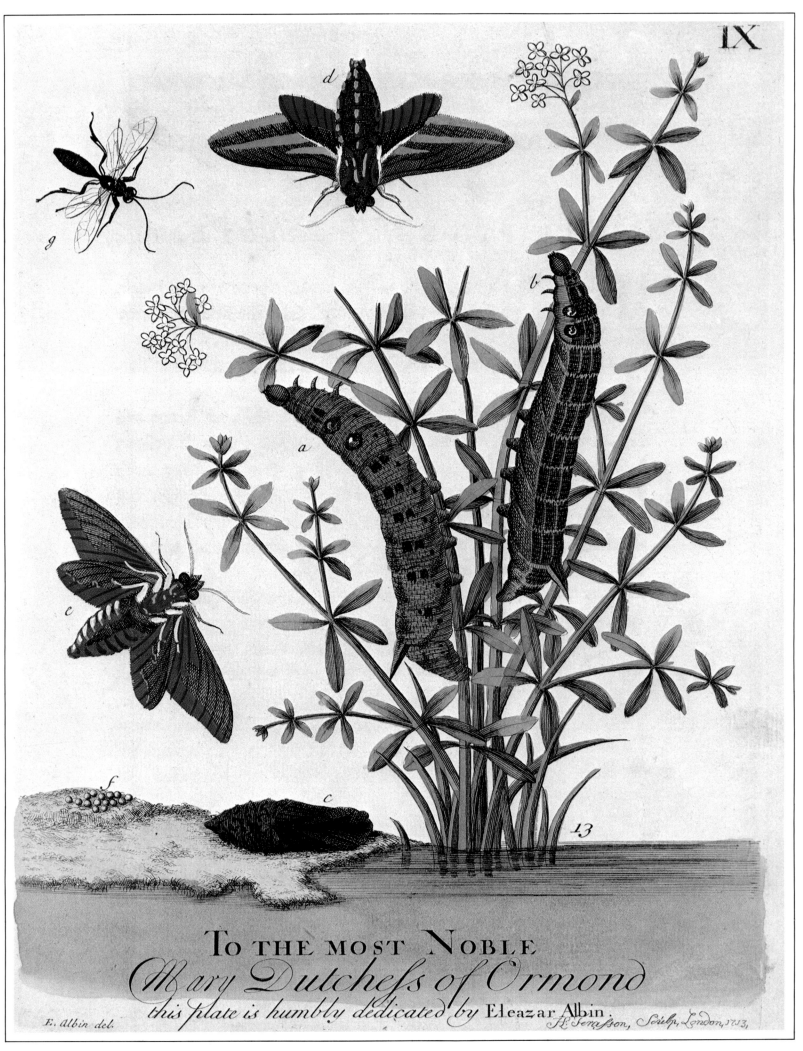

To the most Noble
Mary Dutchess of Ormond
this plate is humbly dedicated by Eleazar Albin.

E. Albin del.

H. Terasson, Sculp, London, 1713,

It was above all Thomas Bewick who demonstrated that a book does not have to be imposing in size or exquisitely coloured to impart useful or novel information or to convey truth, pathos and wisdom. Bewick revived the lost art of wood engraving in England and developed it along a very personal channel. In particular, he was responsible for initiating

Elephant Hawk Moth and Ichneumon Fly. Hand-coloured copper engraving from Eleazar Albin's *History of Insects*, 1720.

Papilio Archippus.

Asclepias Curasavica

a new approach to the illustration of animals, especially birds. To his mastery of the engraving technique he added qualities which had been seldom evident in the copper engravings of animal subjects published throughout the seventeenth and eighteenth centuries: sympathy, love and understanding.

The *General History of Quadrupeds* (1790), which made him famous, and the *History of British Birds* (1797–1804), which made him unique, are the main memorials to Bewick's genius. While his quadrupeds are sometimes stiff and lifeless—many were copied from an edition of Buffon —his birds are vital and charming. With one magnificent exception— the picture of the Chillingham Bull, his masterpiece and one of his rarest woodcuts—his animal engravings are small and often appear as tail-piece vignettes in his books.

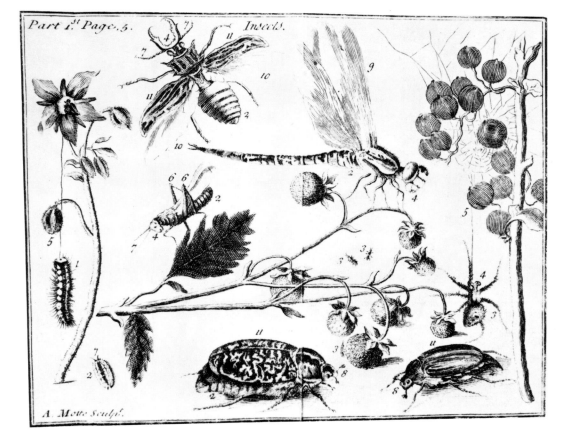

Male Elephant and American Bison. Copper engravings from Thomas Pennant's *History of Quadrupeds*, 3rd edition, 1793.

'The Faceated Couroucou'. Hand-coloured copper engraving by P. Mazell from Thomas Pennant's Indian Zoology, first edition, 1769. In 1791, a smaller edition of this work was published and the title of the subject illustrated has been taken from it.

In his own day, Bewick was most appreciated for the technical accomplishment of his woodcuts, but today the qualities of tenderness, warmth, charm, sincerity and naturalness in his work affect us more profoundly than the most perfect technique ever could. He may not have been the first engraver of animal subjects to imbue his work with such endearing qualities—J. E. Ridinger's animal engravings in the *Betrachtung* of B. H. Brockes also have them—but his is the name we automatically associate with those qualities.

Bewick's personal view of the animal kingdom helped to bring new insight into animal portraiture and inspired some of the greatest animal artists who have ever lived. Not until Joseph Wolf began to translate his own personal view of the animal kingdom into graphic art was Bewick finally outdistanced. By bringing humility into the art of animal portraiture, he helped raise it to new heights, and the finest zoological illustrations of the nineteenth century are touched with Bewick's humility.

Five wood engravings from Thomas Bewick's *General History of Quadrupeds*, 1792. *Left:* Hyena and Walrus. *Right:* Long-Tailed Field-mouse, Tenrec and Capybara. The three exotic animals are based on plates in Buffon's *Histoire Naturelle*. The Walrus is very similar to illustrations of the same subject in early editions describing the voyages of Captain Cook. These, in turn, were based on original drawings by John Webber, the artist who accompanied Cook during his third circumnavigation.

'The Great Owl Moth of Brazil', *Thysania agrippina*, the world's largest moth. Handcoloured engraving from James Wilson's *Illustrations of Zoology, being new, rare or remarkable subjects of the Animal Kingdom,* vol. 1, 1827.

Left: 'The Yellow Owl' (Barn Owl) and Redwing. Wood engravings by Thomas Bewick from his *History of British Birds,* 1847 edition.

Right: Cicada and two other bugs. Handcoloured engraving from Edward Donovan's *Epitome of the Natural History of the Insects of India,* 1800.

CHAPTER V
The Nineteenth Century Background

The first two decades of the nineteenth century offered few signs of radical change from the traditions of animal illustration which had been established before 1800. At first, little interest was shown in lithography, an invention of the late eighteenth century, and none in its application to the portrayal of animals. There were few artists capable of producing life-like pictures of birds and beasts, and it is doubtful if the engravers of the period could have reproduced such pictures satisfactorily. Imitators of Bewick chiselled their wood blocks, while others scratched away at their metal plates or laboured at the more complicated if more rewarding aquatint or mezzotint processes. The effects they were striving for and the means employed to obtain them were not calculated to bring out the vibrant qualities of living animals. It was an unadventurous beginning.

At its best, the zoological art of the time is distinguished by tightness of drawing and brightness of colouring. It is seldom spirited or vital and shows none of the nervous excitement which often characterises the work of a sensitive artist. Lithography was to change all this, but not yet. Its potential for the lively portrayal of at least the larger animals was not realised for a surprisingly long time.

The remarkably industrious Edward Donovan typifies the mentality of the still largely dilettante world of descriptive zoology in the early nineteenth century. His numerous, gaudily illustrated tomes epitomise the taste of the period. In several multi-volume books he described and illustrated the birds, fishes, insects and molluscs of the British Isles; his work on birds was remarkable for the high quality of its many hand-coloured plates. Donovan was an inveterate collector of natural objects, and we learn from the covers to each part of his *Natural History of British Birds* (1794–1819) that the original drawings were made from birds in his own museum. It is certain, however, that most of his preserved specimens could never have looked like his illustrations, which are not always well drawn and are often inaccurate. Furthermore, the hand colouring is simply too magnificent to be true.

In this book, as in his *Epitome of the Natural History of the Insects of China* (1798), the paint is laid on so thickly that it is frequently impossible to see the engraved lines underneath. The already rich colouring is heightened by the addition of burnished highlights, albumen overglazes and metallic paints to give an overall effect reminiscent of the work of a miniaturist. Surprisingly, these techniques often combined to produce a very pleasing and delicate effect: the multiple ruses of the colourist triumph over the draughtsman's numerous failures. Donovan overreached himself and died penniless after trying to raise enough money to take his booksellers to court for holding on to most of his stock. It was an ignominious end to a career which had always been colourful.

It would be wrong to assume that the majority of zoological illustrations then were issued from the press hand coloured. At no time has hand colouring been cheap, and books issued with hand-coloured pictures would usually have been looked upon as luxury productions. Booksellers would sometimes issue brochures publicising the imminent publication

'Le Tocard', Toucan. Engraving from François Levaillant's *Histoire Naturelle des Oiseaux de Paradis et des Roliers, suivie de celle des Toucans et des Barbuts*, 1806, after a drawing by Jacques Barraband of a unique specimen in Levaillant's own collection.

Left: Butterfly, '*Papilio phalaris*'. Hand-coloured line and stipple engraving from Edward Donovan's *Naturalists' Repository*, vol. 2, 1824.

yprinus Carpio. LINN. Syst. Nat. Edit. n. 2 .

Carp. Hand-coloured copper engraving from Carl von Meidinger's *Icones Piscium*, 1785–94.

Fish, *'Blepsias ventricosus'*. Hand-coloured engraving from Johann Friedrich von Eschholtz's *Zoologischer Atlas enthaltend Abbildungen und Beschreibungen neuer Thierarten, während des Flottkapitäns von Kotzebue*, 1829–33.

of such books and calling for subscribers to them. The exclusive character of the bookselling profession then is obvious from the wording of one of these brochures: 'Noblemen and Gentlemen wishing to become subscribers to the above work, are requested to forward their names, through their respective Booksellers, to the Publishers . . .'—no room for ordinary men and women to get on the list. Subscribers often had the choice of a coloured or a cheaper uncoloured copy. From the mid eighteenth century onwards, it was common practice to add a printed list of subscribers to the text of the book, and sometimes the list indicated the kind of copy or copies each subscriber had opted to take. If the subscribers included a liberal sprinkling of royalty and nobility, the list was almost sure to be published.

The heyday of ornithological art in Britain was still more than a quarter of a century away when the travelling naturalist François Levaillant began producing his superb books on exotic birds. 1801 saw the appearance of the first instalments of no less than three, of which the magnificent *Histoire Naturelle des Perroquets* and the *Histoire Naturelle des Oiseaux de Paradis* are the most outstanding. In his illustrations to these works, Levaillant's favourite artist, Jacques Barraband, combines artistic ability of a high order with good taste and a rare aesthetic sense. In almost every way, the illustrations to Donovan's book on British birds are outdistanced by those in Levaillant's various productions, and the comparison serves to show how superior the French were to the English in this branch of animal art at the beginning of the nineteenth century. It is worth noting, however, that neither provided more than the merest indications of ancillary detail, such as a portion of a tree for a perch. Neither came anywhere near providing naturalistic scenic surroundings for their subjects.

The clear superiority of French artists in the period immediately before use of lithography became widespread seems to be connected, to a certain extent, with the art of miniature painting, an art to which the French had long been devoted and at which they excelled. Some proofs of this are to be found in the National Museum of Natural History in Paris in the shape of more than 6,000 sheets of parchment on which animals and plants have been portrayed with an astonishing degree of accuracy and delicacy. The beginnings of this collection date from the seventeenth century, when Gaston of Orléans recruited several artists to paint pictures of the rare animals and plants in his private menagerie and museum. One of these artists was Nicolas Robert, an unusually talented miniaturist who saw the importance of portraying animals in natural attitudes. When Louis XIV acquired Gaston's collection of animal and flower paintings, he continued Robert's employment. Working in close collaboration with the botanists of the Jardin du Roi and the zoologists of the menagerie at Versailles to whom he submitted his work for checking, Robert went on producing his exquisite pictures. In this way, a collection of paintings remarkable alike for beauty and accuracy was built up.

The King made a provision for the curation and enlargement of the collection; after the Jardin du Roi had been turned into a museum, artists were trained to reproduce the appearance of animals and plants exactly, particularly of the specimens which had been studied professionally at the museum. Thus there was an unbroken tradition, securely founded on the miniaturist's art, of portraying natural objects exquisitely and accurately. The names of Robert's successors—an impressive list— sufficiently indicate the quality of the paintings in the royal collection: Pierre-Joseph Redouté and his brother Henri-Joseph, Jean Joubert, Nicolas Maréchal, Nicolas Huet, Pancrace Bessa, Paul-Louis Oudart, Léon de Wailly, Alfred Riocreux and Jean-Charles Werner. Virtually all

Bivalve Shells. Hand-coloured aquatint from George Perry's *Conchology*, 1811, the only published book on seashells which has aquatinted plates.

Tragopan and Vulture. Hand-coloured engravings from C. J. Temminck and Baron M. Laugier de Chartrouse's *Nouveau receuil de planches coloriés d'Oiseaux*, 1820–39.

the French artists whose paintings were reproduced in fine animal books must have known of the existence of this remarkable collection of paintings on parchment, the *vélins*. Most of them had probably been brought up in the tradition which these pictures represent.

This may go some way towards explaining why French zoological publications of the nineteenth century are illustrated with such close attention to detail and why they are so exquisitely coloured. The tradition embodied in the brilliant dynasty of miniaturists, whose work was controlled by scientists, gave zoological art in France an overall uniformity and distinction that was not equalled elsewhere. The illustrations in such books as the *Histoire Naturelle des Singes et des Makis* (1799–1800) by J.-B. Audebert and *Les Pigeons* (1811–43) by C.-J. Temminck and F. Prévost had few serious rivals outside France in the early years of the nineteenth century. No expense was spared in obtaining special effects including colour printing. A coloured engraving of an animal adorning a high-class French book was a work of art, a jewel set down on the page, whether its subject was a tree squirrel or a buprestid beetle.

If anything, it was too artistic, too jewel-like, too minutely observed, too obviously the work of a miniaturist or of someone steeped in that tradition. A few pages of minutely exact pictures of animals can be very stimulating, particularly to the scientist, but a bookful of them is likely to be boring. The desire for perfection in published zoological art was not just a vice of the French. Even Bewick, the most natural of animal artists, presented his subjects in an idealised way: there are no ruffled feathers in his *British Birds*, no matted fur in his *Quadrupeds*. The marvellously talented French illustrators may dazzle us with their exquisitely accurate animal studies but they seldom engage our feelings.

Indeed, there is often much pleasure to be derived from illustrations that are far from accurate. Many early animal pictures were the charming results of imperfect knowledge, but in later publications poor draughtsmanship or colouring was more often to blame for inaccurate representation. George Perry's *Conchology* of 1811 is a fine example of drawing and colouring which has gone pleasingly if inexcusably awry. In this unique

Parra cordifera. (*Lesson*)

JACANA CORDIFÈRE.

folio production—it is the only shell book illustrated with aquatinted plates—the shells are so badly drawn and so garishly coloured that they have become caricatures. Perry was accused of dreaming up extraordinary shells and transferring them to paper on waking, of publishing a panto-mimic display of figures and of being a charlatan in the scientific world. Although professional jealousy was behind some of the criticism meted

'*Parra cordifera*', a Jacana. Hand-coloured lithograph by P. Oudart from M.-A.-P.-O. Des Murs's *Iconographie Ornithologique*, 1849. The long feet enable a Jacana to walk on water lily leaves.

Head of an Andean Condor. Hand-coloured engraving from C. J. Temminck and Baron M. Laugier de Chartrouse's *Nouveau receuil de planches coloriées d'Oiseaux*, 1820–39. Except for the incorrect configuration of the beak, which is more sinuous than it should be, this is a faithful reproduction of one of Nicolas Huet's superb *vélins*.

out to him, even he must have been aware that his figures looked very odd. What Renard had done for fish at the beginning of the eighteenth century, Perry did for shells at the beginning of the nineteenth. Both are rather isolated figures who seem to have seen in their respective subjects what would now pass as surrealist elements and, flouting convention, allowed their imaginations free rein. Perry's book is remarkable for having been published at a time when zoology was becoming more and more of a science. To slip up on an occasional picture was still excusable, and still a regular occurrence, but to get nearly all the pictures wrong, expensively wrong too, was unforgivable.

It was certainly a far cry from Perry's self-indulgent *Conchology* to the magnificent publications which were then emanating from France. Perry's was not the sort of enterprise that any government body would have backed. In any case, the British Government was not in the market for supporting such ventures. In principle, at least, the French Government would have been sympathetic to the idea, as it encouraged the sciences with some generosity and listened to its scientific advisers with respect. French voyages of exploration were accompanied by competent zoologists, botanists and artists, all working together efficiently. The scientific results of these voyages were then enshrined in substantial publications illustrated with splendid coloured plates produced at Government expense. Without such support, it is certain that far fewer sumptuously produced natural history books would have been published in France.

The lack of state support for expensive illustrated books was felt very seriously by at least one Englishman, William Swainson, a prolific author of zoological works during the first half of the nineteenth century. He complained that the British Government, far from underwriting the printing and publication costs of scientifically important books, placed a tax on them—actually a tax on paper, but virtually a tax on knowledge. The tax levied on a book containing only letterpress was small enough, but it was multiplied considerably if the book was furnished with hand-coloured illustrations. In addition, each copy of the book had to receive individual attention, and the hand colouring was particularly expensive and time consuming. All of this had to be reflected in the published price.

Although he was justifiably incensed by the seeming illiberality of the British Government, Swainson would have gained more than most from any aid because he was the author of many lavishly illustrated books on animals, and his sales figures could have been much improved. Between

'Virginian Eared Owl' and Whip-poor-will. Engravings from Louis-Jean-Pierre Vieillot's *Histoire Naturelle des Oiseaux de l'Amerique Septentrionale*, 1807.

94

CARRULUS STELLERI.

London, Printed for John Murray, Bookseller to the Admiralty, January 1st 1829.

LANIUS EXCUBITORIDES.

London, Printed for John Murray, Bookseller to the Admiralty, Jan.y 1st 1832.

Steller's Jay and (right) Great Northern Shrike. Hand-coloured lithographs by William Swainson from William Swainson and Sir John Richardson's monograph on birds in *Fauna Boreali-Americana*, 1829–37.

Overleaf: Portuguese Man-o'-War. Colour engraving from the *Voyage autour du Monde, exécuté par Ordre du Roi, sur la Corvette La Coquille, Atlas de Zoologie* by R.-P. Lesson, P. Garnot and F.-E. Guérin-Méneville, 1826–30. Based on an original by Lesson and Pancrace Bessa, this is perhaps the finest nineteenth-century representation of a Portuguese Man-o'-War.

1829 and 1837, however, there appeared the first natural history work to be subsidised by the British Government. This was the *Fauna Boreali-Americana* by Sir John Richardson and Swainson, for which the Government allocated £1,000 towards the cost of printing the plates. For the book, Swainson executed 49 hand-coloured plates of birds which would certainly not have been published without the grant. The British Government subsidised similar books during the nineteenth century; the scientific results of Darwin's researches during the voyage of the Beagle would probably never have appeared in print if the State had not underwritten the whole venture. But the future of zoological iconography was to remain firmly in the hands of private enterprise. Had it been otherwise, it is doubtful that such a remarkable succession of impressively illustrated zoological books would have emerged in nineteenth-century Britain.

John Gould, for one, needed no subsidies, but his contributions to ornithological literature will be examined later in the context of what may be called the Lithographic Revolution. First, we must meet the one undoubted nineteenth-century hero of our story. He may not be everyone's idea of a hero, but his achievements and his life style have qualities bordering on the heroic.

In 1826, a handsome, simply dressed man alighted at Liverpool from a ship newly arrived from America. He carried with him a few personal belongings including a large portfolio. Penniless and unknown, he had arrived in the Old World to sell his personal vision of the New. The quintessence of that vision was contained in his portfolio in the form of some large coloured drawings of North American birds. He had been born near New Orleans, but had spent much of his youth in France, and his reason for returning to Europe was to seek encouragement and support for a great project which had preoccupied him for several years. His name was John James Audubon.

From the beginning, he was a man possessed. In 1820, he had already decided to produce a large work on the ornithology of North America. In October of that year, he boarded a flatboat as a working passenger. He had few possessions apart from his drawing materials, a gun, the clothes

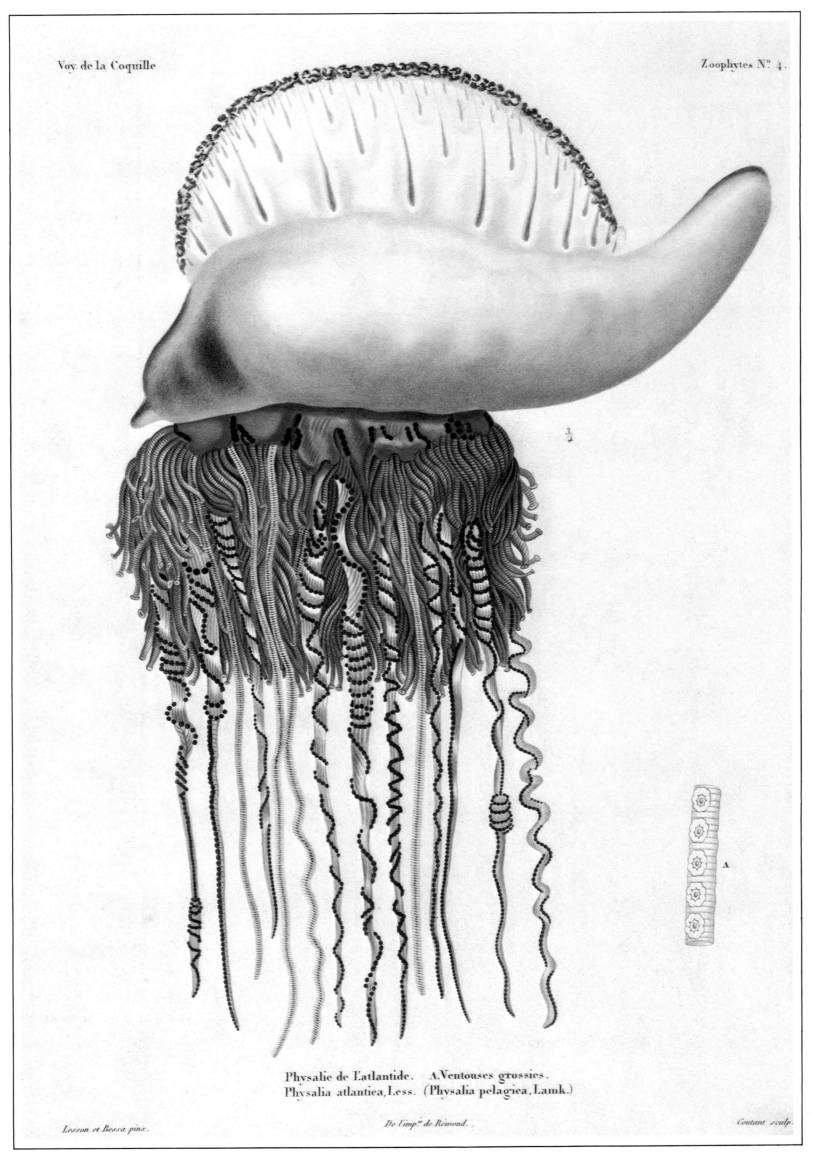

Physalie de L'atlantide.   A. Ventouses grossies.
Physalia atlantica, Less. (Physalia pelagica, Lamk.)

Lesson et Bessa pinx.

De l'imp.ᵉ de Remond.

Contant sculp.

he wore, and his flute. Drifting down the Mississippi, a highway for myriads of migrating birds, he saw and sketched the objects of his passion until he arrived at New Orleans, which became his work centre for the next six years.

At first, he worked only from living birds, for he had resolved never to draw from a stuffed specimen. As the work progressed, however, he was obliged to copy from preserved material, and all the West Coast species in his book were necessarily drawn from skins obtained from other ornithologists. But with the incredible variety of bird life which filled the forests of Louisiana, his project was off to a good start. In these early years, he substantially developed his complicated methods of drawing or painting birds. At first, he drew in pencil and used pastels or chalks for the colouring. Later, he included the habitat details in watercolour. By 1824, he was working largely in watercolour but, to capture special effects, he would also apply pastel over the watercolour or use ink, oil or egg white. Sometimes he scratched through the paint to the paper surface to reveal the underlying whiteness, a technique often used by Turner for his very different pictures. By these various subterfuges, he was able to simulate the appearance of downy feathers, the gleam of an eye or the gloss on a beak. Only a few of the paintings he executed before 1824 were utilised for the book, and most of these were redrawn or improved upon in some other way; several were cut out and pasted down on sheets containing later drawings. From such high-class botching was to grow the world's most expensive published natural history book.

He needed to be tireless in his efforts to capture the likeness of a bird before the colours of its eyes and feet faded and to obviate the need to spend precious hours preserving it in a life-like attitude. Sometimes the bird began to decay before the sketching was finished, but still Audubon would often open up the carcass, a necessary procedure to determine sex and eating habits. His adventures in a largely unexplored country in search of birds read like a novel, and it is remarkable how often he escaped serious injury or worse. Like so many men with a mission, he survived and actually seemed to thrive on adversity. No successful artist has ever served a more rigorous apprenticeship, and few have lived to see their artistic ambitions fulfilled so magnificently. But, like others who were inspired by the natural wonders of the New World, he had to turn to the Old World for support, encouragement and technical assistance. Although his work represented nothing less than the beginning of realism in bird portraiture, he was compelled to go, cap in hand, to Paris and London to seek out people who could duplicate images, provide finance, and find a market for an expensive publication.

Before Audubon, birds had been represented in books as static creatures perched on tree stumps and branches. Illustrators had attempted to give their lifeless figures the kiss of life by applying dazzling colours and smothering them under layers of varnish, egg-white and other substances. Thus Audebert's illustrations to Louis-Jean-Pierre Vieillot's *Oiseaux Dorés ou à Reflets Mètalliques*, which had appeared in all their shining magnificence in 1802, were lavish if futile attempts to animate their subjects by using the tricks of the colourist's trade. Although it may have been justifiable to apply layers of gilt to illustrations of birds remarkable for their metallic sheen, no picture in the book recognises that it is the suggestion of movement and not the richness of the surface which imbues stationary objects with life. This was a lesson which Donovan, Audebert and most others involved in the business of bird portrayal in early nineteenth-century Europe were in no position to learn. They hardly ever saw exotic birds in their living splendour.

It was because Audubon had learned this lesson and realised its importance that he sailed for England in 1826. He was still a very long way from the end of his self-appointed task, but he was impatient to see a start made on his book. Could anyone have suspected then that this plainly dressed figure clutching his portfolio was the apostle of what may

Overleaf: Fishes from Indonesian waters. Colour engravings from the *Voyage de la Corvette L'Astrolabe, Atlas de Zoologie* by J.-R.-C. Quoy and J.-P. Gaimard, 1832–35. Many of the most beautiful and most accurate nineteenth-century zoological illustrations are to be found in the reports of scientific voyages. The French ones, such as those of the Astrolabe and the Coquille, are especially noteworthy for their accuracy of line and delicate colouring.

'Fresh Water Marsh Hen'—King Rail. Hand-coloured aquatint by Robert Havell The Younger after an original painting by John James Audubon, from *The Birds of America*, 1827–38.

may be called 'the new ornithography'? It would not have been immediately obvious to a modern observer from his portfolio, which contained work that was inferior to his later efforts, though remarkable enough in comparison with anything that had so far been seen in Europe, as visitors to his exhibitions in Liverpool and Edinburgh were quick to realise. They must have been amazed and delighted to see pictures of birds so full of animation, so obviously the work of a man who had observed them lovingly and at first hand in their native woods, streams and hills.

In Edinburgh, the engraver Lizars undertook to translate these originals into engravings and had made a start on them before Audubon encountered the young Robert Havell in London. It was Havell who was finally entrusted with the Herculean task of producing all the plates for *The Birds of America*. Working with his father, who owned a highly reputable aquatinting and engraving business, Havell, an excellent artist in his own right, began producing the impressive aquatinted plates upon which Audubon's fame rests so securely. Before the job could be finished, however, Audubon had to make several long excursions back into the North American wilderness to obtain sketches of many more birds, most of which he later worked up into finished paintings in London.

Audubon was extremely fortunate in his choice of interpreter. Havell was very sympathetic to the whole endeavour and indeed to things American in general. Inspired by Audubon's accounts of America, he moved there and ended his days publishing exquisite American landscape plates. Havell had a lot of interpreting to do because, particularly in the later stages, Audubon left him to fill in many details of birds, foliage and scenery on the basis of sketches or written instructions; Havell often had almost nothing to guide him except his own judgment and imagination. *The Birds of America*, published between 1827 and 1838, owes a great deal to this young man who obviously did much more than the most important engraving work and the first colouring.

Black-Billed Cuckoo and Stanley Hawk. Hand-coloured aquatints by R. Havell The Younger after original paintings by J. J. Audubon from *The Birds of America*, 1827–38.

To produce the final output of 75,000 hand-coloured plates which made up the 175 copies of *The Birds of America*, he and his father had to supervise a staff of about fifty men and women—no mean accomplishment in itself—and they had to contend with Audubon's volatile temperament. Nevertheless, *The Birds of America* is still uniquely Audubon's and carries the stamp of his personality on every plate. Left to his own devices, Havell could never have achieved such dramatic and life-like ornithological pictures. His own book on birds of paradise, which he published in 1835, is illustrated with plates showing these lively creatures posed stiffly on twigs.

Audubon may have forseen the day when his *magnum opus* would be highly regarded. Perhaps he would not have been surprised to learn that, a century and a half later, it would still be the largest, most sumptuous, most expensive of all bird books. But had he been present at a New York book auction on 20th November 1977, when a copy of *The Birds of America* was sold for $396,000, a world auction record at that time for a printed book, he would soon have appreciated one aspect of his achievement. In the sale room, people would have talked about his book, not as *The Birds of America*, but as the record-breaking Audubon. For them, the book *was* Audubon. The story of the trigger-happy backwoodsman who notched up a hundred or more feathered victims a day and gave his name to one of the world's most prestigious societies for the protection of birds, who nearly died of starvation while working on a book which only millionaires can afford to own, is rich in paradox.

It is worth pausing at this point to examine one aspect of the book trade as it was when the impact of *The Birds of America* was still fresh: the business of selling secondhand books and prints. Finely illustrated books have never lacked admirers. At present, illustrated books are prized more highly than they have ever been and are moving further and further out of reach of the average pocket. Some of these books, though,

Stanley Hawk.

FALCO STANLEII. Aud.

Young Male, 1. Female, 2.

were never easy to obtain and were always expensive. The only way that many of them could be issued in the first place was by the author or publisher advertising before publication for subscribers whose money would help pay the production costs. Large illustrated books always took a long time to be published, and some of the more purely scientific treatises were several decades in the making.

The willingness of dealers to sell plates without their accompanying texts is not a modern phenomenon, nor necessarily an unwelcome one. Then, as now, it was impossible for any but the wealthy to own fine illustrated books, but the flavour of such books could be sampled through owning some of the plates taken from them. Whatever the rights or wrongs of breaking up expensive books, the effects of this practice are apparent in the large number of incomplete illustrated books now in circulation.

We can gain insights into the commercial book world of the nineteenth century from catalogues, particularly those of London booksellers. In May 1839, for instance, Henry Coxhead listed in one of his catalogues several lots of plates extracted from various valuable books. These included: item 254, 'A SERIES of 77 coloured Plates of Birds, with their Descriptions, from the original and esteemed edition of Catesby's "Natural History of Carolina", &c. 18s'; item 321, 'A SERIES, consisting of 35 very finely coloured Figures of Fishes, by Nodder, with Descriptions in Latin and English, by Shaw, 7s 6d. *From Shaw and Nodder's Naturalists' Miscellany.*'; item 427, 'TWENTY-ONE finely coloured Figures of Crustacea, Fishes, &c. &c. by Knorr and others, on 9 folio sheets, 6s 6d'; item 475, 'Ten Folio Sheets, containing about 180 Figures of Shells, (*some coloured*) with Descriptions in English and French, 5s 6d.'

Coxhead was certainly not the only bookseller in those days who had a special line in collections of fine plates. Many illustrated books must have been ruined to make such collections, and it is remarkable that so many complete copies have survived to the present day (in some instances to be dismembered by Coxhead's spiritual descendants). Henry G. Bohn, on the other hand, was a London bookseller who had a very different attitude to fine plate books. He used to buy up the original copper plates, stone blocks or wood blocks which had been used to produce illustrated books on various subjects; sometimes he bought sheets of letterpress and stocks of printed plates as well. He then issued relatively cheap reprints.

INDRI

Indri, the largest of the Lemurs. Engraving from George Shaw's *General Zoology*, vol. 1 (Mammalia), 1800.

Two exotic birds, '*Alcedo atrocapilla*' and '*Epimachus magnificus*'. Steel engravings after original drawings by Jean-Gabriel Prêtre, from René-Primevère Lesson's *Centurie Zoologique*, 1832.

Whip Snake, '*Coluber trabalis*'. Hand-coloured engraving from Anatole Nikolaevich Demidoff's *Voyage dans la Russie Meridionale et la Crimée, Histoire Naturelle, Atlas*, 1842.

Usually his reprints of originally rare and expensive books were advertised 'at very reduced prices'; and sometimes the reductions were indeed considerable.

Many illustrated books with Bohn's imprint were originally issued by other publishers. He can be seen as a remainder specialist who attempted to bring expensive books within the reach of the less wealthy book collector, and he was very successful at this. Some of his reprints were not of as high a standard as the original publications, but a few were actually better. According to Bohn's own advertisements, some if his reprints were far superior. In an 1839 catalogue, he offered: 'HARRIS'S AUREL-IAN . . . To which is now first added, a SUPPLEMENT, containing a complete Modern Nomenclature of all the Species figured in the work, By J. O. WESTWOOD . . . In one volume, small folio, with forty-four Plates . . . EXQUISITELY COLOURED AFTER THE ORIGINAL DRAWINGS. Reduced to £4. 4s. half-bound morocco. This is the original edition of the work printed in 1766, a few copies of which have lately been discovered in an old warehouse. The Supplement, containing the modern nomenclature, is quite new, and has been prepared expressly for the present copies, to which only it will be attached. The colouring is executed with the utmost accuracy and the highest finish, from the original drawings, and is far superior to any copies which have ever been sold, excepting the few coloured by Harris himself, to which these are at least equal'; 'LEWIN'S BIRDS OF NEW SOUTH WALES . . .

PL. XXXVII.

To my Ingenous Friend and Benefactor Mr Dru Drury This Plate is most Humbly Dedicated by his Obliged Servant Moses Harris

Death's Head Hawk Moth. Hand-coloured copper engraving from Moses Harris's *The Aurelian*, 1766.

Right: Globe Fish and inappropriate plants. Hand-coloured copper engraving from Mark Catesby's *Natural History of Carolina, Florida, and the Bahama Islands*, 1731–43.

An Phaseolus &c.

Orbis &c.

With Twenty-six Plates, beautifully coloured, Finished like Drawings. Third greatly improved Edition . . . Folio, originally published at £4. 4s. REDUCED TO £2. 2s. Neatly half-bound morocco. This beautiful and interesting volume, although now offered at a reduced price, has for a long time been considered very scarce. The colouring of the present copies is so infinitely superior to what have hitherto been sold, as scarcely to be recognised for the same plates'; 'LATHAM'S GENERAL HISTORY OF BIRDS . . . THE SECOND ENLARGED AND IMPROVED EDITION . . . 11 vols. 4to. reduced to the extremely low price of £12. 12s. Elegantly half-bound morocco . . . This celebrated work was published at twenty-five guineas in boards, with the plates coloured in a very inferior manner. The present copies are all COLOURED LIKE HIGHLY FINISHED DRAWINGS, with studious accuracy, under the direction of several eminent Ornithologists, and most of the subjects have been compared with living or preserved specimens in the Museums and Gardens of London. Copies coloured in this manner would not have been published at less than FIFTY GUINEAS.'

Although the lithographic revolution was well under way in the 1830s, Bohn and Coxhead listed only one or two lithographically illustrated items in their catalogues. Their wares, in 1839 anyway, were still primarily the products of engraving on wood or metal. For a time, indeed, it seemed as though steel engravings were in just as much demand in early and mid Victorian times as they had been previously. The work of the Sowerby dynasty shows how old habits die hard. Since the last quarter of the eighteenth century, members of the Sowerby family had been a dominant influence in zoological (and botanical) iconography, illustrating, writing and publishing books on most animal groups. They concentrated their efforts upon the lower animals, especially upon molluscs and their shells, and were among the last to abandon steel engraving for other methods of graphic reproduction. True, George Brettingham

A living Volute and Volute shells. Hand-coloured steel engraving from Louis-Charles Kiener's *Spécies Générale et Iconographie des Coquilles Vivantes*, 1834–79.

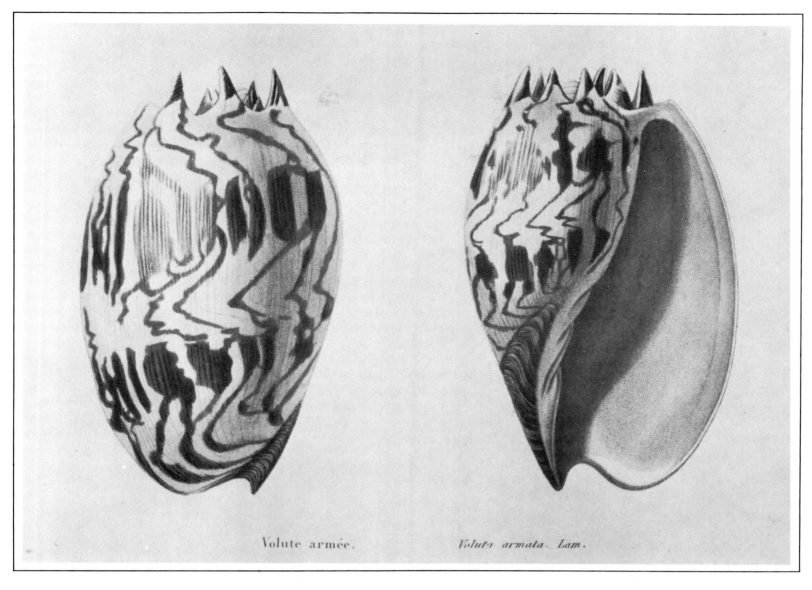

Volute armée.   *Voluta armata. Lam.*

Sowerby (second of the name) did many drawings on the stone for Lovell Reeve, the publisher and conchologist, but at the same time he continued to engrave on steel the many illustrations for his own *Thesaurus Conchyliorum* and other shell books.

In France, too, many books on insects, shells and other invertebrates were still being illustrated with steel engravings well into the second half of the century. The two finest shell books ever produced there are illustrated throughout with hand-coloured steel engravings, although both were produced during the period when lithography had become a favourite reproduction process for zoological enterprises. Louis-Charles Kiener began to issue his *Spécies Générale et Iconographie des Coquilles Vivantes* in 1834 and continued to mesmerise conchologists with the beauty of his immaculately coloured steel engravings up to 1879, three years before his death (the last volume being prepared by P. Fischer). Between 1843 and 1853, Jean-Charles Chenu, who followed Kiener as the curator of Baron J. P. B. Delessert's huge natural history collection at Lyon, published his impressive *Illustrations Conchyliologiques*, possibly the finest of all illustrated shell books. Never has steel engraving and hand colouring been more exquisitely combined. Kiener's and Chenu's plates show conclusively that shells, and by inference most other invertebrates, were more satisfactorily illustrated by steel engravings than by lithographs.

We may use the subject of conchology to introduce another aspect of zoological art. Many men and women have felt an irresistible urge to write and illustrate their own books, an urge which is usually satisfied, if at all, through the medium of a publisher. Occasionally, however, someone decides to go it alone and writes, illustrates and publishes his own brainchild. Such a person was Thomas Gray of Glasgow, an amateur conchologist who produced two books which have the doubtful distinction of being unrecorded in any major bibliography or book catalogue.

Overleaf: Shells of the genus *Strombus*. Hand-coloured and colour printed engraving from J.-C. Chenu's *Illustrations Conchyliologiques*, 1843–53. The exquisite colouring of Chenu's shells has never been surpassed.

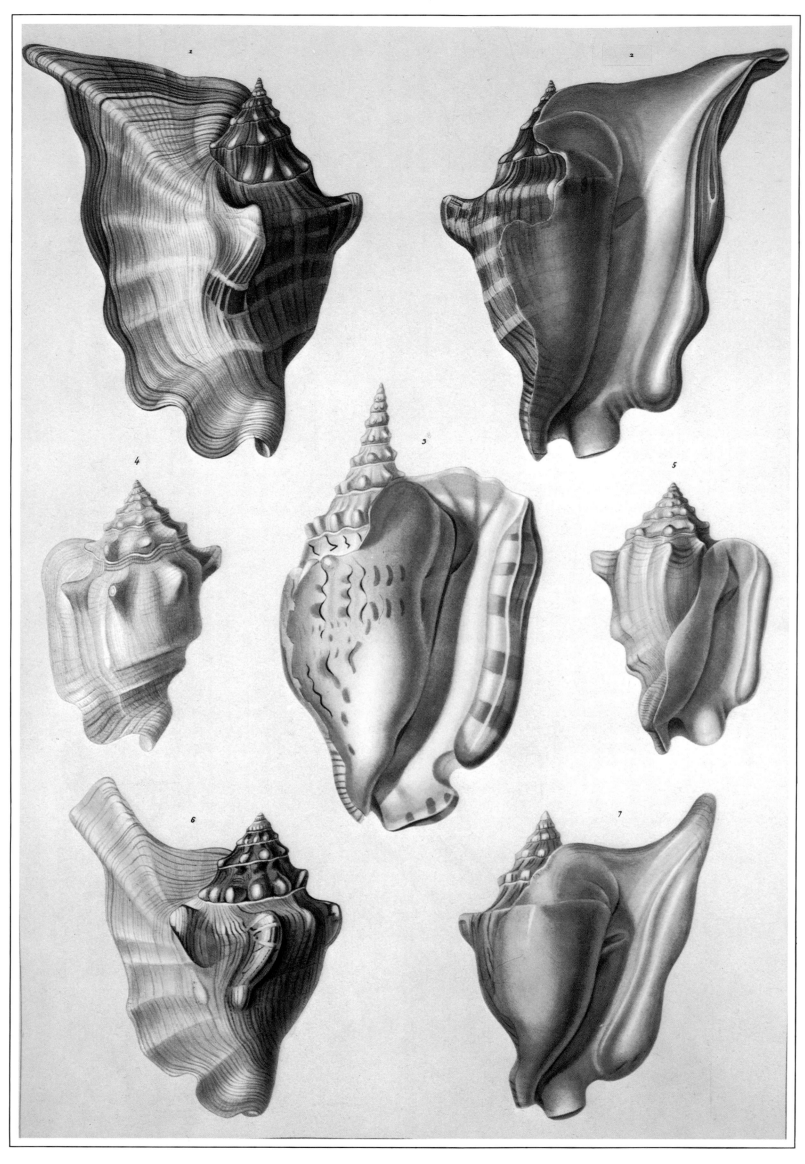

Pteropus samoensis. Peale.

T.R.Peale del.

Rawdon, Wright, Hatch & Edson.

In 1841, he wrote and printed *Illustrations of Conchology* containing 53 plates of watercolour drawings which he painted himself. He followed this, in 1848, with his two-volume *Icones Conchyliorum Terrestrium* containing a further 164 plates of his own watercolours of shells with accompanying letterpress written and printed by himself. Gray obviously produced these books for his own private pleasure, as he was satisfied to print only one copy of each, a rather extreme interpretation of the principle of limitation.

But such solo performances become almost masochistic exercises when the author decides to issue more than one copy of a book. Back in the late eighteenth century, William Lewin had given the personal touch to every copy of his *Birds of Great Britain* (1789–94) by embellishing each of its 323 plates with an original watercolour drawing. His enthusiasm for his ambitious venture must have waned considerably by the time he had finished illustrating the sixtieth and final copy for, by then, he had provided a total of nearly two thousand original watercolours. Understandably Lewin's book is one of the rarest, and most unequal, of all illustrated books on birds.

Other, much later examples of this self-imposed artistic torture are provided by the work of Theo Johnson who produced several privately printed books on natural history subjects. His *Illustrations of British Hawk Moths*, published in 1874, was illustrated with 35 original watercolours. Half a lifetime later, in 1906, his *Illustrations of Exotic Conchology* appeared, embellished with 45 original watercolours which were more noteworthy for their gaudiness than their accuracy.

If this outline of the background to zoological art in the nineteenth century seems sketchy, it is partly because the nineteenth century produced such an untidy profusion of individual activity in every sphere that its zoological literature lends itself less to a neatly ordered, overall treatment than to a series of literary vignettes. Partly, though, it is because one of the most important aspects of nineteenth-century zoological literature, the application of lithography to animal illustration, has been deliberately circumnavigated.

Great Snipe. Hand-coloured engravings from C. J. Temminck and Baron M. Laugier de Chartrouse's *Nouveau receuil de planches coloriés d'Oiseaux*, 1820–39.

Overleaf: Fruit-Eating Bat from Samoa, 'Pteropus samoensis'. Hand-coloured engraving after an original drawing by T. R. Peale from J. Cassin's monograph on mammalogy in *The United States Exploring Expedition, during the Years 1838–42*, under the command of Charles Wilkes, 1845–76.

CHAPTER VI
The Lithographic Revolution

The development of zoological art was advanced immeasurably, though not immediately, by a simple discovery made by Alois Senefelder at the end of the eighteenth century He found that printing ink would adhere closely to lines drawn on a limestone slab with a greasy crayon but not to the rest of the slab if it had been dampened with water. With the concomitant discovery that a piece of paper laid on the treated surface would take up a faithful impression of the inked lines, a new graphic reproduction process, lithography, was born. Quick to exploit his new process, Senefelder set in motion the Lithographic Revolution.

Though lithography was sometimes employed to illustrate insects and other creatures where fine detail was required, the method proved to be most suitable for portraying animals large enough to obviate the need for showing very delicate features Above all, it was an admirable process for reproducing pictures of mammals and birds, especially birds. It was appropriate, therefore, that the first book about animals to be illustrated by lithography was Karl Schmidt's *Beschreibung der Vögel*, published in 1818, the modest precursor of all the handsome and costly folios showing

Crested Shortbill and Hawk Moth. Hand-coloured lithographs by William Swainson from his *Zoological Illustrations* (First Series), 1820–23.

birds from all parts of the globe that are the chief glories of nineteenth-century zoological art.

William Swainson was one of the earliest converts to the lithographic process in England and used it for his *Zoological Illustrations* (1820–23). At the same time, he brought out his *Exotic Conchology* (1821–22) which showed that lithography could be a suitable medium for illustrating fairly large shells. In the illustrations to another shell book published a few years later, Edmund A. Crouch's *Illustrated Introduction to Lamarck's Conchology* (1827), two of the method's strong points, softness and delicate tonal gradations, are shown to perfection; in coloured copies the excellence of the lithography tends to be hidden, while the market value is disproportionately high. A master lithographer—and Crouch's work in this medium would be difficult to better—could produce un-coloured lithographs that are much more pleasing to discerning eye than most uncoloured steel engravings.

But at all times the book-buying public has wanted colour, and the lithographic print was, above all, a vehicle for colour. All the great folios and most of the memorable zoological books of lesser size issued during the last two-thirds of the nineteenth century were coloured. The authors of those books were clearly as much seduced by colour as were the book buyers. And in the context of the period, this is scarcely surprising. The world of nature can never before have seemed so colourful: from all parts of the globe came a seemingly endless succession of animals, brilliant, iridescent, fantastically shaped, plumed, scaled, spiny, striped, spotted, hairy, horned, glossy, hideous or breathtakingly beautiful, but, above all, colourful.

Each newly arrived expedition and each traveller fresh from adventuring in far-away places seemed intent upon bringing back ever more

Great Crested Grebe. Hand-coloured copper engraving by W. H. Lizars from Prideaux John Selby's *Illustrations of British Ornithology*, 1818–34. It may justly be claimed that this book contains the finest copper engravings to be found in any ornithological work.

Lobster. Hand-coloured steel engraving by James Sowerby from William Elford Leach's *Malacostraca Podophthalmata Britanniae*, 1815–75. Because the figures in this book were drawn actual size, it was necessary for some, like this one, to be on fold-out plates.

exotic creatures to Europe's capitals. With this revelation of the bewildering kaleidoscope of natural colours, the portrayal of zoological exotica in their full splendour became the overriding passion of many who saw them. Most magnificent of all were the birds, which had always been favourites with artists and naturalists.

Heron, '*Ardea speciosa*'. Hand-coloured lithograph from Thomas Horsfield's *Zoological Researches in Java and the Neighbouring Islands*, 1824.

ARDEA SPECIOSA.

Hoatzin, 'Opisthocomus cristatus'. Hand-coloured lithograph from George Robert Gray's *Genera of Birds*, 1844–49.

The practice of keeping unusual animals alive in zoological gardens helped the artist enormously. With a live subject in front of him, he now realised how much had been lost when only the skin or the set-up carcass had been available for study. He could see how vibrant and ever-changing were the feathers and plumes, how much more brilliant the colouring was in life than in death. He was dazzled by colour and, in turn, wanted to dazzle others.

An American, Dr Thomas Horsfield, tried to convey something of the beauty of living colour he had seen on the island of Java between 1799 and 1819 by having some of the animals he had collected there illustrated with coloured lithographs in his *Zoological Researches in Java and the Neighbouring Islands* (1824). As lithography was then considered un-suitable for showing fine detail clearly, some of the illustrations were engraved on copper (they certainly look better for it) and so the book was a hybrid affair. A few years later, however, Benjamin Waterhouse Hawkins was hired to make lithographs of a collection of drawings by native artists who had worked for Major-General Hardwicke in India. *Illustrations of Indian Zoology* (1830–34) was noteworthy for its many hand-coloured plates of birds looking impressively large in a folio format.

Nearly all the great bird books illustrated by lithography were to be published in folio, and the birds were shown natural size whenever possible, a development in which Audubon was the leading pacemaker. As the standards of lithographic reproduction improved, the process attracted the attention of gifted artists who between them effected the last great revolution in zoological art. Several of them were associated with John Gould who, more than anyone else, succeeded in using lithography to celebrate the beauties of the bird world.

Goose, '*Anas arcuata*'. Hand-coloured litho-graph from Thomas Horsfield's *Zoological Researches in Java and the Neighbouring Islands*, 1824.

ANAS ARCUATA.

Audubon may have been the author of the largest and most expensive of all bird books, but Gould, whose total output far exceeded Audubon's, did more to make men and women bird conscious. Significantly, it was Gould and not Audubon who was dubbed 'The Bird Man', even though Audubon's ornithological knowledge was much the greater. Enlisting the help of some very fine artists, Gould wrote, designed and published a series of lavishly illustrated folios. He covered the birds of Australia, the

'*Chauna derbiana*', a Screamer from South America. Hand coloured lithograph from George Robert Gray's *Genera of Birds*, 1844–49.

Right : Red-Breasted Toucan. Hand-coloured lithograph from J. Gould's *Monograph of the Ramphastidae or Toucans*, 1834.

birds of Europe, of the Himalayas, of New Guinea, of just about everywhere. He also published monographs of particular groups, big birds or small birds, but always colourful birds. He was directly responsible for the publication of three thousand (less one) hand-coloured lithographs of birds in 41 folio volumes, and he wrote most of the text to go with them. He also bought or captured most of the birds and mounted them. As if this were not enough, he saw to the publishing and distribution of the parts, obtained subscribers and looked after their interests personally. But, apart from designing all the plates and providing rough pencil sketches of their subjects, he did comparatively little finished artwork and seldom, if ever, executed a lithograph. First and foremost, he was an organiser of others' talents. He was to the iconography of birds what Lovell Reeve, his contemporary, was to the iconography of shells.

Gould took his first intelligent step up the ladder of fame in 1829 when he married Elizabeth Coxen, an artistic young lady of his own age, whose drawings were accomplished and charming. A year later, he acquired a large collection of birds from the Himalayas and took his second step by deciding to issue an illustrated book describing the rarest of the species whose skins he had stuffed and mounted. Being unversed in the scientific aspects of descriptive ornithology, he engaged N. A. Vigors to write the text. And he told his wife that she was going to learn how to transfer his sketches to lithographic stones, much to her surprise, no doubt. Vigors and Eliza did their work well, but Gould failed to find a publisher and reluctantly decided he would publish his own book. *A Century of Birds* was published in parts in 1831 and 1832. The birds were shown life size, and the impressions from the lithographic stones were taken by Charles Hullmandel, an excellent printer. The profitability of the venture set Gould off on his remarkable career.

He lost no time furthering that career. Before all the parts of his first book had been published, he had begun work on his second. *The Birds of Europe* was produced over a five-year period from 1832, with the feverishly busy Eliza now being assisted by Edward Lear, whose own exquisitely illustrated *Parrots* (1830–32) had been almost a solo affair. Lear sketched in some of the foregrounds and thus helped to develop the characteristics of the later Gould plates. Lear played a more vital part when he contributed nine of the thirty-four plates illustrating Gould's first book on a particular bird group, the *Monograph of the Ramphastidae or Family of Toucans* (1833–35). Then followed the *Monograph of the Trogonidae* (1836–38) in which about two-thirds of the species described and illustrated were then new to science.

Like his book on the toucans, the monograph on the trogons (which include the quetzal) dealt with brightly coloured birds. The gaudier the birds, the more Gould loved them, and so apparently did his clientele, for each of these monographs went into a second edition. And that is how his career might have continued, with his magnificently illustrated books following one another with almost monotonous regularity, the plates in each becoming more and more sophisticated and Gould himself becoming more confident, more authoritative, more respected, wealthier and ambitious for more fame. But there was one thing that he could not do: he could not organise the supply of birds to allow the completion of some of his more ambitious books.

Only two parts of his *Birds of Australia* had been issued when he was compelled to abandon it for lack of material. But he did not abandon it for long. Having made £7,000 over the previous eight years by the sales of his books, he decided to go to Australia with his wife and a paid assistant to collect the specimens he needed. He left England in May 1838 and returned in September 1840, leaving his assistant behind in Australia to continue collecting for him. Typically, Gould had made up a list of subscribers for the projected book before leaving England and had enlarged the list during his stay in Australia. Typically, too, he organised everyone so efficiently that the first part of the new version of

Birds of Australia, containing eighteen plates and associated text, was issued in December 1840, only three months after his return to London.

For this project, the most ambitious he ever undertook, he employed Henry Constantine Richter, a very competent artist and lithographer, who worked on the plates of most of his subsequent books. It is with Richter's arrival that the bird plates begin to take on their distinctive, uniquely Gouldian appearance. From this time onwards, each plate shows a pair of the particular species (if it is a large species, the male is shown on one plate and the female on another) carefully posed for an attractive effect. If the male and female have similar plumage, they are shown from above and below. Foreground and background scenes are nearly always subordinate to the birds, although sometimes the plants and foliage are prominently displayed when they have a close association with the birds. Richter was very good at the composition and arrangement of the botanical embellishments and took more trouble than Gould's other artists over the foreground scenes. Whether or not the representations of birds on these plates are very exact and lifelike, the plates themselves are always well composed and aesthetically very satisfying.

Unfortunately, the effect of Gould's plates in quantity is not so pleasing, as the eye appreciates variety. Gould adhered to his formula rather too rigidly, and his style became mannered. Too often, the exhilaration that can be induced by a few Gould plates is succeeded by a sense of ennui at their sameness when they are seen in quantity. Gould did not learn one very important lesson: if you are intent on giving the world three thousand hand-coloured plates of birds in folio, be sure that every so often you introduce the unexpected, the occasional surprise, something new. After the first half dozen Gould plates, there are no surprises—only more Gould plates.

Gould's five-volume *Monograph of the Trochilidae, or Family of Humming-Birds*, a dozen years in the making and one of his best sellers, deserves close scrutiny here, even though no-one could be blamed for a reluctance to inspect every one of its 360 dazzling plates. Before 1849, when Gould issued the first part of his gigantic offering, there had effectively been only one illustrated monograph on humming birds: the three-part *Histoire Naturelle des Oiseaux-mouches* by Réné-Primevère Lesson, produced in an octavo format—quite sufficient to display these tiny creatures—between 1829 and 1833. Each of its many plates, nearly all of them by Jean-Gabriel Prêtre, illustrates a single specimen perched on a twig.

In a note to 'the amateur and subscriber' prefacing the third part, Lesson says, 'For bibliophiles and ladies it is an album of elegant drawings; for everyone an unusual book, executed with care, full of graceful figures, dainty in its format, elegant in its execution. It has nothing of the heaviness of the in-folio, nothing of the pretention of academic memoirs.' Except

Humming Birds: '*Le Rivoli, Ornismya rivolii*' and (right) '*Oiseau-mouche à petit bec, Ornismya brevirostris*'. Hand-coloured steel engravings René-Primevère Lesson's *Histoire Naturelle des Oiseaux-mouches*, 1829–30.

for a few examples showing outspread wings, all the birds are shown in profile, stiff, lifeless, unreal and brilliantly coloured. There is not a spark of life or movement in any of them—they might as well be pieces of dress jewellery. If Gould was familiar with these dainty confections, and it is highly probable that he was, he would have been aware of their shortcomings by the time he became immersed in his own monograph.

Gould's humming birds could hardly be more different from Lesson's. Nearly every Gould plate shows one or two humming birds in flight as well as one or two at rest. Gould's main reason for showing so many of them flying was his desire to reveal the different aspects of their plumage, even though he must have been aware of the impossibility of capturing the evanescent beauty of humming birds on the wing. We may well be inclined to side with W. H. Hudson's view that Gould should not have shown them flying because of the artistic impossibility of the task. Whether or not we agree with him, there cannot be the smallest doubt that Gould's representations of humming birds are infinitely more satisfying to look at than Lesson's.

This is not the place to examine the whole voluminous output of 'The Bird Man'; we must pass over in silence such works as his *Birds of Great Britain*, his *Birds of New Guinea*, his *Birds of Asia*, his *Partridges of America*, even his *Monograph of the Kangaroos*—and much else besides. After all, he was not the only man who produced impressive folios which glamourised the more spectacular members of the animal kingdom. His unique gift was for making a very profitable business out of producing them; he alone had the energy and the organising ability to get three thousand different plates of birds sketched, lithographed, coloured, bound, subscribed and sold.

We are now set on a course which will bring us into contact with most of the other great names in Victorian zoological iconography. Several of them worked for Gould at one time or another; and most of them were able to take advantage of the demand for sumptuously illustrated books which he helped to create. But, in spite of the seemingly endless succession of published animal illustration in Britain, we should not forget the other, equally gifted men who were working away energetically, if less productively, at zoological subjects in other countries. It is only the sheer weight of the British achievement which suggests that little of significance was happening elsewhere. If an assessment were to be made on the basis of quality, we should have to adopt a more sober view of that achievement.

It is all too easy to enthuse over the well-publicised, continually auctioned and often reproduced products of the Gould factory while remaining ignorant even of the existence of many zoological treatises of equal or superior artistic merit. The magnificent hand-coloured lithographs of the *Oiseaux Brillans et Remarquables du Brésil* by J.-T.Descourtilz, dating from 1835, surely deserve the highest praise, but they were almost totally overlooked for a long time. Here the reason for the oversight was excusable because only two copies were produced. Indeed, rarity as often as not is the principal reason why some excellent illustrated zoological books have been overlooked. It must be the main reason, for instance, why more people have not noticed the existence of A. F. A. Wiegmann's *Abbildung und Beschreibung merkwurdiger Saugethiere*, a folio work dating from 1831–32. The fine plates by O. Bürde, among the earliest to illustrate mammals by means of lithography, do not appear to have been known to any bibliographer of zoological works (though they have not escaped the lynx eyes of the book-selling profession).

On the other hand, the plates issued under the title *Gleanings from the Menagerie and Aviary at Knowsley Hall* will be well known to anyone who appreciates fine illustrations of larger zoological subjects and has access to a well-appointed library. J. E. Gray of the British Museum, a jack-of-all-zoological-trades, supervised the publication of this two-volume pictorial record of the Earl of Derby's zoo at Knowsley, near

Overleaf: 'Chlamydera maculata', Spotted Bower Bird. Hand-coloured lithograph from J. Gould's The Birds of Australia, Part 4, 1841.

Liverpool, and the services of two excellent artists were obtained. One of these artists was Edward Lear, who paid special attention to the Earl's bird collection, and the other was Benjamin Waterhouse Hawkins, who concentrated on the mammals.

Lear, who was to become well known for his travels and watercolours and famous for his nonsense, had embarked on a career as a zoological illustrator at an early age. In 1830, when only 18, he conceived the idea of publishing a series of plates depicting members of the parrot family. In November of that year, the first two parts of his *Illustrations of the Family of Psittacidae or Parrots* were issued, and ten further parts followed before the project was prematurely abandoned in the spring of 1832. Lear drew the parrots from life, mostly in the Parrot House at the Zoological Society of London's gardens. He then re-drew them in reverse on the lithographic stones from which the prints were taken. These prints were then coloured by hand and despatched to the few people prepared to subscribe to the book's publication. Lear had preceded Gould in choosing to illustrate a book on birds with hand-coloured lithographs, in supervising the prints at every stage of the printing process and in deciding to be his own publisher. In transferring his own designs to the stone, he went further than Gould. Despite their similar aims, Lear and Gould were totally unlike each other; Lear was a more sensitive and far better artist. It is scarcely surprising that Lear eventually helped to illustrate some of Gould's books. The great organiser was not one to let a talent like Lear's go to waste.

Lear was introduced to Lord Stanley (later to succeed to the title of Earl of Derby) by Gray, who asked the artist to draw some of the creatures at Knowsley Hall. Lear agreed and completed over a hundred drawings at various times from 1832 to 1836. His work, once again, was of a high standard and the large size of the plates enhanced it. Waterhouse Hawkins also excelled at large-scale lithographs. His plates for the *Gleanings* include some of the finest representations of mammals ever executed. The soft lines of the lithograph are admirable for capturing the contours and texture of fur; the hand colouring of these plates was so well applied at least in the most select copies of the book, that the final results are wholly admirable. The composition of the mammal plates is always pleasing; the animals are usually represented as part of a scene in which foreground and background details never obtrude but merely set off the main subjects. Waterhouse Hawkins did not give his mammals human expressions, but he was not averse to making them appealing. The plate labelled 'Korin—*Gazella rufifrons*' shows a group of gazelles which could have provided models for Walt Disney's 'Bambi'. Although it would be incorrect to label the artist a sentimentalist, the way he captures the wide-eyed innocence of these delightful creatures would have wrung the heart strings of Disney himself.

One of the effects of lithography was to bring artists who utilised it more prominently to public attention. The new artistic freedom they acquired by drawing direct on the stone made their work seem more vital and more individual than before. The value and interest of an expensive illustrated book could now be seen to depend so much on the quality of the illustrations that it was as important for the intending purchaser to know who illustrated it as to know who wrote it. If the artist was someone of recognised stature, the book stood a good chance of selling well. Most high-quality books were nevertheless still subscribed for, just to make sure that they would not be produced at a loss. Once an author had found good artists, he was reluctant to let them go. This was particularly true of the artists who worked on the larger natural history subjects, for there was never a glut of them in their specialised field.

Gould was good at finding, cultivating and keeping such artists. When his wife died, he enlisted the services of Waterhouse Hawkins to help him with the quarto plates illustrating his account of the birds in the *Zoology of the Voyage of H.M.S. Sulphur* (1843–44), but it was Conrad

TERRAPENE CLAUSA.

J.D.C Sowerby del. E.Lear lithog.   Printed by C.Hullmandel.

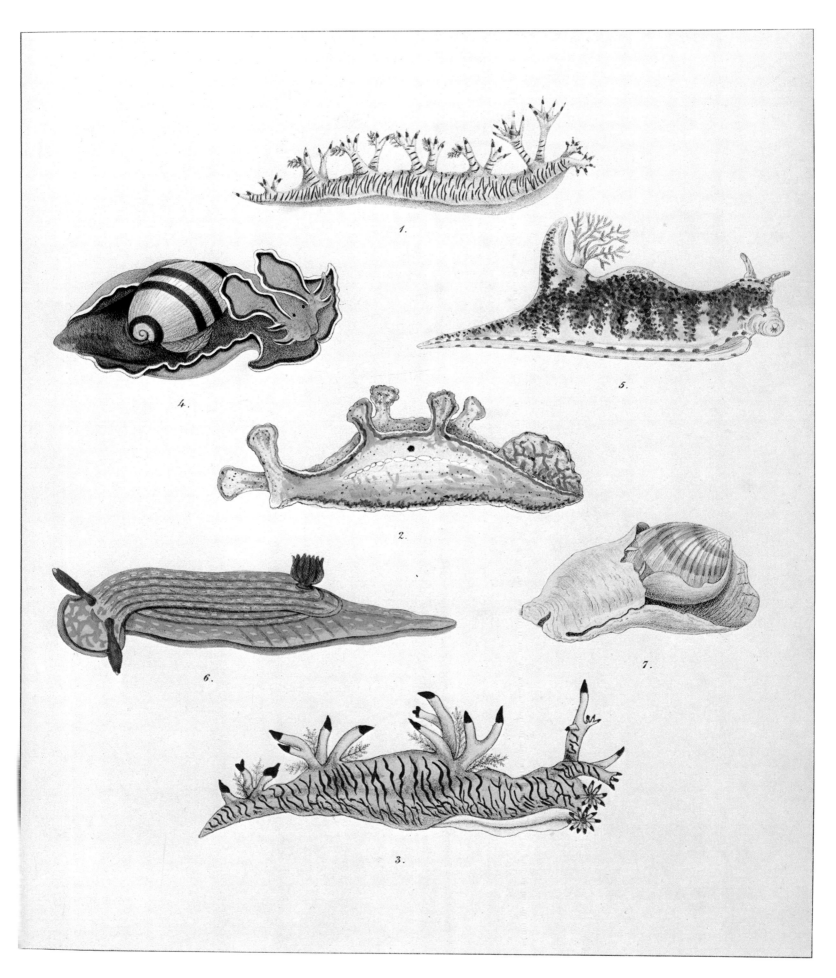

Sea Slugs and other gastropod molluscs. Hand-coloured lithograph after drawings by Arthur Adams from *The Zoology of the Voyage of HMS Samarang, Mollusca*, 1848, by Adams and L. A. Reeve.

Left : Chequered Tortoise, '*Terrapene clausa*'. Hand-coloured lithograph by Edward Lear after an original drawing by James de Carle Sowerby, from Thomas Bell's *Monograph of the Testudinata*, 1836–42.

Richter who really made it possible for him to issue most of his more ambitious works. Richter lithographed hundreds of Gould's plates and also painted many full-scale watercolours of birds for him. He lithographed all the 360 plates illustrating the monograph on humming birds, an indication both of his industry and of Gould's ability to harness it. William Hart was brought into the fold in 1851; he was at work on *The Birds of New Guinea* when Gould died in 1881. Hart not only made many original watercolour drawings and drew them on the stones, but he also coloured the prints. Gould certainly had his money's worth out of Hart. But there was one man Gould could not capture, at least not for as long as he would have wished. This man was Joseph Wolf, whose work includes some of the finest creations in zoological iconography.

We know a great deal about this artist, largely from a detailed biography of him by A. H. Palmer, the son of a very different artist, Samuel Palmer. Because of his achievements as an artist, because almost all his waking hours were dedicated to the close observation and truthful portrayal of animals, and because by general consent his work is considered to represent all that is best in animal art, Wolf's life deserves more than a passing note here.

Born in the German village of Mörz in 1820, he spent his boyhood in and around the fields of the family farm where he devoted rather more time to watching animals and plants than his father would have wished. Even in these early days, he sketched living animals. He reared birds at home as well as in the wild and came to know them intimately by observing them closely. Birds of prey soon became his special favourites and were to remain his lifelong passion. He devised a means of trapping them so that he could observe them closely without harming them. Merlins and kestrels were often caught in his spring trap, and on one occasion a buzzard was trapped but by sheer wing-power loosened the whole contraption and flew away with it. This did not deter Wolf, who was rarely without living subjects for study. In various other ways he showed that he was no ordinary farmer's boy, as when he made his own brushes out of the longest and most elastic hairs pulled from the tails of beech martens and set in the quills of various birds' feathers.

In his youth, he acquired more knowledge of the appearance and ways of animals than most men acquire in a lifetime. In 1836, however, the sixteen-year-old Wolf was apprenticed to a firm of lithographers in Coblenz, where he spent the next three years picking up the rudiments of a craft in which he was later to excel. Returning to his father's farm for a year, he painted a series of miniature watercolours of birds for his own amusement. This modest collection was to be the stepping stone to his future career: it was shown to Eduard Rüppell of Frankfurt who was so impressed by it that he commissioned Wolf to illustrate a book on the birds of North-East Africa for him (with results that, for various reasons, were disappointing).

These miniature watercolours were to lead to something much more exciting for Wolf, because they were also seen by Hermann Schlegel of Leyden, an authority on falconry, who immediately asked the young artist to do some drawings for a treatise on that subject. The first part of the *Traité de Fauconnerie* by Schlegel and A. H. Verster von Wulverhorst

Left: Grant's Gazelle. Wood engraving after Joseph Wolf from P. L. Sclater and M. R. Oldfield Thomas's *The Book of Antelopes*, vol. 3, 1897–98.

Right: Woodcock carrying its young. Wood engraving after an original drawing by Joseph Wolf from James Edmund Harting's *Sketches of Bird Life*, 1883.

Polar Bear climbing a floe. Wood engraving after Joseph Wolf from *The Royal Natural History*, edited by Richard Lydekker, vol. 3, 1894–95.

was published in 1844, the last in 1853. Eleven of its huge lithographed plates were executed by Wolf (though he was not responsible for the indifferently drawn backgrounds). In spite of the rather stiff and formal attitudes of some of the falcons on these plates, their overall impact is stunning. Certainly no other book on falconry has illustrations to rival them in accuracy, and only Wolf's own later work excels them in artistry. Further commissions inevitably followed, and thereafter Wolf, who had never had a formal art lesson, found no difficulty obtaining work to his liking.

Realising that he still had much to learn about the profession into which his natural gifts had led him, he began to attend an art school. He drew outlines from antique models, copied portraits, applied himself to oil painting and generally tackled the aspects of art which he had previously ignored. Had he been subjected to this 'school discipline' at the outset, he told his biographer, his animal subjects would have been 'knocked out of his head', a telling indictment of contemporary art education. While he was being 'educated', he continued to sketch and paint his beloved birds and mammals. But it was not enough for him to sketch and paint them; he had to know them, understand them, sympathise with them.

He made many outline sketches of the animals he shot (a desire to gun down the objects of their passion has characterised the early careers of many animal lovers besides Wolf) and from these outlines he compiled a scale of comparative measurements, subdivided under such headings as Foot, Tail, and so on. He also noted the exact positions, shapes and areas of various patches of feathers as well as the shape of each kind of feather, and drew diagrams of heads and other parts, filling many pages of his meticulously ordered notebooks with information for future reference. He could therefore dispense with constant visits to museum collections to check on these features. His knowledge of the arrangement and appearance of plumage went beyond that of any previous bird artist.

Wolf was a fanatic for work; as opportunity allowed, he drew trees, foliage, flowers, tangled thickets of brambles—he loved these—and anything else which could be incorporated into his animal pictures. He made it his business to learn as much as he could about the animals' environment, because its make-up and colouring, he realised, contributed both to their concealment and their beauty. Everything he did had an artistic purpose and in everything he was methodical. When he was not drawing, painting or measuring, he was watching.

Even his methods of field work were carefully organised. Once, having been shown a good hiding place in the Odenwald, he made preparations to watch the assembly of the Black Grouse. He dug himself a hole, made a screen of fir branches and, clutching his binoculars (actually opera

Dessiné par M.WOLF, accessoires par C.SCHEUREN   Publié chez A.ASNZ et Comp à MINZ

LE TIERCELET HAGARD DE FAUCON D'ISLANDE.

Gyrfalcon. Hand-coloured lithograph by Joseph Wolf (the bird only) from H. Schlegel and A. H. V. von Wulverhorst's *Traité de Fauconnerie*, 1844–53. This book contains some of the largest and possibly the finest plates of falcons ever published; they include some of Wolf's most outstanding animal illustrations.

Purple Guan, *Penelope purpurascens*, a member of the Curassow family from South America. Hand-coloured lithograph after an original drawing by Edward Lear, from J. E. Gray's *Gleanings from the Menagerie and Aviary* at Knowsley Hall, vol. 1, 1846.

glasses), crept into it just before dawn. 'There is a great enjoyment in watching these birds day after day,' he told A. H. Palmer. 'When they fight, the combs of the males are inflated, so that they look as big as strawberries. These combs are chiefly developed in the breeding season, and are therefore not much known to sportsmen. Nor do sportsmen know the size of the comb of a Red Grouse, which, when courting is going on in the spring, is three-quarters of an inch high.' It is almost unnecessary to point out that Wolf's fellow artists knew even less of these things than sportsmen did, or that such observations are the hallmarks of a first-rate ornithologist.

Wolf's bird portraits had captivated more than one British ornithologist. Inevitably, their excellence had not gone unnoticed by 'The Bird Man' himself who commissioned him to do a small watercolour of partridges. Soon afterwards, in 1848, Wolf packed up his belongings and boarded a steamer for London.

Once in England, he found, to his amazement, that his knowledge and instincts as an artist did not stand for much in the eyes of the artists and naturalists he met. 'Among the naturalists,' he told Palmer, 'there are some who are very keen about scientific correctness, but who have no artistic feeling. If a thing is artistic they mistrust it. There must be nothing right in perspective. There must be nothing but a map of the animal, and in a side view. They are like those other naturalists who only know a bird when they handle the skin. It is impossible, for instance, for a mere museum man to know the true colour of the eyes.' An acid view, perhaps, but probably a true enough picture of the situation as it was in England—and most of Europe, too—in the 1850s. From this quotation alone it can be seen that Wolf brought a new kind of vision to bird art and showed future generations of bird artists the road they should follow.

It was not long before Wolf was called upon to provide illustrations for the publications of the Zoological Society of London, in whose Gardens he was to spend many happy and industrious hours sketching. His 27 contributions to the Society's *Transactions*, lithographed by other hands, include some of his finest work and mostly depict mammals. Gould tried

E. Lear del.   J. W. Moore lith.

PURPLE GUAN.   PENELOPE PURPURASCENS.

Hullmandel & Walton Lithographers.

hard to get hold of Wolf, but, apart from extracting some watercolours of birds of prey from the unwilling artist which were eventually reproduced in his *Birds of Great Britain*, he was not very successful. One of the reasons for his failure to secure the lasting services of an artist recognisably superior to any other of the time was Gould's love for bright colours; Wolf was much more attuned to birds with muted colouring. In any case, the two men were incompatible in temperament and could not have worked together harmoniously.

Wolf's own *The Poets of the Woods*, published in 1853, was illustrated with nine chromolithographs of birds. As these were the first chromolithographs of birds ever published, it is hardly surprising that they were a disappointment to him. In the following year, he published a similar volume entitled *Feathered Favourites*, again with disappointing results. Like so many artists, he was often at the mercy of reproduction processes over which he had no control. He was luckier with his *Zoological Sketches*, a collection of 100 plates illustrating various exotic animals in the Zoological Society's Gardens at Regent's Park. Published between 1856 and 1867, this substantial work was based on Wolf's original designs, which were then lithographed and coloured by Joseph Smit, a Dutchman who had come to England in 1866 and had been befriended by Wolf. Smit worked well with Wolf and the result of this happy collaboration was one of the finest collections of scenes of animals in their natural surroundings ever published. As only 94 copies were subscribed, it is also one of the rarest.

In the 1860s, Wolf was engaged in designing the plates for two books written by a wealthy American authority on birds, Daniel Giraud Elliot.

Cape Hartebeest. Hand-coloured lithograph by Joseph Smit from an original by Joseph Wolf, from P. L. Sclater and M. R. Oldfield Thomas's *The Book of Antelopes*, 1894–1900.

'Maternal Courage'. Wood engraving (reproduced here larger than its original size) after design by Joseph Wolf from Daniel Giraud Elliot and Joseph Wolf's *The Life and Habits of Wild Animals*, 1874.

The *Monograph of the Phasianidæ* (1872) and *Monograph of the Paradiseidae* (1873) are hardly noteworthy for the muted colouring of the plates, but even Wolf would have admitted that pheasants and birds of paradise demand the brightest colours in an artist's colour box. Evidently Wolf

did his best work when the company was to his liking. In Elliot he had a generous and sympathetic patron and in Smit a kindred, if less gifted, spirit.

But for all Wolf's originality and vision, he was very much a Victorian whenever he stepped beyond the bounds of scientific illustrating. Nothing could have been more Victorian than his two chromolithographed

Elliot's Bird of Paradise. Hand-coloured lithograph by Joseph Wolf and Joseph Smit from Daniel Giraud Elliot's *Monograph of the Paradiseidae,* 1873. The plates in this work, almost as magnificent as the birds they portray, were the fruits of Eliot's considerable wealth, Wolf's great artistry and both men's profound knowledge and love of birds.

Desert Cat. Hand-coloured lithograph by Joseph Wolf and Joseph Smit from Daniel Giraud Elliot's *Monograph of the Felidae or Family of Cats*, 1883.

monstrosities, but there the make-up of the books was largely responsible. It was otherwise with his own 'set pieces' showing animals in scenes which 'point a moral or adorn a tale', such as 'Surprise' (two rabbits confronting a snow-covered scarecrow), 'Peace and War' (a turtle dove perched meaningfully above a discarded soldier's helmet), 'Inquisitive Neighbours' (a pair of squirrels glared at by a discomfited ring dove).

Burmese Stork-Bill Kingfisher. Hand-coloured lithograph by John Gerrard Keulemans from Richard Bowdler Sharpe's *Monograph of the Alcedinidae, or Family of Kingfishers*, 1868–71.

'The Island Sanctuary'. Wood engraving after an original design by Joseph Wolf from Daniel Giraud Elliot and Joseph Wolf's *The Life and Habits of Wild Animals*, 1874.

'Mrs Gray's Waterbuck'. Hand-coloured lithograph by Joseph Smit after an original by Joseph Wolf, from P. L. Sclater and M. R. Oldfield Thomas's *The Book of Antelopes*, 1894–1900.

The Victorian side of Wolf can be seen in the illustrations for *The Life and Habits of Wild Animals* (1874), which was written by Elliot and illustrated with engravings by J. W. and Edward Whymper from Wolf's designs. It hardly matters that Wolf considered the engravings pale shadows of his original artwork. The very titles of his subjects—'Bruin at Bay', 'A Happy Family', 'Maternal Courage', etc.—are sufficient to indicate their triteness. The book enjoyed considerable popular success and was universally praised by the critics, another indication that a great and original artistic talent had been overwhelmed by the bad taste of the age. Wolf, who died in 1899, is remembered now only for his achievements, which were many; it is easy to forgive his occasional lapses. The only way Wolf (or any other artist) could have been entirely true to the best in himself would have been by lithographing all his own designs, colouring all his own plates and shutting his eyes to social trends and dictates. Even the capable and self-sufficient Wolf could not manage that. Fortunately it was the best aspects of his art which influenced other artists.

Among those artists, besides Smit, were Keulemans and Thorburn. John Gerrard Keulemans, like Smit, came to England from Holland to earn his living as a bird artist. Like Wolf and Smit, he had worked for Schlegel but had found the prospect of working in London too alluring to resist. It was Richard Bowdler Sharpe who persuaded him to leave his native soil in 1869. Sharpe's *Monograph of the Kingfishers* was by then well advanced, and Keulemans had already supplied some of the drawings for it. He went on to execute many hundreds of original drawings for various authors of bird books and for contributors to ornithological journals. In the latter part of his career, he also transferred most of his drawings, as well as those of other artists (including Wolf), to the stones.

It was Keulemans, for instance, who executed most of the lithographs from Wolf's drawings for Elliot's monograph of the pheasants. He lacked Wolf's profound knowledge of birds but was able to instil life into his subjects even though he had to work largely from preserved specimens. Even if there had been living models available, he might not have taken much advantage of them. No man who turned out so many drawings and lithographs could have afforded the time to sit in an aviary to obtain lifelike impressions of unco-operative birds. Having hit upon a suitable formula, which was unashamedly modelled on Gould's, he sped through plate after plate, with his compositions varying little from first to last. Keulemans may not have been much of an innovator but at least his customers knew what they were going to get and were not kept waiting.

In view of his prolificacy, the plates are generally of high quality; few are less than pleasing. But it is only the beauty of the birds themselves which saves much of his work from seeming pedestrian. To say that he was little more than an honest journeyman in ornithological graphics might seem harsh but it would not be far from the truth. In any case, with so many new or poorly known birds flooding in from freshly explored territories in Africa, South America, Australasia and elsewhere, such a man was a godsend. He supplied his customers with bird pictures in quantity. That he was able to bring so much quality into his work at the same time must be considered a bonus.

The work of Archibald Thorburn spanned the years of the late nineteenth century and the first three decades of the twentieth. His distinctive and immaculate art was, like Wolf's, the outcome of natural artistic talent backed up with knowledge obtained along the sights of a gun and from close observation and frequent handling of animals, both alive and dead. Birds were his favourite subjects, too, and he had a remarkable ability to draw the small species. He is most famous, though, for his vivid

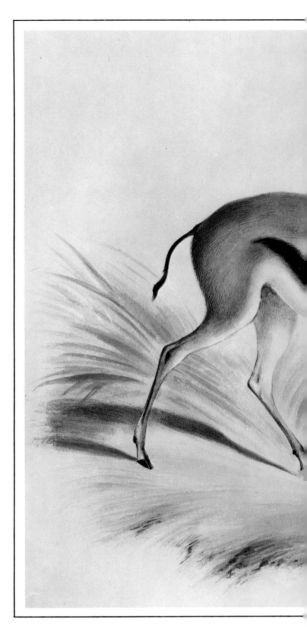

'Korin — *Gazella rufifrons*'. Hand-coloured lithograph by Benjamin Waterhouse Hawkins from J. E. Gray's *Gleanings from the Menagerie and Aviary at Knowsley Hall*, vol. 2, 1850.

'*Dicotyles labiatus*', the White-Lipped Peccary. Hand-coloured lithograph by Joseph Wolf and Joseph Smit from Edward Alston's monograph of the Mammalia in *Biologia Centrali-Americana*, vol. 2, 1879–82.

Right : 'Esquimaux Dog' — Husky. Hand-coloured lithograph by J. G. Keulemans from St G. J. Mivart's *Dogs, Jackals, Wolves and Foxes, A Monograph of the Canidae*, 1890.

Three wood engravings from James Edmund Harting's *Sketches of Bird Life*, 1883. Blue Tits (from an original drawing by Archibald Thorburn), Teal (from an original drawing by J. G. Keulemans) and Curlew.

portrayals of birds of prey and game birds. The master of every aspect of animal art, Thorburn has never been surpassed in the delineation of feathers, conveying the softness of their texture and the delicacy of their markings with a skill which has been the despair of bird artists ever since.

Unlike Smit and Keulemans, he placed great emphasis on setting his subjects in suitable scenery. The environment, for him, was as important

'Magellanic Dog'. Hand-coloured lithograph by J. G. Keulemans from St George Jackson Mivart's *Dogs, Jackals, Wolves and Foxes, a Monograph of the Canidae*, 1890.

a part of an animal picture as the animals themselves. Even Wolf's scenic backgrounds are seldom as pleasing or as effective; but if anyone may be considered Wolf's spiritual descendant, it is Thorburn.

Many of Thorburn's designs were produced by chromolithography, including those he did for Lord Lilford's *Coloured Figures of the Birds of the British Islands* (1885–98) which is generally considered to contain some of the finest pictures of birds ever reproduced in colour. The *Supplement* to H. E. Dresser's *History of the Birds of Europe*, however, contains a handful of plates by Thorburn which are hand-coloured

Squirrel, '*Sciurus variegatus*'. Hand-coloured lithograph by J. G. Keulemans from Edward Alston's monograph of Mammalia in *Biologia Centrali Americana*, vol. 2, 1879–82.

A.Thorburn

2/7

Litho. W. Greve, Berlin.

lithographs. Perhaps Thorburn is best known today through many fine reproductions of individual plates of birds and mammals produced in limited and often signed editions and by his own *British Birds* (1915–18) and *British Mammals* (1920–21) which were published long after the period covered by this book.

It would be misleading to end this chapter without reference to the use of lithography for illustrating invertebrates. Probably the first time it was employed to cover a complete invertebrate group was in 1821, when J. S. Miller's *Natural History of the Crinoidea, or Lily-shaped Animals* was published in Bristol, around which city Miller found most of his specimens.

Most of the fifty plates depict fossil examples of this predominantly fossil group but one or two show species which are found in modern seas; one of them, *Comatula fimbriata*, forms the frontispiece. It was singularly appropriate that Miller should illustrate his book lithographically because crinoids are common fossils in the kind of limestone used for lithography. Hardly anyone else in England had used lithography to illustrate natural history subjects, but Miller had lived for some time in Danzig (now Gdansk), where German had been his everyday language, and it is more than likely that he was familiar with the art of lithographic illustration. The preface to his book indicates another reason for his choice of lithographs rather than steel engravings. Finding that his monograph had grown too large to be published by the Linnean Society

$\frac{1}{3}$

A. Thorburn

Litho. W. Greve, Berlin.

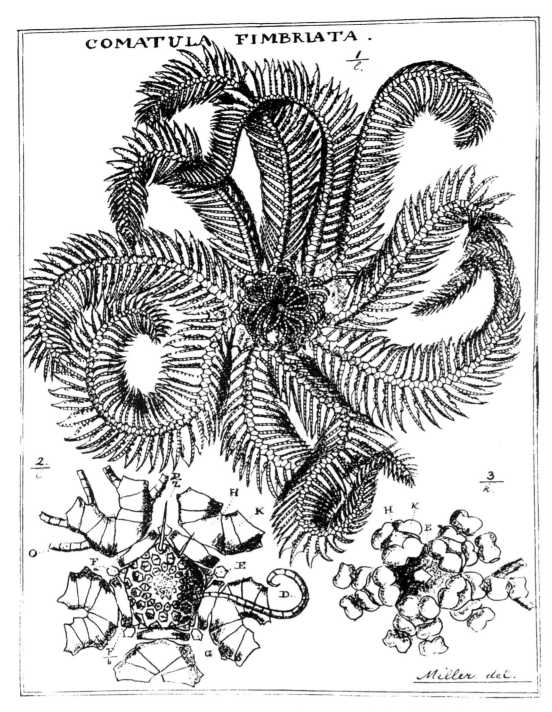

COMATULA FIMBRIATA.

Miller del.

'*Comatula fimbriata*', a Feather-Star. Lithograph, frontispiece to J. S. Miller's *Natural History of the Crinoidea*, 1821.

Right : Basilisk, '*Basiliscus vittatus*'. Lithograph from the Reptiles and Amphibia section of *Biologia Centrali-Americana*, edited by Frederick Ducane Godman and O. Salvin, 1879–1910.

in its Transactions, as he had originally intended, he decided to publish it himself. Because 'regular engravings' would have been too expensive he decided to produce 'the necessary illustrations in a series of Lithographic Plates, as the only mode in which a private individual could bring forward such an undertaking, and one which, if less consistent with its beauty as a work of art, might yet, it was observed, bestow an additional degree of fidelity and precision on its anatomical details.' Miller's objective assessment of his performance on the stone was sound, for his plates are noteworthy for their scientific clarity and lack of artistic pretension. Only the accident of its subject's intrinsic beauty makes his frontispiece pleasing in other respects. Miller's words also throw some light on Swainson's early predilection for lithography: it was cheaper.

Lithography had pleasing results when applied to the illustration of at least the larger species in that mammoth compendium of shell portraits, the *Conchologia Iconica* of Reeve and Sowerby, a book which no customer was able to own in its entirety until thirty-five years after the appearance of its first instalment in 1843. But when Kiener adapted some of its illustrations for his own *Spécies Générale*, he demonstrated the superiority of steel engravings for showing fine detail and diminutive species.

Steel engravings were also much more suitable for displaying the minute features of most insects, but lithography has been used effectively for showing off the beauties of the larger species, particularly of Lepidoptera. J. O. Westwood's *Arcana Entomologica, or Illustrations of New, Rare, and Interesting Insects* (1841–45) is illustrated by lithography, with

Turban Shells. Hand-coloured lithograph by G. B. Sowerby (second of the name) from L. A. Reeve's *Conchologia Iconica*, 1843–78.

Right : Four species of '*Phyllomorpha*', heteropterous bugs. *Far right :* '*Deroplatys desiccata*', a Mantis. Hand-coloured lithographs from John Obadiah Westwood's *Arcana Entomologica*, 1841–45.

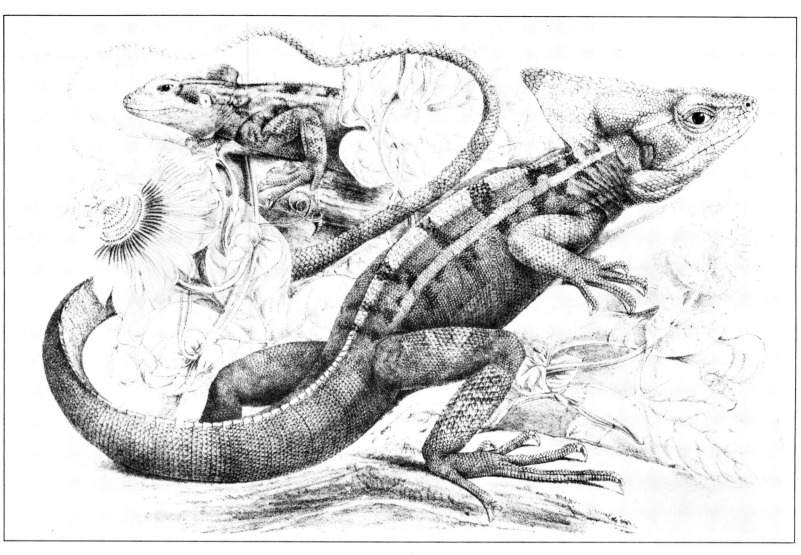

BUCEPHALUS CAPENSIS. Var A.
(Reptilia Plate II.)

pleasing results whenever the species are large and showy. R. H. F. Rippon's *Icones Ornithopterorum* (1898–1906) is among the best, though one of the least known, examples of a book in which lithography is employed to illustrate an insect group. This two-volume, privately published work has nearly a hundred plates, most of them exquisitely hand coloured, displaying those most gorgeous of all insects, the birdwing

Snake, '*Bucephalus capensis*'. Hand-coloured lithograph by G. H. Ford from Sir Andrew Smith's *Illustrations of the Zoology of South Africa*, 1838–49.

Bird-Wing Butterflies of the genus *Troides*. Hand-coloured lithographs from R. H. F. Rippon's *Icones Ornithopterorum*, 1898–1906. Perhaps no more than 30 copies of this privately published book were issued with the complete complement of plates.

butterflies. Here, of course, the large and colourful wings are the eye-catching features, while the nature and quality of the lithographed lines are swamped by the riotous colouring. It may be more correct to say that these books succeed in spite of rather than because of the lithographic process. In a zoological context, lithography achieves its finest effects only when its subjects are large and beautiful.

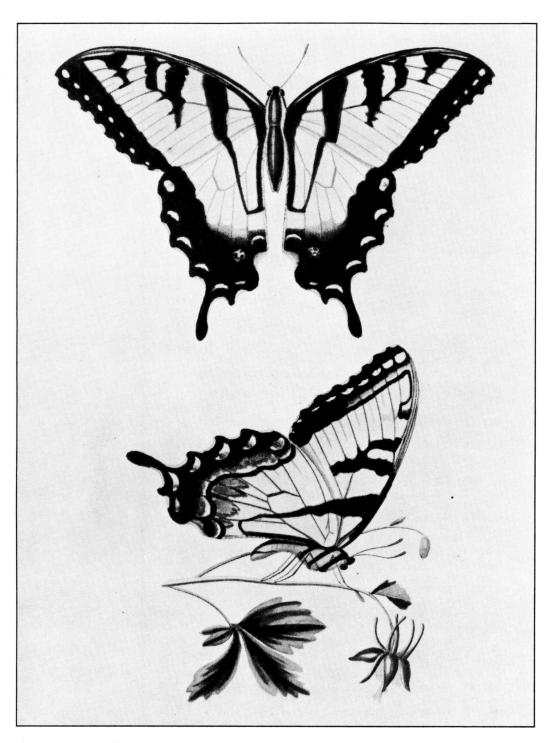

Butterflies, 'Papilio turnus'. Hand-coloured engraving from Say's *American Entomology*, 1824–28.

There is a boldness, a largeness if you like, about the lithographic process and it attracted men—though not, it seems, women—who revelled in bold, large subjects. Gould's humming birds may have been neither bold nor large, but these qualities were supplied by the dimensions of the plates in which they were set: the process demanded the size which the subjects lacked.

The Lithographic Revolution may be said to have ended with Thorburn. Another revolution in animal illustration, made possible by the camera, was well under way long before his death in 1935. The appearance of animals could now be recorded with great clarity and accuracy. No longer was it inevitable that a picture would be marred by large or small infidelities introduced into it by the fallible pencil of an artist, the erring crayon of a lithographer or the over-zealous brush of a colourist. The photographer was ousting the illustrator.

Zoological iconography had taken a long time to reach the impartiality of the photograph. But the thirty-thousand-year interval between cave scribble and photographic fidelity had been illuminated from time to time by men and women who gave us something much more fascinating and precious than impartiality. In their very different ways, Mu Ch'i, Dürer, Pisanello, Renard, Merian, Catesby, Bewick, Audubon, Wolf and many others gave us their personal visions of the animal world, legacies for which we should be eternally grateful.

Right: A South American scene with Rheas and Cavies. Wood engraving after G. Mützel from *The Royal Natural History*, edited by Richard Lydekker, vol. 3, 1894–95.

PART TWO

CHAPTER VII
Mirrors to Ourselves

The author of an illustrated book needs to bear in mind the kind of public he is trying to satisfy. If he has produced a scientific zoological treatise, the illustrations must be accurate and clear; they do not have to be aesthetically pleasing. If the book is meant for a more popular audience then it is more important for the illustrations to be appealing than to be accurate.

To show an animal as it really is would seem to be a reasonable artistic objective, but it is one that is not often attained. The most faithful and most sensitive studies of higher animals have often had a sporting context. Ironically, the most sympathetic understanding of animals has often been found in people who derive pleasure from hunting and killing them.

The sporting artist, who specialises in depicting the chase, the kill, the bag and so on, has several distinct advantages over artists who merely draw animals intermittently. He sees his subjects many times and in many different poses. He often sees them moving about in their native haunts—a very different experience to seeing them in a zoo—and he is constantly handling them when they are freshly killed, before they lose the colour and lustre of life, becoming set in the inflexible attitudes of death. That this close and constant acquaintance with hunted animals can have a salutary effect on art is strikingly evident from the earliest of all graphic art forms: prehistoric cave painting.

To a considerable extent, the sporting artist achieves his best effects (as does any good artist whatever his special field of endeavour) by unconsciously introducing a great deal of himself into his work. There are many ways an artist's personality creeps into his work. In his book, *Animals and Men*, Sir Kenneth Clark compares two sporting pictures, one by J.-B. Oudry and the other by Oudry's compatriot and contemporary Alexandre-François Desportes, both of whom painted in a similar manner. Oudry's picture shows a group of slain animals being guarded by two hounds; on a wall out of reach of the dogs, a live pheasant spreads its wings; a gun leans conspicuously against the wall. We get the impression that Oudry had a great sympathy for animals, loved them alive or dead, and was so much their master that it was enough merely to show his gun amongst them. The other picture is dominated by a portrait of Desportes himself as a hunter with a gun. Like Oudry, he has a pile of slain animals in the foreground, and two dogs are there as well; but no live wild creature is to be seen. Desportes, apparently, was less interested in living animals than dead ones and saw them, in this picture at any rate, as objects against which he could set off his own Olympian presence.

There is more humility, sympathy and understanding represented in Oudry's picture than in Desportes's. The slaughtered animals in Desportes's picture are mere decorative elements, well-groomed components of a still-life. Those in Oudry's humbler masterpiece have been flung down untidily, their limbs, heads and wings at all angles; a roe deer in the foreground is remarkable for the dishevelled state of its fur, a heron in the background for the inelegant attitude of its splayed legs. Even when Desportes, in another picture, indicated the hunter's presence by a solitary gun, he posed the victims of that weapon elegantly in front of it.

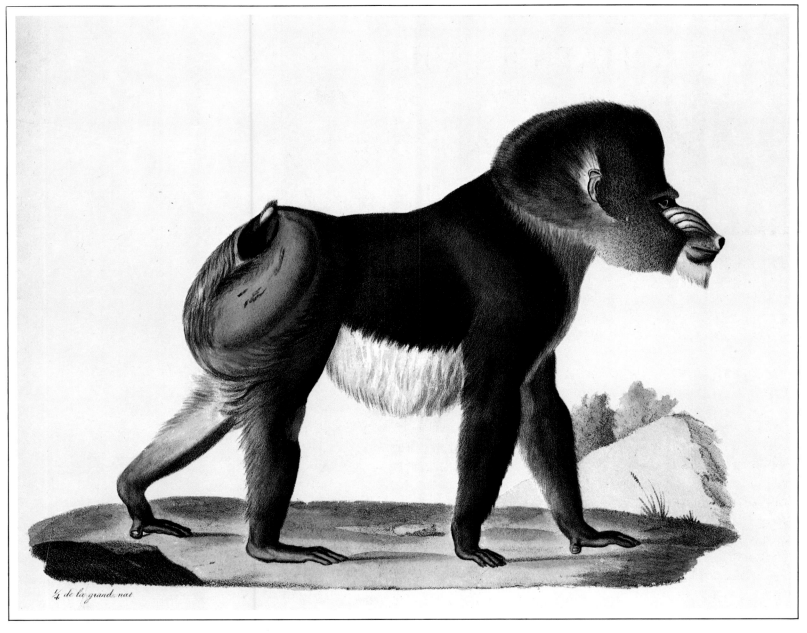

Male Mandrill. Hand-coloured lithograph from Frédéric Cuvier and Etienne-Geoffroy St Hilaire's *Histoire Naturelle des Mammifères*, 1824–25.

An artist whose talent is allowed free rein, who satisfies himself before he satisfies anyone else, is more likely to produce an imaginative and pleasing picture than an artist who must adhere rigidly to an ideal imposed from outside.

It is very difficult for an artist, no matter how conscientiously and rigorously he tries to keep within the limitations imposed upon him, to curb his imagination completely. The true artist is imaginative by nature. Without imagination, he would be more of a draughtsman, a very different creature. In the early days of zoological art, indeed, it was a positive necessity for the artist to use his imagination to fill gaps in his knowledge of some of the animals he wished to portray. Nowadays even the rarest animals from the remotest parts of the globe have been made familiar to us by television, cinema and zoo. A wide variety of animals have been kept in captivity since the mid-eighteenth century and, before photography came into its own, artists who were unable to travel could sketch living animals in zoos and menageries.

The practice of keeping exotic animals in captivity for various purposes has ancient origins, of course, and was an important part of life in the Roman world. Hundreds of years before the Renaissance, there had been a fine animal collection at Istanbul, which was in contact with countries that abounded in rare and savage animals; oriental potentates were extremely fond of owning and training these beasts. From very early times, lions could be seen caged up all over Europe. Elephants were often displayed at court from the time of Charlemagne onwards and Henry I, King of England, had many foreign beasts in his park at Woodstock, among them a porcupine; his procession at Caen included ostriches, a cheetah and a camel.

In the fifteenth century, Charles VIII of France had a chimpanzee, Louis of Orléans a parakeet, and Counte René of Anjou a fine collection housed in his various castles; this included leopards, lions, elephants, dromedaries, civets, monkeys and rare water fowl. In the thirteenth century, Frederic II, King of Naples and Sicily, had exchanged a polar bear for a giraffe with the Sultan at Cairo, and a zebra was to be seen in fifteenth-century Naples. By the sixteenth century, there were many fine zoos in Europe, particularly in Italy, where that of Lorenzo the Magnificent was remarkably well stocked. The majority of the animals in these early zoos came from Africa or India; even when commerce between Europe and the two Americas began to flourish, there was much less call for animals from across the Atlantic than from the East and South. Most of the animals brought from the Americas were small and not very striking to look at.

Consequently, we can expect to find illustrations of exotic animals, especially those native to Africa and Asia, appearing in books at an early date. We should not, however, expect all these illustrations to be accurate simply because there were living models available. Many things conspired to make an artist's representation of an animal differ from its actual appearance. It was still far easier to copy an existing illustration of an uncommon animal than to seek out a specimen of it to draw. There was also no very obvious line which separated fact and fable; legendary animals were as numerous as real ones. At a purely practical level, there was the ever-present difficulty of converting an artist's original drawing into a published illustration without to some extent losing the artist's original conception along the way. An engraver's main concern was with

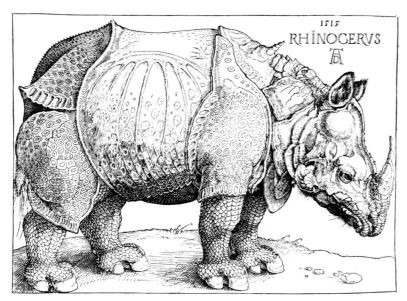

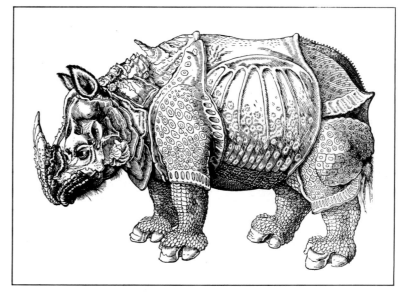

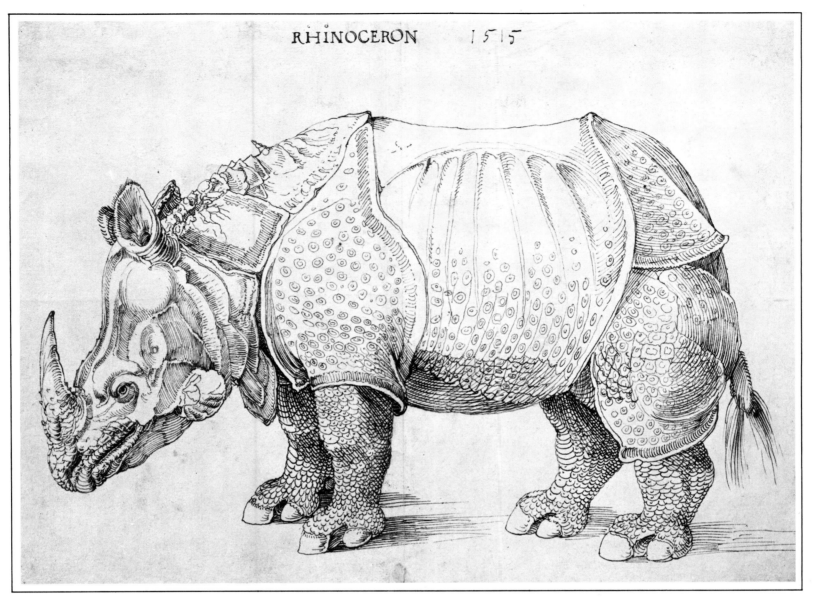

RHINOCERON 1515

Dürer's Rhinoceros and its descendants. *Above:* Dürer's original drawing, dated 1515, based on a sketch and a brief description by a Portuguese artist of the animal exhibited in Lisbon in that year. British Museum. *Far left:* Dürer's woodcut executed from the drawing and also dated 1515. This was the foundation of most representations of the Indian Rhinoceros until the mid 18th century, including the following three. *Left:* one of the earliest copies, a woodcut from Conrad Gessner's *Icones Animalium*, 1560. *Below:* a copy of Gessner's illustration, a woodcut from Edward Topsell's *History of Four-footed Beasts and Serpents*, 1658. *Right:* a crudely stylised version in a copper engraving from Gaspar Schott's *Physica Curiosa sive Mirabilia Naturae et Artis*, 3rd edition, 1697.

making a satisfactory engraving rather than faithfully preserving an original artistic idea.

Whether the engraving was accurate or not, it existed for anyone to copy. Sometimes it was copied *ad nauseam*, particularly if it was well drawn or of a seldom seen creature. In, say, a seventeenth-century book dealing with animals, it is rash to assume that all, even any, of the engravings are appearing for the first time. The illustrations from Topsell's *Historie of Foure-footed Beastes* first published in 1607, reappear in many popular books, thinly disguised or merely copied, for well over a century afterwards. But Topsell himself had already purloined most of them from earlier works, principally those of Gessner.

The example of Dürer's Indian Rhinoceros shows how far uncritical plagiarism could be taken in zoological iconography. In Topsell's book,

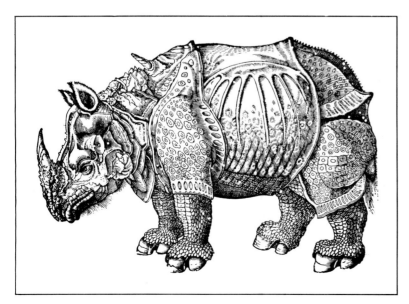

there is a figure purporting to be that of a rhinoceros which had been sketched from the life in Lisbon before many witnesses. Topsell's engraving is a very close copy of one reproduced in 1551 in Gessner's *De Quadrupedibus Viviparis*, which is itself acknowledged by Gessner to be a copy of a Dürer woodcut. Dürer himself never saw a rhinoceros—his knowledge of it was based on a sketch and a brief description by a Portuguese artist of a live Indian rhinoceros which arrived in Lisbon in 1515.

Dürer's woodcut, dated 1515 and similar in nearly all respects to his original drawing (now in the British Museum), shows a rhinoceros, but a curiously anomalous one. On its back, a short distance from its head, is a small twisted horn rather like that depicted in early representations of the fabulous unicorn, a creature which still seemed a reality to many in 1515. The body of the rhinoceros is covered with stylised folds of thick hide, which resemble sheets of armour, and circular and oval markings; its legs are sheathed in scales. In spite of these fanciful attributes, Dürer's creature still manages to look essentially like a rhinoceros. Strangely enough, another, more correct, version of the same rhinoceros was engraved by Hans Burgkmair, Dürer's friend, but only a single copy is known. This version, though a more accurate portrayal of an Indian rhinoceros, did not stand a chance against Dürer's.

Subsequently Dürer's rhinoceros, usually unacknowledged, reappeared in book after book, print after print, and it was even carved on doors, painted on porcelain, carved in marble, cast in bronze, modelled in shells and woven into tapestries. One of its last appearances in printed form as a fully accepted and genuine rhinoceros was in 1775. In that year, John Boydell published a print called 'Africa' copied from a painting by Paul

Giraffes. Hand-coloured lithograph after an original painting by Robert Hills, from *Transactions of the Zoological Society*, vol. 3, 1839–48.

'Ielerang or Javan Squirrel'. Hand-coloured lithograph after an original drawing by Edward Lear, from J. E. Gray's *Gleanings from the Menagerie and Aviary at Knowsley Hall*, vol. 2, 1850.

Brill. Dürer's misconception of the Indian rhinoceros, which had haunted European art in various forms for at least two and a half centuries, ended up in Africa. In a way, it still haunts us because it continues to appear in such guises as pictures on shopping bags and table mats. It is still with us because it is such a good untrue picture.

We can expect fiction to be muddled with fact in many early illustrations. Most of Topsell's, for instance, contain unnatural features. There is also the example of the Great Auk in the *Museum Wormianum* (1655). The engraving of this bird, which was still abundant during the seventeenth century, shows a conspicuous 'collar' around its neck. This was not a normal feature of the Great Auk but was peculiar to the specimen engraved which had been a pet kept by Ole Worm, the Dane who formed the museum and wrote the book. The collar was real enough but not natural to the bird. Nevertheless, some later engravings of the Great Auk are obviously based on Worm's picture because in them the bird sports a collar of white feathers

Other inaccuracies which were perpetuated through successive books and prints were usually the result of initial misunderstanding of the objects observed. They are also more common the further back we go in time. We would not expect to find animal fictions masquerading as animal facts in the work of a giant of nineteenth-century zoological illustration such as the incomparable Audubon.

As we have seen, Audubon spent a long time seeing his *Birds of America* through the press and was fortunate enough to find, in Robert

TAB. LXV.

Penguin Worm.

Alka Hoieri.
The Razor-bill or Auk.

Anas Arctica Clus.

Lomvia Hoieri.
The Guillemot.

Great Auk, Razorbill, Puffin, Guillemot. Brass engraving from Francis Willughby and John Ray's *Ornithology*, 1678. The Great Auk, now extinct, was then known as a Penguin. Its name here, 'Penguin Worm', and the white ring around its neck show its origin in the *Museum Wormianum* engraving (opposite).

Havell, an engraver who could translate the original paintings and sketches into finished aquatints with remarkable fidelity. Havell sometimes placed the birds in appropriate landscapes, but he did not modify the bird paintings appreciably. Although Audubon enlisted others to help him complete the original watercolours, the birds themselves were always his own work.

The Birds of America has a well-nigh unassailable position as the greatest bird book ever produced. It is both a magnificent work of art and an important scientific treatise. One might conclude that it is so popular, even among people who are untutored in art and uninterested in science, because the author has managed to show off birds in a distinctive, compelling and, above all, lifelike manner.

Audubon's aim, at least in the beginning, was to produce the best illustrations of birds ever made, and the earlier illustrations in the book are generally more attractive and better finished than the later ones. Audubon had a great feeling for texture and great ability to draw fine detail. He could show the wrinkles on a vulture's head, capture the gloss on a woodpecker's claws and convey the softness of a fledgling's feathers. More than anything else, he had a genius for showing birds in action: their dramatic attitudes and movements enliven every page. *The Birds*

Great Auk. Copper engraving from Ole Worm's *Museum Wormianum*, 1655. Worm kept the bird as a pet, hence its white collar, which reappears in copies such as Willughby's as if it were a ring of white feathers.

of America is deservedly famous. But there is a peculiar quality about some of the pictures; they are not always convincing when you look at them closely. This could be in part because Audubon sometimes mounted dead birds in supposedly authentic poses by piercing them with wires and fixing them to blocks of wood. But something else is strange. As the colours seem to be accurate enough, the peculiarity must lie in the expressions and attitudes adopted by the birds.

Many of them have postures and expressions which may best be described as human. Most human of all are the eyes. Take the picture of mocking birds, for instance. A rattlesnake is being attacked by mocking birds, two of which seem to be showing human fear while another two evince human determination; the expressions are concentrated in the eyes. Even the snake glares expressively at one of the birds, and its pupils are shown, quite erroneously, as round. But, as a whole, the picture is still masterly, a composition of textures and human emotions. In another picture, the eyes of the Barred Owl bulge menacingly, and the bird advances in a threatening way along a branch towards a Grey Squirrel whose eyes beg for mercy, whose paws are clasped in a recognisably human act of submission. To juxtapose an owl, a nocturnal predator, with a squirrel, a mammal which is active only in daylight hours, and

Huet pinx. Chromolith. G. Severeyns

Kookaburra, *Dacelo gigas*. Hand-coloured lithograph by J. G. Keulemans from R. B. Sharpe's *Monograph of the Alcedinidae,' or Family of Kingfishers*, 1868–71. See page 135.

to transform both animals into characters in a ballet may be taking artistic licence a little too far. Audubon's flying hawks and owls are performing in some aerial dance rather than flying through the air, and his Arctic Tern is surely about to alight safely on a stage rather than on the sea. The Roseate Spoonbill seems to have emerged straight from a Disney film, and a Brown Thrasher, lying limp and helpless over a coil of a snake is nothing but a lady in distress. Some of the mammals in Audubon and Bachman's *Quadrupeds of North America* also exhibit the symptoms of anthropomorphism. Their expressions are often human; one creature, a Carolina Squirrel (but labelled Eastern Gray Squirrel in the book), is shown sitting on a branch, smiling.

Perhaps, then, the reason why Audubon's illustrations have always been so popular with naturalists and laymen is not that they depict animals accurately and in natural, true-to-life postures. As Audubon had more dead birds to hand than live ones when he set about a painting and he was not very good at taking notes in the field for future reference, he had to do his best to visualise how his subjects had looked in life, frequently relying on his imagination to fill in the details of a bird's appearance as a living creature. What could be more natural than for his human imagination to endow birds with human expressions and human postures? It seems as though their popularity comes from reaching out to a human audience in recognisably human ways. Audubon does not, as some of his many admirers insist, teach us to see birds as they really are. Rather, he lets us see something of ourselves and our behaviour in his animal portraits. Other illustrators were undoubtedly as anthropomorphic in approach as Audubon, but only he has been so richly rewarded by posterity.

Squirrel. Chromolithograph after an original drawing by Nicolas Huet, from Henri and Alphonse Milne Edwards's *Recherches pour servir à l'Histoire Naturelle des Mammifères*, 1868–74.

Tarsier. Copper engraving from an article by
B. S. Nau in *Der Naturforscher*, 1791.

Perhaps the ultimate fusion of human and animal attributes in biological
art was the man-ape. The idea of a 'wild man' had already been current in
Europe for centuries when Edward Tyson published his famous *Anatomy
of a Pygmie* in 1699. The true nature of the creature he anatomised was
correctly interpreted by Tyson: 'Our *Pygmie* is no *Man*,' he said, 'nor
yet the *Common Ape*; but a sort of *Animal* between both.' Tyson's
Pygmie was actually a young chimpanzee, as is obvious from his excellent
illustrations. It was the first of the higher anthropoid apes to be examined
anatomically and to have its apparent kinship to man demonstrated.

The orang outang was also dissected in the late eighteenth century,
but the gorilla was not discovered until about 1847. Between 1699 and
1847, however, various kinds of man-ape made their appearance in books.
Travellers' tales and existing knowledge about chimpanzees, orangs and
some of the larger monkeys combined to support the notion that creatures
existed which looked very like humans. As most of the artists who drew
apes and monkeys in the early eighteenth century often did so without
seeing them alive and sometimes without seeing them at all, they had to
imagine how those animals looked in the wild. Their imaginations took a
familiar and predictable course. Their apes became man-apes, and some
of their less advanced simians also took on human characteristics.

By paying special attention to its face and by showing it standing up,
artists could easily make an ape or a monkey into a man-ape. Sometimes
They went even further and gave their subjects the limbs and other
attributes of humans. In the *Descrizioni degli Animali* (1773–75) of
Alessandri and Scattaglia, two gibbons illustrated on a plate in the third
volume have 'human' legs and heads; their facial expressions are easily
recognisable as those of *Homo sapiens*.

158

Human characteristics in 18th century depictions of apes. *Below:* '*Le Jocko*' and '*Le Grand Gibbon*'. Copper engravings after original drawings by de Sève, from Buffon's *Histoire Naturelle, Générale et Particulière*.
Right: '*Le Jocko*' and '*Le Pongo*', the former obviously copied from Buffon and both displaying an exaggerated degree of anthropomorphism in both facial expression and stance. Copper engravings after Scattaglia from *Planches de l'Encyclopédie Methodique*, Padua, 1787.

But it was the orang outang which seems most to have inspired artists to use their imaginations. Few Europeans had seen this retiring creature before the middle of the nineteenth century, and so all sorts of legends had accreted around it. To some artists, an orang differed considerably from a human only in its rather abundant hairy covering. The supposed similarity was at its most complete in a picture of a fine-limbed orang standing upright, wearing a benign expression on its simple human face, holding a long stick and looking for all the world like an unconventional hiker. This version of the orang crops up rather frequently in literature during the early nineteenth century. One of the most artistic renderings of it is found in a monumental scientific work, J.-C. Temminck's *Monographies de Mammalogie* (1827–41). In the second volume of this work,

there are several illustrations of orangs, and the one holding a stick, 'an old female', has her face turned towards the observer as though she is posing for a photographer. A 'very old male' pictured in another plate is noticeably less humanoid in appearance.

There was one man-ape whose resemblance to a human, as represented in the one contemporary engraving of it, was not just close but absolute. In the frontispiece to the early editions of Charles Waterton's *Wanderings in South America*, first published in 1825, it looks just like a rather grumpy old man with a very hairy face. The artist, T. J. Foljambe, drew only the

Three species of bird in hand-coloured lithographs by J. G. Keulemans from Osbert Salvin and Frederick Ducane Godman's monograph of birds in *Biologia Centrali-Americana*, vol. 4, 1879–1904. *Above*: '*Grallaria dives* and *G. perspiculata*'. *Right*: '*Muscivora mexicana*', male and female.

head and shoulders of what Waterton called his 'Nondescript' because that was all there was to draw. Waterton, according to his own account, had not been able to carry any more of it out of the Guiana forest where he had shot it.

Sydney Smith, who reviewed the book when it came out, was quick to notice a strong resemblance between the features of the Nondescript and those of a certain Member of Parliament. Eventually, after much speculation, it transpired that Waterton, a master taxidermist, had exercised his talents on the features of a Red Howler Monkey to make them resemble

'A Nondescript'. Steel engraving after an original drawing by T. Foljambe, frontispiece to Charles Waterton's *Wanderings in South America*, 2nd edition, 1828. The engraving represents the head and shoulders of a Red Howler Monkey which Waterton had cleverly manipulated to resemble a human being.

those of a certain J. R. Lushington who, as a Treasury official, had made things difficult for him when he wanted to import wild animals into England from South America.

That arch-populariser of natural history, the Revd J. G. Wood, was a friend of Waterton's and had studied the Nondescript minutely. Writing of it in his edition of the *Wanderings*, he said: 'The drawing of the head ... scarcely does justice to the original, for Waterton made the nose much more aquiline and thinner than is shown in the engraving, which also makes the face look as if it were hairy, whereas it is absolutely bare.' This implies that the artist may have been party to the elaborate send-up of the parliamentarian and may have modified his drawing to further Waterton's purpose. If he did so, then the frontispiece to the *Wanderings*, representing the total conversion of ape into man, is without parallel in the history of zoological art. Anthropomorphism could go no further.

On the other hand, Joseph Wolf's illustration of a magnificent live gorilla from the collection of M. du Chaillu (the man who first made this animal known in Europe), published in the fifth volume of the *Transactions of the Zoological Society of London*, makes no concessions to anthropomorphism. If anything, Wolf was determined to make the creature look bestial. But at least it was a timely corrective to the practice of making men out of apes.

Left: 'The Oran-Outang, or Wild Man of the Woods'. Wood engraving from Thomas Bewick's *General History of Quadrupeds*, 1792.

Below: 'Long-Armed Ape', i.e. Gibbon. Copper engraving from Thomas Pennant's *History of Quadrupeds*, 3rd edition, 1793.

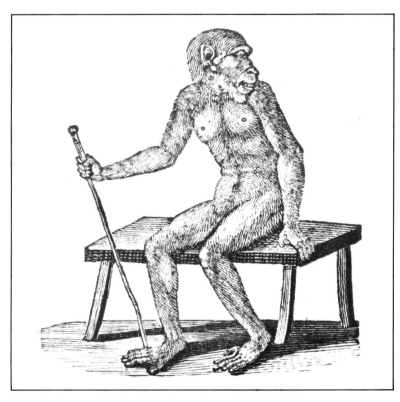

Whether or not Dürer's tongue was in his cheek when he added a little unicorn's horn to his rhinoceros, we may never know, although it seems as though his intention was serious enough. Undoubtedly, Audubon's anthropomorphic birds and mammals were meant to be taken seriously. At various times, however, books on animals have been published with illustrations which were intentionally playful or sentimental. Manetti's *Ornithologia Methodice Digesta*, that mid-eighteenth-century collection of impossibly foppish birds, is the classic example of the playful genre, and its considerable size and length place it almost in a category by itself. Most other examples of the tongue-in-cheek approach to zoological graphics are much slighter affairs. One or two of them are curious enough to deserve a place here, although none can be considered to belong rightly in the domain of natural history.

In 1681, long before Manetti was born, the author of the first conchological manual, a Jesuit priest, saw fit to publish among its illustrations of shells a few 'portraits' made from assorted shells. Such trivia do not enhance the scientific value of P. Buonanni's *Ricreatione dell'occhio e della mente*, but they do help to enliven its dry-as-dust technical content. Earlier still, Michael Rupert Besler in his *Gazophylacium Rerum Naturalium* (1642) had included some illustrations of shells arranged in the form of human heads, complete with hats. The most extravagant examples of this conchological picture-making, however, are to be found in the third volume of Seba's *Thesaurus* (the name by which his *Locupletissimi*

'Orang-Outang, vieux mâle'. Engraving from C. J. Temminck's *Monographies de Mammalogie*, 1827–41.

Overleaf: Gorilla. Hand-coloured lithograph by Joseph Wolf from *Transactions of the Zoological Society*, vol. 5, 1851–65.

Wolf. lith.

M. & N. Hanhart imp.

TROGLODYTES GORILLA mas adult.

1. The White Admirable Butterfly, to be taken in the Fly State about the 20.th of June, in Comb-Wood. 2. The Drinker Moth. The Caterpillar feeds on long Grass, changes to Chrysalis the end of May, the Fly appears the end of June. 3. The Lime Hawk Moth, the Caterpillar feeds on Elm, Lime &c. changes to Chrysalis in July, the Moth comes forth in April. 4. The Eyed Hawk Moth, the Caterpillar feeds on Willow, changes to Chrysalis in August, the Moth appears in May. 5. A White Striped Moth, taken by beating the Hedges in May. 6 The Mottled Umber, a Moth. The Caterpillar feeds on Oak, changes to Chrysalis about July, the Moth appears in October.

Setts Plain (or Colourd from the Real Flyes) Sold by B. Wilkes against the Horn Tavern in Fleet Street, Where any Gentleman or Lady may See His COLLECTION of INSECTS.
Published by Benj.n Wilkes April y.e 21, 1742, According to Act of Parliament.

Design'd by B. Wilkes.   Engrav'd by H. Roberts.
8.th Plate.

White Admiral Butterfly and various moths. Hand-coloured copper engraving from Benjamin Wilkes's *Twelve New Designs of English Butterflies*, 1742. To produce the design, the same view of each species is reproduced two or four times. Coloured copies are exceedingly rare.

Rerum Naturalium is generally known). One illustration shows an assortment of exotic shells arranged in ornamental motifs, of which the most outlandish simulates a satyr's head complete with coral beard and tuskshell horns. The motifs were merely copies of shell arrangements to be seen in the drawers of his specimen cabinets and reflect contemporary taste among collectors rather than a predilection for the bizarre by the artist who drew them. Having fun with natural objects in this way represents the very nadir of zoological art because it leads nowhere, has no practical application beyond a capacity to amuse, and has little aesthetic appeal. This kind of art was fortunately never produced in sufficient quantity to be a real annoyance.

Several eighteenth-century zoological treatises are noteworthy for the odd arrangements of subjects in their illustrated plates. Sometimes it seems as though the artist must have been at a loss to know how to present his subjects in an attractive manner. The butterflies on plate 27 of Cramer and Stoll's *Uitlandische Kapellan* (1775–84) are shown with their wings conventionally outspread, their antennae pointing forwards and outwards. This is the stiff and lifeless position of insects pinned out in a collector's cabinet. Instead of presenting the butterflies in an attractive and imaginative way, the artist has placed one in each corner so that their antennae point towards the centre of the page; two others occupy most of the central area, one facing up and one down, with the tips of their antennae almost touching and delimiting a lozenge-shaped area. Although both art and science enter into the composition of this plate, the overall effect is completely artificial, as the butterflies merely make a simple pattern.

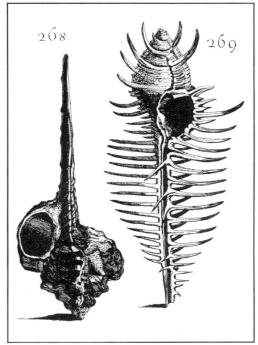

Decorative title page and two Murex shells. Copper engravings from Philippo Buonanni's *Ricreatione dell 'Occhio e della Mente*, 1681. Despite the playful decorations, Buonanni's book is accepted as a pioneer conchological treatise.

Decorative arrangement of shells in a collector's cabinet. Copper engraving from Albert Seba's *Locupletissimi Rerum Naturalium*, vol. 3, 1758. Similar arrangements of natural objects appear on the walls of the museum interior shown in the engraving in Levin Vincent's *Wondertoonel der Nature*, 1706 (see p. 7).

Unless an artist was dealing with higher animals, such as mammals or birds, it was difficult for him to bring variety and interest into his illustrations. Merian had shown how a few insects could be made to form part of an attractive composition by mixing them up with beautiful plants and foliage, and this device was adopted by some other artists. After all, if you are going to show an insect on a page and wish to give it a realistic pose or make it seem attractive, it is a good idea to rest it on its food plant or a pretty flower. Donovan posed his gaudily painted insects in this way for the plates in his *Epitome of the Natural History of the Insects of India* (1800) and one or two other entomological books, although he was sometimes mean with the foliage and usually made a leafy sprig suffice. John Curtis did likewise in his *British Entomology* (1823–40), but he was more interested in showing the food plant associated with a particular insect than in creating a pleasing composition (although the plant which is illustrated often has no obvious reference to the juxtaposed insect).

Robert Hooke had shown in 1665 that even a picture of a flea could be an arresting subject when it was enlarged many times, but no-one took the opportunity to publish large illustrations of highly magnified insects or other minute organisms in the Hooke manner until comparatively recent times. In the early days of entomological iconography, when insects were typically shown life size, it made sense to fill out a plate with botanical as well as entomological detail.

The subsequent discovery of almost astronomical numbers of previously unknown species of insects changed all this. The need to make

Drawn from Nature by A. Wilson)   Great-Footed Hawk)

'Great-Footed Hawk', i.e. Peregrine Falcon.
Hand-coloured engraving from Alexander
Wilson's *American Ornithology*, vol. 9, 1814.
Right : Bath White Butterfly and Oleander
Hawk Moth. Two hand-coloured steel en-
gravings from John Curtis's *British Entomology*,
1823–40.

these insects known to science meant that there was no longer room for
botanical padding in the reports which brought them to the attention of
the scientific community. Some nineteenth-century illustrated reports of
scientific expeditions are noteworthy for the monumental dullness of
their entomological sections. Too often, the plates show serried ranks of
tiny insects which differ from each other only in microscopic details. As
well as being unattractive and repetitious, the illustrations are frequently
useless from a scientific viewpoint. As with so many of these scientific
publications, the attractiveness of a plate diminishes as the number of
subjects engraved on it increases.

A similar problem was encountered with other small invertebrates,
many of which are diminutive and remarkably alike. But it is not just
small size and dull colour which pose problems for an artist who wants
to make an attractively composed picture. Most, if not all, invertebrates
lack the human interest which birds and other animals high in the
evolutionary scale often have. You cannot extract a meaningful expression from a beetle's eye, and a spider is always a spider, a creature as
remote in all its physical attributes from the human animal as it is possible
to be. You cannot anthropomorphise a sea anemone or a jellyfish. No
matter how beautifully formed or how colourful they may be, these
lowly creatures can never be, as birds and mammals sometimes are,
mirrors to ourselves. There is nothing familiar, nothing an artist can
recognise as even distantly anthropomorphic about an invertebrate. In no

way can he identify himself physically with a sea-slug or a wood-louse.

A similar problem is encountered with fishes. An artist can establish no easy empathy with them unless, like Renard, he can subjugate his awareness of their predominantly expressionless physiognomies and their essential aloof coldness to allow himself to revel in the delights of their bizarre forms and riotous colours. Only Chinese and Japanese artists have been able regularly to endow the portrayal of fish with grace, charm and flowing movement. Until modern times, European artists usually portrayed them as though they had just been removed from a fishmonger's slab, an indication of the depth of feeling they had for them. In European artists, at least, it seems that empathy could be achieved only with animals which are warm blooded or are capable of imparting warm feelings through certain activities indicative of advanced evolutionary development, such as nest building or singing.

We come across more overt attempts to anthropomorphise the animal kingdom, or parts of it, in certain playful publications, particularly those

"Sipping their cups of dew."

The classic Cicada, the grassy Gryllus,
and the deep-toned Dor.

of the nineteenth century. One of the most delightful and most attractive of these attempts is found in the three-volume *Episodes of Insect Life* by 'Acheta Domestica' (M. L. Budgen) which was published between 1849 and 1851. The exquisite vignettes in this popularising exposition of entomology include many of insects engaged in various activities natural to insects and some in which they are seen performing conspicuously human activities, such as eating and dining at table and playing musical instruments. Apart from the unlikely attitudes and actions of some of the insects, they are engraved and coloured with consummate skill and were obviously adapted with care from real specimens. To some extent, perhaps, these vignettes are the spiritual descendants of the illustrations to a children's book which was very popular in its day, *The Butterfly's Ball and the Grasshopper's Feast* by William Roscoe, one of the lesser, but more successful, literary productions of 1808.

If the posturings of Manetti's birds and Acheta Domestica's insects represent a playful approach to zoological art, then the illustrations to Jules Michelet's various books on natural history represent a supremely sentimental one. In *The Insect*, one of the books he wrote in the middle of the nineteenth century, Michelet said that he wrote 'wholly from the heart. Nothing has been given up to the intellect, nothing to systems.' Speaking of that volume in particular, he described it as a book 'which puts forward no scientific pretensions, the book of an unlearned writer dedicated to unlearned readers.' Unscientific it may have been, un-systematic it certainly was, but like his other books it succeeded very well in its main aims. The writing, at once beautiful, poignant and emotional, is matched to perfection by the engraved plates and vignettes. In each of his books, the engravings, based on drawings prepared by Hector Gia-comelli, are executed with close attention to detail and are faithful to the physical appearances and attitudes of their subjects. Often the subjects are set amid scenes reminiscent of those associated with the name of Birkett Foster—pastoral, domestic and idyllic. But the animals, correctly drawn though they always are, often seem unreal. It is almost as if they are humans transformed into lesser creatures. This is especially true of the engravings of insects where we are taken, so to speak, into the insect world.

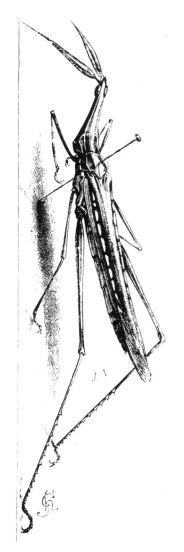

These skilful engravings help us to imagine we are at one with a stricken butterfly lying helpless on the ground, with a group of beetles burying a mouse, two armour-plated and horned beetles roaming through the jungle of leaves and grass stems like foraging rhinoceroses, with a hum-ming-bird hawk moth sipping at a flower. Having established a rapport with Giacomelli's insects, we are almost physically hurt each time we

come across a picture of one impaled on an entomological pin. There are several such illustrations scattered through the book, evidence that Giacomelli sometimes drew from cabinet specimens. A vignette showing a stag beetle lying on its back with its legs at all angles and a tell-tale bottle of ether positioned behind it is almost as painful for the more tender hearted of us to look upon as it was for Michelet and his wife who, unwillingly and by way of experiment, tried to take the life of one of these large beetles by repeatedly smothering it with ether. The vignette amply illustrates Michelet's words: 'His punishment—and, reader, you may justly call it *ours*—endured for fully fifteen days.'

Giacomelli compels us to look at the world from the point of view of an insect or a bird by the very subtle expedient of reducing us to the level of an insect or a bird. Few other artists have succeeded in this endeavour. A twentieth-century example is the work of Julius Detmold whose illustrations of insects have something of the sensitivity and sympathy of Giacomelli's, but it is difficult to find any nineteenth-century counterparts to place beside these. There are many examples of sentimentality in animal art, with subjects that are predominantly mammalian and usually domestic: Landseer was not the only artist who rode to success on the backs of pet dogs and cats, but there was only one Giacomelli.

Dead stag beetle, impaled stick insect and two chapter title pages. Wood engravings by Hector Giacomelli from, Jules Michelet's *The Insect*, (18—).

III.—WORLD-BUILDERS

IV.—LOVE AND DEATH.

CHAPTER VIII

Life! Life! Life!

One of Joseph Wolf's favourite sayings, which appears on the title page of Palmer's biography of him, was 'We see distinctly only what we know thoroughly.' He applied that idea to his art at all times. He could do such wonderful things with nature as it really is that the addition of imagined or inferred details would have spoilt the veracity and thus the very meaning of his art. Wolf seems to have been constitutionally unable to invent. It has to be admitted, however, that there can be useful scope for inventiveness in the portrayal of live animals.

Many illustrations, particularly those in encyclopedic works such as Buffon's and Goldsmith's, would have benefited from the touch of an imaginative or inventive artist. The gain would not have been in truth to life but in liveliness. The animals portrayed in early books look all too often as though they had been set up by an unskilled taxidermist who had no idea of their appearance in life. That was precisely what many early animal portraits were based on, and the artists followed

Imaginary and real animals. Hand-coloured woodcuts on a double spread from the *Hortus Sanitatis*, 1517. The crude colouring is typical for the period. See p. 211.

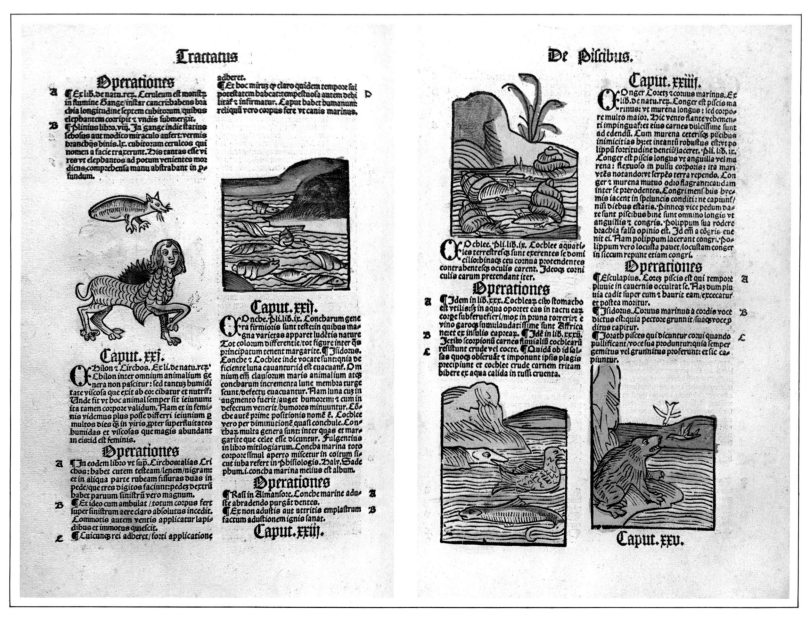

slavishly what they had before them when they were not copying previously published and even more wooden illustrations. Early book illustrators, on the whole, did not know how to put life into their animal portraits and did not try to do so; their job was to produce a likeness of the animal, not to infuse it with life.

Well-stocked menageries and improved standards of zoological knowledge gave nineteenth-century artists such as Wolf, Waterhouse Hawkins and Lear advantages denied to their predecessors in the field of zoological art. Each could follow his own artistic star. From the first, Wolf did just this. The subject of his second commission from Gould was 'Woodcocks seeking Shelter', which was hung in the Royal Academy in 1849. He subsequently received commissions from others for more woodcocks, but always he showed them on their nests. 'I didn't want to do them on their legs, and I wanted to do them as well as possible, as I had actually seen them.' It did not occur to him to 'invent' legs for them; if his patrons wanted woodcocks with legs, they would have had to go to some other artist. Speaking to Palmer generally about his work, Wolf once said, 'The great thing I always aimed at was the expression of *Life*. In animals the ear is the great organ of expression—but Life! Life! Life!—*that* is the great thing!'

This sentiment, so passionately expressed, must have been shared at

Mediterranean species of *Cerianthus,* a solitary polyp that differs from true sea anemones in living in a mucous tube rather than having a basal adhesive disc for attachment. Chromolithograph by A. Andres from his monograph *Le Attinie* in *Fauna und Flora des Golfes von Neapel,* vol. 9, 1884. Like Gosse, Andres showed off the beauty of his subjects by placing them in submarine landscapes.

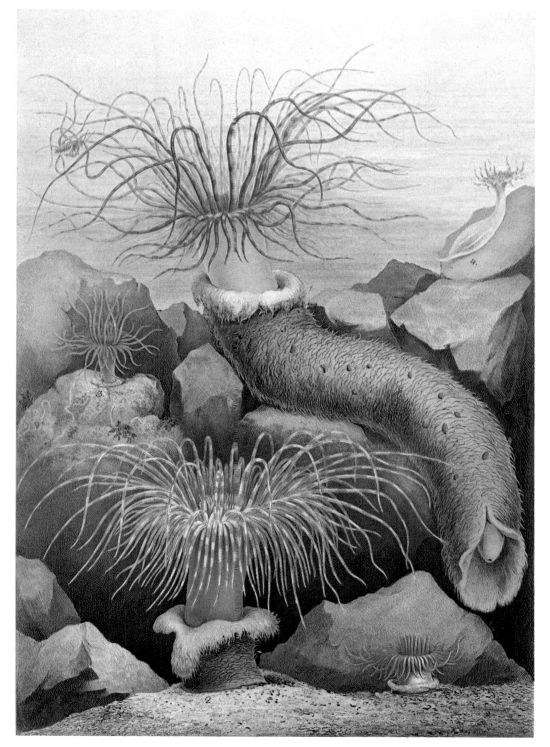

Plumose Anemone and Serpulid Worms. Chromolithograph from P. H. Gosse's *The Aquarium,* 1854. It was with illustrations like this that Gosse brought the wonders of sea life to public notice and helped to popularise the scientific study of marine biology. See p. 196.

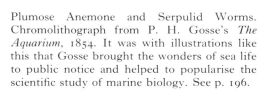

some time by every great or exceptionally gifted animal artist. But life shows itself in different ways to different people. For one artist, it is all colour; for another, it is all expressed in the organs of the higher senses— Wolf refers specifically to the ear although for many the eye would be more significant. For most artists, however, life is movement. And as the power of movement is what separates animals from the vast majority of plants, that is a very reasonable definition of the essence of animal life. It is also precisely this quality of potential or actual movement in an animal that separates zoological art from botanical art.

Relatively few zoological artists before the twentieth century tried consistently to show animals in motion; the most obvious exceptions were the sporting artists. As few of them understood the principles of animal locomotion and fewer still were interested in animals except for their use as props in a socially acceptable genre of the graphic arts, the sporting artists remain as obvious but not very significant exceptions. When artists tried their hand at depicting movement, they frequently went astray—which is hardly surprising in view of the difficulties inherent in observing animal movement by the eye alone. Wolf, well aware of the dangers of invention, rarely showed an animal actually moving. Some of his most memorable pictures are studies in tension, of animals about to move or at the completion of a movement, or caught by surprise at some activity. It is then that we see what he means about their ears, which are often most expressively raised at moments of discovery or of being discovered. Perhaps an animal picture is made more exciting by introducing tension of this sort into it than by attempting to freeze a moment of actual movement.

The horse presented a particular problem as artists could never get it to gallop correctly until Eadweard Muybridge analysed its movements with his perceptive camera in the late nineteenth century. Before then, it seems to have been axiomatic, among artists at least, that the galloping horse moves its front legs forward together and then its back legs together so that it repeatedly assumes the stance traditionally associated with a child's rocking horse.

During the eighteenth century, this 'rocking-horse' notion was almost universally accepted by sporting artists such as James Seymour. The work of this painter shows fully the absurdity of the idea. In nearly all his fox-hunting scenes, every horse and every dog is portrayed in an identical 'rocking-horse' position. Absurd though it seems to us now, it was still a standard feature of all the banal equestrian aquatints of the early nineteenth century based on paintings by Henry Alken, F. C. Turner, C. Hunt and many others. These prints, as popular as they are insipid, are a far cry from the superb studies of horses for which George Stubbs is renowned. Although Stubbs did not solve the problem of

Elephant vignette and Nylghau (which is clearly the same species and taken from the same source as Pennant's illustration, opposite). Wood engravings from Thomas Bewick's *General History of Quadrupeds*, 1792.

Dorcas Gazelle. Wood engraving after Joseph Wolf, from *The Royal Natural History*, edited by Richard Lydekker, vol. 2, 1894.

equestrian locomotion, it does not seem to matter. Almost everything else Stubbs did in the name of animal art came so wonderfully close to perfection that one can overlook the occasional improbable canter.

Putting life into zoological art in the early days presented the obvious problem of where to put it. Western artists with their eyes firmly riveted to classical models—not, as a rule, the most lively of subjects—did not begin to tackle the problem, let alone solve it, until the nineteenth century. Capturing the correct movement of an animal or giving it a realistic pose did not seem to matter to them. If the animal was one which lived in close association with men and women it was portrayed in a manner pleasing to them. If it was introduced into a rustic scene then it was made to look rustic. The pigs and horses of George Morland or Paul Potter are often accurately portrayed but they are seldom on the move and are never rushing about.

'White-Footed Antelope'. Copper engraving after George Stubbs, from Thomas Pennant's *History of Quadrupeds*, 3rd edition, 1793.

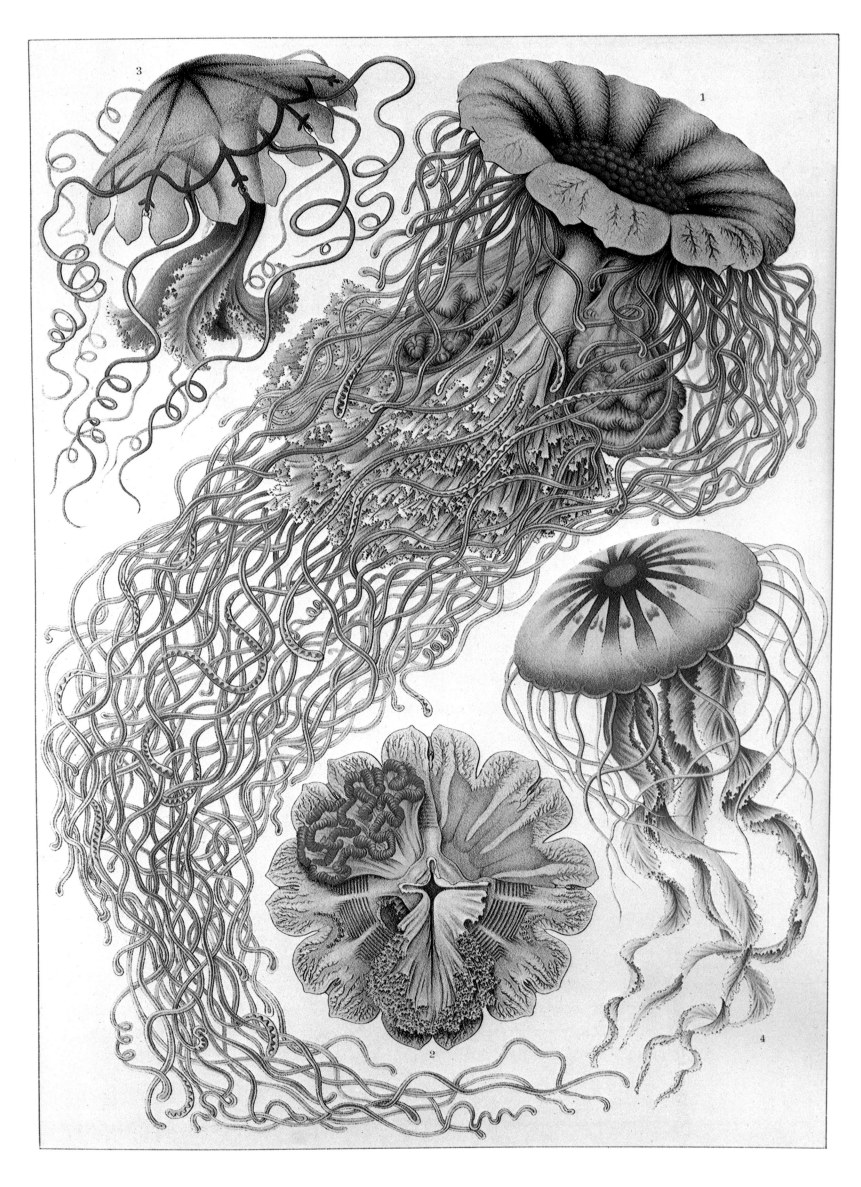

Sometimes an artist was required to emphasis certain physical attributes of domestic animals. In late-eighteenth and early-nineteenth-century Britain, there was a spate of pictures of overweight cows, sheep and pigs. The artists commissioned to paint these pictures were obliged to depict the animals with small heads, short legs and huge rectangular-sided bodies. Their object was to display prime cuts on the hoof and to demonstrate the abilities of the animal breeder.

The influence of classical art did not encourage qualities of movement and realism in animal portrayal. Greek horses are heroic but too idealised to be very much like flesh-and-blood horses; they often seem as capable of aerial flight—what we might call the Pegasus syndrome—as they are of trotting or galloping. But classical ideas were not always to blame for the perpetuation of rather static images of animals. Even Thomas Bewick, who was no product of academic classicism, seems to have had little interest in movement in art. His exquisitely and accurately engraved birds remain on the ground, on the water or on a branch. Not more than one or two, except in some of his background skies, are on the wing, and most of them are not doing anything. Similarly, his other animal subjects, except those in his superb tail-piece vignettes, are not exactly pulsating with life and movement.

Few artists successfully infused life and movement into their portrayals of birds before Audubon came on the scene. Before his giant, aquatinted plates were published, few artists had represented birds in flight or even with their wings outstretched. Mark Catesby, a century earlier, had made

'Kate', a Norfolk Polled Heifer which won the First Prize at the Smithfield Club Show in 1867. Print, from a painting dated 1868 by A. M. Gauci, Animal Painter. This is a typical sample of 19th century livestock portraiture with its emphasis on the marketable portions of the animal at the expense of the head and legs.

Sheeted Somerset Cattle, a breed that is now extinct. Hand-coloured lithograph after an original painting by William Shiels from David Low's *Domesticated Animals of the British Isles*, 1842.

Left: various species of Semaeostomae, a group of jellyfish. Chromolithograph from Ernst Haeckel's *Kunstformen der Natur*, 1904.

some brave attempts in this direction, but his poor draughtsmanship and poorer understanding of the mechanics of flight were not equal to the task.

A few flying birds are represented in Alexander Wilson's *American Ornithology* (1808–24), but they are not very convincing. Wilson's pictures are seldom very convincing anyway; he illustrated his own book only because no-one else was available to do the job, at least no-one he could afford to pay. Even Audubon, although his birds were certainly lively, also had a poor understanding of avian flight. His Arctic Tern is, if anything, even more improbable than Wilson's Common Nighthawk; both birds are hurtling through the air like demented ballet dancers. Even in the seventeenth century, Barlow had shown a greater ability to capture the essence of bird flight with his drawings of flying herons.

Some animal movements are too rapid for the human eye to follow, among them the wing beats of humming birds in flight. John Gould did not discover this for himself until 1857, when he saw his first live humming bird in Philadelphia. By that time, he had issued a large part of his monograph on the Trochilidae. He did so in the knowledge that these tiny creatures are among the loveliest of all living things, with plumage colours that are almost impossible to describe. To display their finery adequately, Gould showed some of them with their wings outspread, as if frozen in mid-air. Few would have thought to question this course of action, but one man, at least, thought that Gould had deceived the spectator and done the humming bird a disservice by revealing its iridescent charms in this manner. He was William Henry Hudson, author of *Green Mansions, Birds of La Plata* and many other books in which natural history is an important element. He was also an ornithologist with a profound knowledge of birds.

As a corrective to the unctuous verbiage which swills around everything Gould manufactured and as an insight into something most of us never experience, or even think about, the following quotation on humming birds from Hudson's *Naturalist in La Plata* could not be more appropriate. 'Doubtless many who have never seen them in a state of nature imagine that a tolerably correct idea of their appearance can be gained from Gould's colossal monograph. The pictures there, however, only represent dead humming-birds. A dead robin is, for purposes of bird-portraiture, as good as a live robin; the same may be said of even many brilliant-plumaged species less aërial in their habits than humming-birds. In butterflies the whole beauty is seldom seen until the insect is dead, or, at any rate, captive . . . The special kind of beauty which makes the first sight of a humming-bird a revelation depends on the swift singular motions as much as on the intense gem-like and metallic brilliancy of the plumage.

'The minute exquisite form, when the bird hovers on misty wings, probing the flowers with its coral spear, the fan-like tail expanded, and poising motionless, exhibits the feathers shot with many hues; and the next moment vanishes, or all but vanishes, then reappears at another flower only to vanish again, and so on successively, showing its splendours not continuously, but like the intermitted flashes of the firefly—this forms a picture of airy grace and loveliness that baffles description. All this glory disappears when the bird is dead, and even when it alights to rest on a bough. Sitting still, it looks like an exceedingly attenuated kingfisher, without the pretty plumage of that bird, but retaining its stiff artificial manner. No artist has been so bold as to attempt to depict the bird as it actually appears, when balanced before a flower. The swift motion of the wings obliterates their form, making them seem like a mist encircling the body; yet it is precisely this formless cloud on which the glittering body hangs suspended, which contributes most to give the humming-bird its wonderful sprite-like or extra-natural appearance. How strange, then, to find bird-painters persisting in their efforts to

Goosanders (male and female), Pintail, Blue-Winged Teal, Snow Goose. Hand-coloured engravings after original drawings by Alexander Wilson, from his *American Ornithology* (completed by George Ord), 1808–24.

Domestic and wild birds and mammals in a rural setting. Copper engraving after an original drawing by Francis Barlow, from *Barlow's Birds and Beasts in Sixty-Seven Excellent and Useful Prints*, 1775 (the first edition appeared in 1655). Barlow was one of the first artists successfully to integrate animal studies into well-designed landscapes. Some of the engravings for the first edition of these plates were prepared by Wenceslaus Hollar.

show the humming-bird flying! When they draw it stiff and upright on its perch the picture is honest, if ugly; the more ambitious representation is a delusion and a mockery.

'Coming to the actual colouring,' continues Hudson, 'the changeful tints that glow with such intensity on the scale-like feathers, it is curious to find that Gould seems to have thought that all difficulties here had been successfully overcome. The "new process" he spoke so confidently about might no doubt be used with advantage in reproducing the coarser metallic reflections on a black plumage, such as we see in the corvine birds; but the glittering garment of the humming-bird, like the silvery lace woven by the Epeira, gemmed with dew and touched with rainbow-coloured light, has never been and never can be imitated by art.'

But Gould, not a man to admit defeat, evidently considered that art could imitate the humming bird's 'glittering garment'. At the Great Exhibition of 1851, where he had a display of humming birds set up, he demonstrated how he copied their iridescent colours by overpainting and varnishing pure gold leaf. He did not adopt this method of capturing their colours on the plates of his monograph, presumably because of the expense and the technical difficulties. Half a century earlier, however, Audebert and Vieillot had brought out their *Oiseaux Dorés ou à Reflets Métalliques*, a book dealing mostly with humming birds and birds of paradise, and the plates were printed in colours, including gold. The results, as might have been expected, were not very convincing, although the humming birds were at least 'honest, if ugly'.

If an animal's beauty can be fully appreciated only when it is moving rapidly and the essence of that beauty resides in its constantly changing coloration, then you need more than gold print to capture it. You need a movie camera.

Moose. Hand-coloured copper engraving from John Frederick Miller's *Cimelia Physica, Figures of rare and curious Quadrupeds and Birds, &c., together with several of the most elegant Plants*, 1796.

CHAPTER IX
Through
the Microscope

The appeal of the larger members of the animal kingdom, especially the birds, is such that artists have given disproportionately little attention to the smaller animals. An artist who tackles the job of portraying a tiny creature has either to be very interested in it or to be well remunerated, for it is unlikely that he will have any intuitive feeling for a water flea or an amoeba.

This is not to say that it is essential for an artist to identify with an animal in order to draw or paint it, but it seems to help enormously if he does. Wolf or Lear, for example, would have found it difficult if not impossible to enjoy drawing a jellyfish, a barnacle or a foraminiferan, none of which showed obvious or recognisable forms of expression and which probably had nothing to express anyway. On the other hand, Gosse certainly enjoyed drawing such creatures at least as much as he enjoyed drawing larger ones, and his work was at its best when his subjects were very small or microscopic. It was as if his mission was to reveal beauties and truths which would otherwise have remained hidden.

Wolf and Lear had an emotional involvement with most of their subjects; Gosse apparently had not, although some students of his life and work would certainly argue that no-one could love animals more than he loved the tiny creatures which danced around in a drop of pond water. Probably every artist who has depicted microscopic animals has been, in some degree, interested in them scientifically. Before the nineteenth century, though, few skilled microscopists were also skilled artists, which was a pity as their subjects can be conveniently shown to others in graphic form. Most early attempts to illustrate minute animals are disappointing. Antony van Leeuwenhoek, the doyen of microscopists,

Fleas. Copper engraving from Antony van Leeuwenhoek's *Arcana Naturae*, 1695.

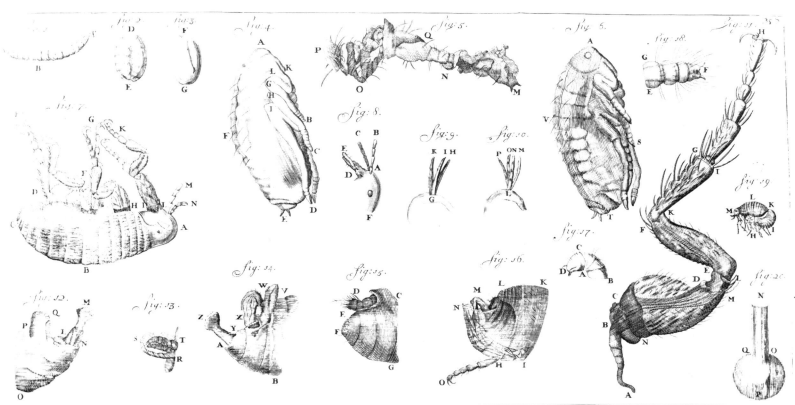

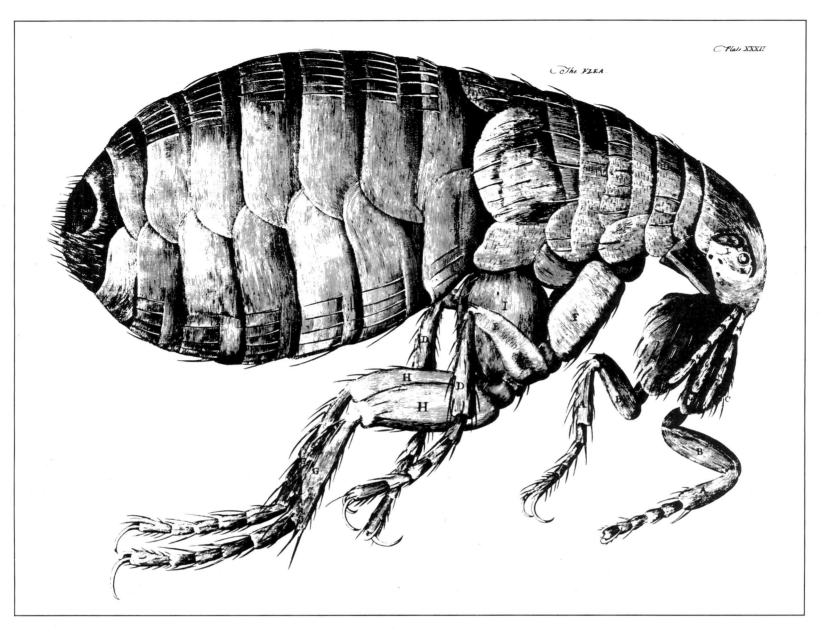

Plate XXXII

The FLEA.

published a mass of interesting but disorganised observations, many of them illustrated, but the figures in his *Arcana Naturae* (1695) show him to have been a poor artist. His illustration of a flea, for instance, is a sad-looking caricature of the real thing. It is totally eclipsed, scientifically as well as artistically, by the enormous flea picture published in Robert

Flea. Copper engraving from Robert Hooke's *Micrographia Restaurata: or the Copper-Plates of Dr Hooke's Wonderful Discoveries by the Microscope*, 1745. This reissue of Hooke's plates appeared 80 years after they were first published in his *Micrographia*.

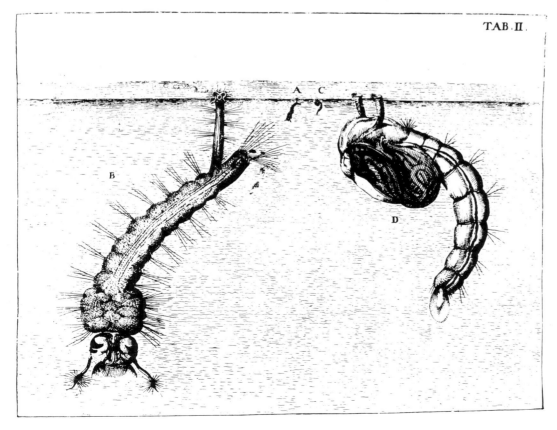

TAB. II.

Mosquito larvae. Copper engraving from Jan Swammerdam's *Historia Insectorum Generalis*, 1693.

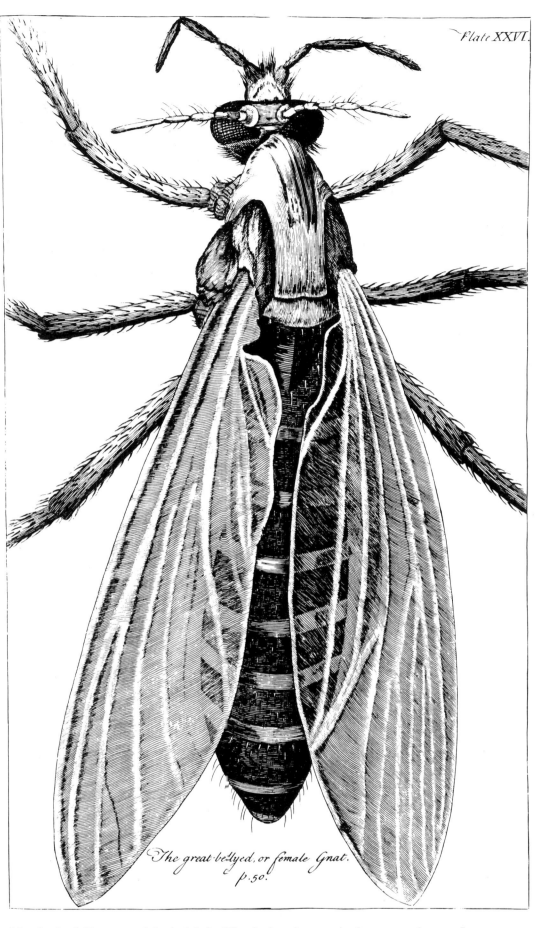

Plate XXVI

The great-bellyed, or female Gnat.
p.50.

Gnat. Copper engraving from Robert Hooke's *Micrographia Restaurata*, 1745.

Hooke's *Micrographia* (1665). Hooke's picture is far superior to Leeuwenhoek's not just because of its size (it is about 45 centimetres long), but also because it has been exquisitely yet boldly drawn.

Many early microscopists seem to have been constrained by the smallness of their subjects to publish pitifully small illustrations of them, an illogical convention when the key to their discoveries was magnification. Hooke's illustrations of insects, spiders, mites and other tiny creatures were unrivalled for a century except by those of the Dutchman, Jan Swammerdam. This tireless, accurate and mentally unstable observer of insects and their anatomy died in 1680 at the age of 43 leaving a great deal of his finest work in manuscript. Much of it was published more than fifty years after his death in the *Biblia Naturae*, a magnificent folio work in two volumes which contains perhaps the finest collection of microscopic studies ever produced by a single observer.

Because so much of Swammerdam's efforts were devoted to insect anatomy—his illustrated account of the honey-bee and its internal organs has never been excelled—the illustrations, wonderful though they are, do not have the simplicity, power and sheer magnitude of Hooke's. This is in part why Hooke's flea and his louse are reproduced more often than any picture by Swammerdam or the other microscopists. Swammerdam's figures are just too detailed to have the immediate and unforgettable impact of Hooke's. The same may be said of the illustrations in the various works of Marcello Malpighi although his were neither as detailed nor as competent as Swammerdam's.

The era of the classical microscopists came to an end with the death of Leeuwenhoek in 1723, and their work was not effectively taken up again until the nineteenth century. The microscope was not abandoned in the interim, but no one person or group produced results which could

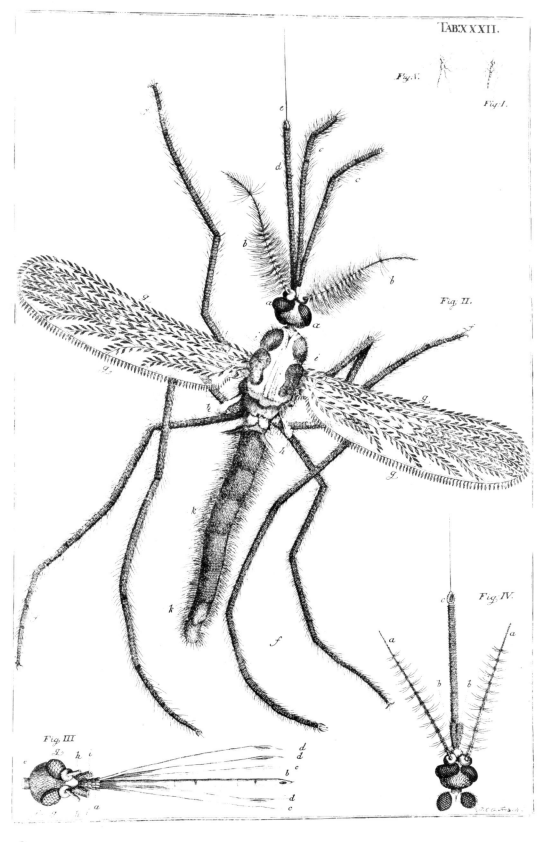

TAB XXXII.

Mosquito and its mouthparts. Copper engraving from Jan Swammerdam's *Bible of Nature* (English edition by John Hill), 1758.

Freshwater Hydras. Copper engraving from Abraham Trembley's *Polypes*, 1744.

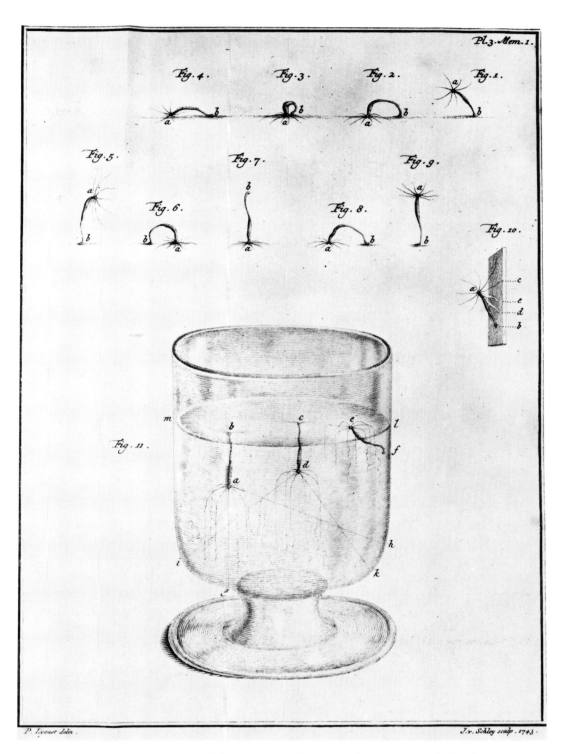

compare in importance with those achieved by a handful of devoted observers during the second half of the seventeenth century. The microscope was used more for amusement than for serious scientific study during the eighteenth century, and this more light-hearted approach is reflected in several publications of that period which dealt with microscopic observations.

Of necessity, Abraham Trembley of Geneva used a microscope to study the fresh-water hydra on which he conducted experiments to do with the regeneration of parts. These were described in his *Polypes*, a memoir of fundamental scientific importance published in 1744. His book sent the curious scuttling to their local ponds to collect specimens of the hydra for study under their lenses. About twenty years after Trembley's memoir was published, the *Amusements Microscopiques* of Ledermüller appeared (although there was a prior edition in German). Among many plates illustrating the delights of studying microscopic creatures is a decorative, though not fanciful, one showing the various attitudes of a creature which can turn itself inside out as well as replace lost parts.

A few years later, the science of microbiology began to come into its own. Leeuwenhoek had detected rotifers, those minute whirling dervishes of the animal world, in water from ponds and rivers, even in water from flower vases. He had actually published some drawings of 'infusoria'—

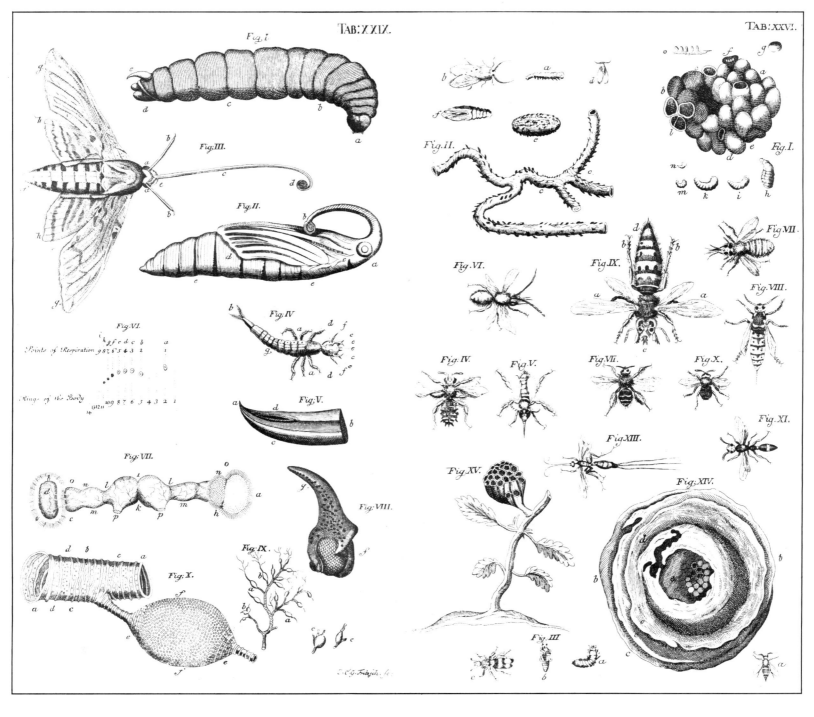

the collective name by which assorted protozoans and rotifers were long known—but it was not until Otto Frederik Müller made a special study of them that any considerable additions were made to our knowledge of them. In 1786, two years after his death, Müller's *Animalcula Infusoria* was published by Fabricius. It was illustrated with many accurate and well executed engravings of them and of other organisms which were then confused with them. More than fifty years later, in 1838, the splendidly illustrated *Infusionsthierchen* of Christian Gottfried Ehrenberg brought the beauties and complexities of various rotifers and protozoans to the wide attention of biologists. Later in the century, others, such as Gosse, published many beautiful figures of these creatures, but it was the combined scientific and artistic abilities of Ernst Haeckel which revealed the most lowly organisms in all their loveliness and variety.

An enthusiastic student of the deep-sea fauna which had been brought to light by the explorations of the *Challenger* and other research vessels, Haeckel was privileged to view under his microscope some of the loveliest and most spectacular of all natural objects, the radiolarians, whose tiny skeletons occur in countless myriads on the sea floor. In his *Challenger* reports and other scientific papers, his artistic and scientific gifts were crystallised superbly. Each plate was filled with illustrations of the astonishingly beautiful, symmetrically organised, incredibly delicate yet durable remains of these lovely organisms. The infinitesimally small have never been displayed with greater sensitivity and delicacy than by

Hawk Moth, Wasps and other insects and their parts. Copper engravings from Jan Swammerdam's *Bible of Nature* (English edition by John Hill), 1758.

Stentor and other ciliate Protozoans, high magnified. Hand-coloured engraving from C. G. Ehrenberg's *Die Infusionsthierchen*, 1838.

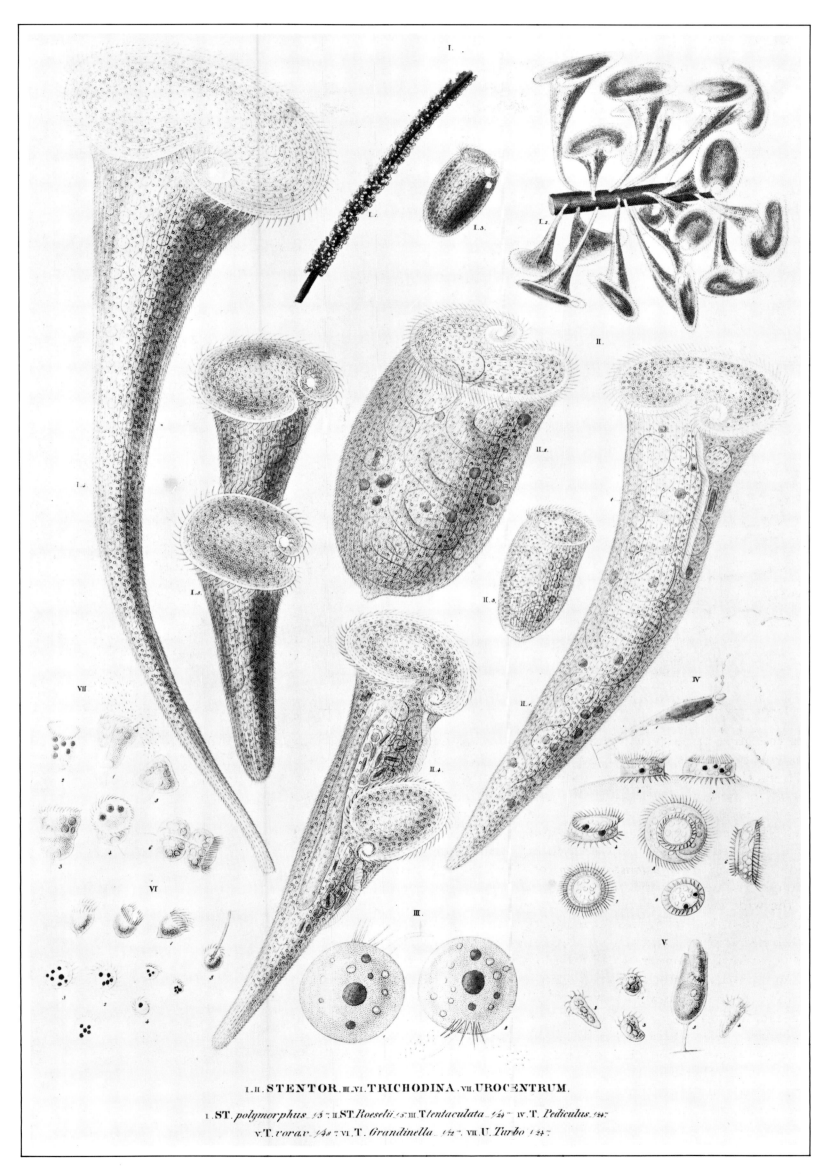

I.II.**STENTOR**.III.VI.**TRICHODINA**.VII.**UROCENTRUM**.

I.ST.*polymorphus* ⅓ ː II.ST.*Roeselii* ⅕ ː III.T.*tentaculata* ⅓₄ ː IV.T.*Pediculus* ₁₄₇

v.T.*vorax* ⅓₈ ː VI.T.*Grandinella* ⅓₂ ː VII.U.*Turbo* ₁₂₄₇

Haeckel. In his *Kunstformen der Natur*, a popular, illustrated exposition of the external morphology of animals throughout the animal kingdom, he showed to perfection the immense variety of forms assumed by different animal groups and brought to each of his designs the same

Foraminiferans, highly magnified. Lithograph, from a report by William Benjamin Carpenter on his specimens of the genus *Orbitolites* collected during the voyage of HMS Challenger, in *Philosophical Transactions of the Royal Society*, 1883.

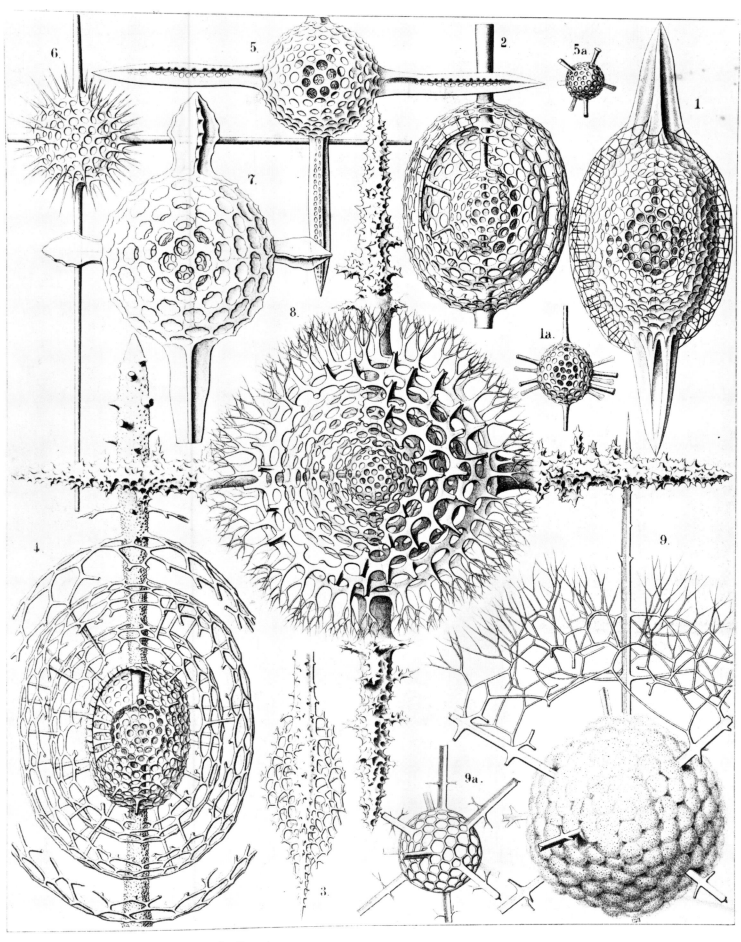

dedication and love which moved him to make such exquisite artistic memorials to the beauty of radiolarians.

The first illustrations of an animal made with the assistance of a microscope, albeit a very primitive microscope, had been published in 1625 by Francesco Stelluti. On a single sheet—the extent of his publication—Stelluti had illustrated the external characters of the honey-bee, including a tolerably accurate representation of the stinging apparatus. Truly microscopic animals were first illustrated by Leeuwenhoek in 1702 (*Polystomella*) and 1703 (*Vorticella, Carchesium*), all of them protozoans. The first published illustration of *Amoeba*, the most famous and least shapely of all protozoans, was given to the world in 1755 by Roesel von Rosenhof in his *Monatlich herausgegebene Insecten-Belustigung*. This author, whose illustrations of amphibia have already been singled out for their high quality, was originally a miniature painter. This may help to explain the excellence of his hand-coloured copper engravings of microscopic organisms; his figures of *Stentor* are beyond criticism.

It can only be a general unfamiliarity with such minute objects which makes us less aware of them than we are of the larger members of the animal kingdom. If rotifers and radiolaria were the size of birds or mammals, they would certainly have attracted the attention of the world's finest animal artists. As it is, the wonderful portrayals of such tiny organisms by artists such as Haeckel deserve a prominent place in any survey of zoological illustrations. To exclude them because they are diminutive would be to ignore some of the most fantastic of all forms of animal life—and some of the most accomplished and memorable achievements in zoological iconography.

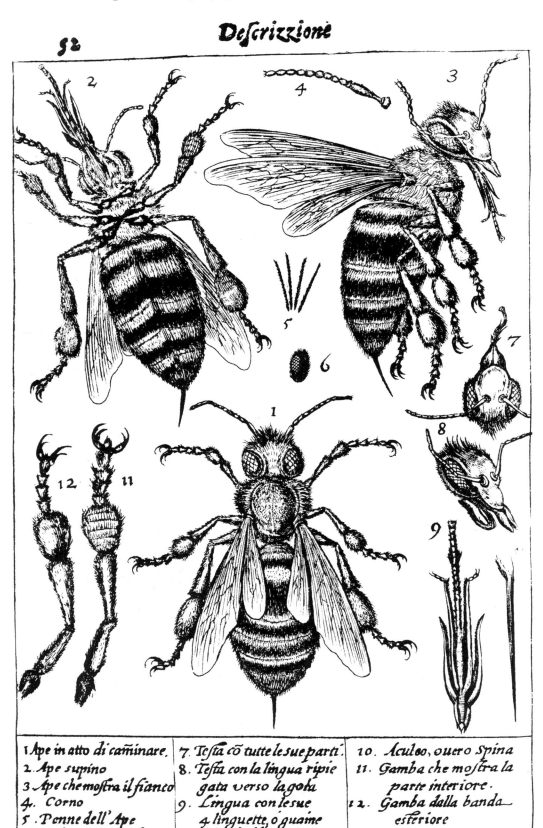

The Honey Bee and its parts. Copper engraving from Francesco Stelluti's *Persio*, 1630. A modified version of the engraving published as a loose leaf by Stelluti in 1625 which was the first published illustration of an animal species made with the assistance of the microscope.

CHAPTER X
Going Popular

From the start, the literature of zoology included works that were intended to have a popular appeal. Conrad von Megenberg's *Book of Nature* was undoubtedly meant to reach ordinary people and to be understood by them. In its period, it was as much a popular work as was the Revd J. G. Wood's *Illustrated Natural History*. Admittedly, Wood's book sold many more copies, but then there were many more literate persons to sell to in the nineteenth century, and technological innovations had made it possible for copies to be produced in greater quantities and at an economical price.

One variety of popular book is the cheap version of a title which has previously been available only in expensive editions. Buffon's *Natural History* is the prime example of an expensive and bulky work which later appeared in numerous cheaper editions and in several languages. Cuvier's *Animal Kingdom* was another extensive work which existed in sumptuous editions as well as cheaper ones. Oliver Goldsmith's *History of the Earth and Animated Nature*, originally published in 1774 with Buffon-type engravings, came to be one of the most popular of all natural history books during the nineteenth century, even though the basic text had become woefully out of date. The hand-coloured illustrations which embellish most of the late editions were the principal reason for the book's continued popularity.

During the second half of the nineteenth century, when publishers first discovered the buying potential of the man in the street, popular encyclopedias dealing with all aspects of nature were produced in many

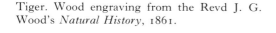

Tiger. Wood engraving from the Revd J. G. Wood's *Natural History*, 1861.

Hartebeest. Wood engraving after Friedrich Specht from *The Royal Natural History*, edited by Richard Lydekker, vol. 2, 1894.

Polar Bears. Wood engraving after Friedrich Specht, from Carl Vogt and Friedrich Specht's *Natural History of Animals (Mammalia)*, English translation by G. C. Chisholm, 1887.

Arabian Camel. Wood engraving after Friedrich Specht, from *The Royal Natural History*, edited by Richard Lydekker, vol. 2, 1894.

countries; they were usually the combined efforts of several different writers and artists. Occasionally, as in *The Royal Natural History* edited by R. Lydekker and published in the 1890s, some at least of the illustrations were specially commissioned rather than being copied from other sources, printed or otherwise. A massive ten-volume work on animal life, Brehm's *Tierleben*, was published in Germany and enjoyed very wide popularity during the late nineteenth century and beyond. Its hundreds of engravings were often used to adorn other books or provided patterns to be imitated.

The most successful popularisers, however, have always been solo performers. Zoological books with a wide popular appeal have been associated with one name, whether of its author or its illustrator. But this is equally true of books for a much more restricted audience: a book written but not illustrated by Gould somehow gains by being associated with his name. It may even gain so much from the association that it is identified with him and becomes known simply as a Gould. In the field of popular animal books, the name of Gosse has a comparable weight.

Family of Hedgehogs, and Common Baboons. Wood engravings after original drawings by Friedrich Specht, from Carl Vogt and Friedrich Specht's *Natural History of Animals (Mammalia)*, English translation by G. C. Chisholm, 1887.

Below left: Philander Opossum. Wood engraving after Friedrich Specht, from *The Royal Natural History*, edited by Richard Lydekker, vol. 3, 1894–95.

Below: Manatee. Wood engraving after Friedrich Specht, from Alfred Edmund Brehm's *Tierleben (Saugetiere)*, vol. 3, 1891.

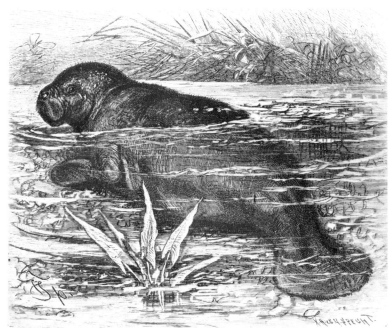

'Hippotragus niger' and 'Hippotragus leuco-phaeus', two species of Antelope. Wood engraving after G. Mützel, from Alfred Edmund Brehm's *Tierleben (Saugetiere)*, vol. 3, 1891.

Top right: Frontal Shrike-Tit. Wood engraving after Friedrich Specht, from *The Royal Natural History*, edited by Richard Lydekker, vol. 3, 1894–95.

Sloth Bears in a forest glade. Wood engraving after G. Mützel, from *The Royal Natural History*, vol. 2, 1894.

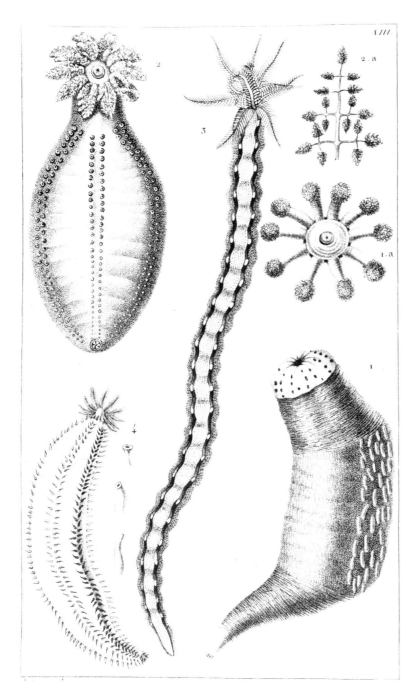

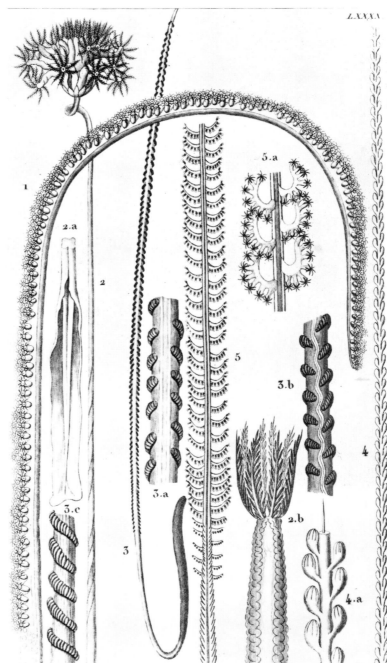

Holothurians (Sea Cucumbers) and details of Sea Pens and other Coelenterates. Engravings after original drawings by Jean-Gabriel Prêtre, from Henri-Marie-Ducrotay de Blainville's *Manuel d'Actinologie ou de Zoophytologie*, 1834.

Philip Henry Gosse was one of the most successful and most prolific popularisers of natural history in nineteenth-century Britain. On his own subject, marine life, he was a leading authority; as the illustrator of his own influential books he was without a near rival. In many ways, Gosse was a most unlikely person to become a famous and occasionally best-selling popular author, as will be evident to anyone who has read Edmund Gosse's *Father and Son*. He made lasting contributions to several branches of zoology but never allowed science to move him from a belief in the literal truth of the Bible—every word of it. Deep-rooted and sincere piety marked the unceasing stream of his writing as it marked his mind. It was different with his artwork.

In January 1852, after several years of exhausting literary work in London, Gosse went with his family to South Devon where he settled down. Soon, he became absorbed in the study of marine life. After being so long immured in the city, he was particularly struck by the bright colours of the animals and plants which lived on the shore below the high tide mark. He began putting down on paper, using a brush as well as a pen, his impressions of the living creatures he encountered in such profusion in the rock pools.

His *Naturalist's Rambles on the Devonshire Coast* was published in 1853. Twelve of the plates, reproduced from his original sketches, were done on the stone by Gosse himself and printed in colours. These plates are good examples of his artistic ability and show some of the objects he studied so long and so lovingly. But it was with *The Aquarium*, which was

Sea-Anemones. Colour print from Philip Henry Gosse's *Actinologia Britannica, a History of the British Sea-Anemones and Corals,* 1858–60.

published in the following year, that he scored his first notable literary hit and cashed in on the craze for keeping natural objects in salt-water aquaria, a craze which his *Naturalist's Rambles* had initiated and which was to last another dozen years before the public began to tire of it. *The Aquarium* sold very well and eventually earned Gosse nearly a thousand pounds. The publishers, M. and N. Hanhart, who specialised in chromo-lithography, were delighted because the plates illustrating the book had been very costly to produce and they had feared a loss on the venture. Gosse had been determined to see his book illustrated with coloured plates of a higher quality than those in his *Naturalist's Rambles*, and the publishers had given in to him reluctantly.

Apart from the additional cost of production, there was a sound, but to us almost inexplicable, reason why Gosse had difficulty in persuading publishers to improve their reproductions of his sketches. Some pundits doubted the veracity of his illustrations. As Edmund Gosse wrote in his *Life of Philip Henry Gosse*, 'So little did people know of the variety and loveliness of the denizens of the seashore, that, although these plates fell

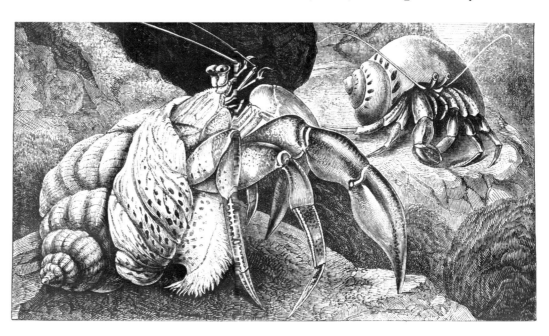

Hermit Crabs. Wood engraving after an original drawing by Philip Henry Gosse from his *A Year at the Shore* in *Good Words for 1864.*

far short of the splendid hues of the originals, and moreover depicted forms that should not have been unfamiliar, several of the reviewers refused altogether to believe in them, classing them with travellers' tales about the hills of sugar and rivers of rum. Philip Gosse himself was disgusted with the tameness of the colours [of the plates in his *Naturalist's Rambles*], to which the imperfect lithography gave a general dusty grayness, and he determined to try and dazzle the indolent reviewers. Consequently, in 1854, in publishing *The Aquarium*, he gave immense pains to the plates, and succeeded in producing specimens of unprecedented beauty. Certain full-page illustrations in this volume, the scarlet Ancient Wrasse floating in front of his dark seaweed cavern; the Parasitic Anemone, with the transparent pink curtain of *delesseria* fronds behind it, the black and orange brittle-star at its base; and above all perhaps, the plate of Star-fishes, made a positive sensation, and marked an epoch in the annals of English book illustration.'

Others, too, have praised the plates in *The Aquarium* which, over a century later, do not seem all that exquisite but which must have been eye-openers in their day. Like those in the copiously illustrated *British Sea-Anemones and Corals* (1858–60), they delighted the public as much as they probably disappointed Gosse. It was undoubtedly his brush rather than his pen which made him a best-selling author.

His biographer son describes the basis of his art: 'Philip Gosse as a draughtsman was trained in the school of the miniature painters. When a child he had been accustomed to see his father inscribe the outline of a portrait on the tiny area of the ivory, and then fill it in with stipplings of

Left: Fifteen-Spined Stickleback and Great Weever. Wood engraving after an original drawing by Philip Henry Gosse, from his *A Year at the Shore* in *Good Words for 1864*.

Above: Sea-Anemones. Colour print from Philip Henry Gosse's *Actinologia Britannica, a History of the British Sea-Anemones and Corals,* 1858–60.

THE SEA-URCHINS.

ECHINIDÆ,

OR CIRRHO-SPINIGRADE ECHINODERMATA.

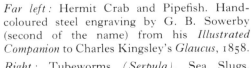

Coral Fishes. Wood engraving after G. Mützel from T. S. Kingsley's *Riverside Natural History*, 1885–88.

pure body-colour. He possessed to the last the limitations of the miniaturist. He had no distance, no breadth of tone, no perspective; but a miraculous exactitude in rendering shades of colour and minute peculiarities of form and marking. In late years he was accustomed to make a kind of patchwork quilt of each full-page illustration, collecting as many individual forms as he wished to present, each separately coloured and cut out, and then gummed into its place on the general plate, upon which a background of rocks, sand and seaweeds was then washed in. This secured extreme accuracy, no doubt, but did not improve the artistic effect, and therefore, to non-scientific observers, his earliest groups of coloured illustrations give more pleasure than the later.'

Gosse was not the first to try to popularise marine natural history, but he was the first to demonstrate to the general public, with his detailed and pleasing pictures, what a wealth of beautiful and fascinating creatures

Far left: Hermit Crab and Pipefish. Hand-coloured steel engraving by G. B. Sowerby (second of the name) from his *Illustrated Companion* to Charles Kingsley's *Glaucus*, 1858.

Right: Tubeworms *(Serpula)*, Sea Slugs, Piddocks *(Pholas)*, etc., also from the *Illustrated Companion* to *Glaucus*.

Left: Two wood engravings from Edward Forbes's *History of British Starfishes*, 1841. 'Spiny Cross-Fish, *Uraster glacialis*.' Compared with such unexciting pictures as this, Gosse's colourful studies of marine life must have seemed astonishing in their day. The vignette which heads the chapter on Sea Urchins is an example of the playful sketches which Forbes often incorporated in his scientific works.

the sea and shore contained. In 1855, Charles Kingsley, already famous as the author of *Westward Ho!* and *Hypatia*, had brought out his engaging *Glaucus*, subtitled *The Wonders of the Shore*. This was enjoyable to read and superior in style to Gosse's books but it did not gain wide public notice until 1858, when G. B. Sowerby (the second of the name) added an *Illustrated Companion* to it. It went into many editions—*The Aquarium* went into only two—and the plates came to look more and more like Gosse's. The Sowerby illustrations, though accurate, are rather lifeless steel engravings coloured by hand and without backgrounds; those in the later editions are colour printed and similar in style to the plates in Gosse's *Year at the Shore* and his *Sea-Anemones*. Gosse achieves a more pleasing effect than Sowerby by harmoniously grouping objects in a single picture and, in his later illustrations, placing them against underwater backdrops. The responsibility for the submarine scenery rested with Mrs Gosse, who had been a student of the landscape painter John Sell Cotman; her assistance is nowhere acknowledged by Gosse.

Egg cases of a Skate. Wood engraving from L. Sonrel's *Le Fond de la Mer*, 1868.

One of Gosse's numerous imitators was H. Noel Humphreys, whose *Ocean Gardens* and *River Gardens* both appeared in 1857. These two small volumes deal essentially with the history and maintenance of salt-water and freshwater aquaria. Each contains several highly coloured engravings which owe much of their inspiration to *The Aquarium*. These engravings, from original drawings by Humphreys, owe almost all their appeal to their colouring which disguises how naive, amateurish and poorly engraved most of them were. Even the vivid colouring is largely inaccurate and suggests that whoever coloured them was aiming for effect rather than accuracy.

In 1868, a decade after the appearance of *Ocean Gardens* and *River Gardens*, the Revd J. G. Wood brought out his *Fresh and Salt-Water Aquarium*. This was a small book illustrated with colour-printed plates, each of which showed many separate subjects and had a similar dullness to Sowerby's work on *Glaucus*. The large number of popular books illustrated in this way makes it seem almost as though the public wanted its natural history presented plainly and dully.

If the plates sold the books in those days, as they still do, J. G. Wood certainly hit upon the right illustrative formula with his *Common Objects of the Country*. It is said that a hundred thousand copies of the first edition were sold within a week of its publication in 1858, making it a worthy rival in its own field to Gosse's *Aquarium*. Admittedly, the illustrations, which were printed in colour by Edmund Evans, are more attractive than those in Wood's book on aquaria, but the subjects on each

Sea Anemones on shell containing Hermit Crab. Steel engraving from George Johnson's *History of British Zoophytes*, 2nd edition, 1847.

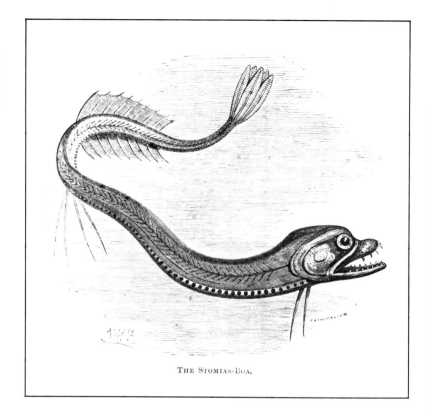

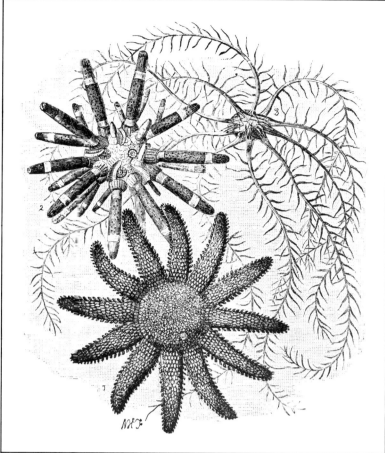

THE STOMIAS-BOA.

Top: Two wood engravings from Arthur Mangin's *Mysteries of the Ocean*, 1875. 'The Stomias-Boa', a deep-water fish, and three Echinoderms—a Sea Urchin ('*Asterias paposa*'), a Feather Star ('*Comatula mediterranea*') and a Starfish ('*Cidarites imperialis*').

Above: '*Gryllus* depositing eggs'. The author notes that this insect, now known as a bush cricket, is also called a 'wart-biter'. Wood engraving from the Revd J. G. Wood's *Homes Without Hands*, 1865.

Right: Swordfish attacking a Whale. Wood engraving from L. Sonrel's *Le Fond de la Mer*, 1868.

plate are not combined into a single picture as they are in some of his larger books. A similar formula was adopted for his *Common Objects of the Microscope* (1861) which had illustrations by Tuffen West. Here the formula is the right one; there is no correct landscape for a fly's tongue or a moth's antenna.

Originality was not a strong point with most popularisers, and the plates often had little more than a decorative function, for example in the work of the Revd W. Houghton, author of a well-known book on British freshwater fishes and numerous lesser books. Like Kingsley, he aimed to reveal the wonders of nature to city folk and their children by guiding them to nature's playgrounds. In his *Sea-side Walks of a Naturalist with his Children* and *Country Walks of a Naturalist with his Children*, both from the 1870s, his own children play a prominent part, asking perceptive questions like, 'Oh, papa, look there! What is that large bird flying over the sea—it cannot be a gull?' Fortunately Houghton interspersed some attractive, if not very relevant, coloured plates between the turgid pages of childish precocity. The most pleasing pictures in these books are basically landscapes in which the most curious specimens are the author and his insufferable progeny.

If a bookseller were asked to name the most popular illustrated book of the Victorian era on any aspect of zoology, he would probably say Morris's *Birds*. From 1851 to 1857, the Revd F. O. Morris—another of the

Microscopic objects under moderately high magnification. Colour print from the Revd J. G. Wood's *Common Objects of the Microscope*, 1866.

Right: Lapwing. Hand-coloured wood engraving from the Revd F. O. Morris's *British Birds*, 1864.

energetic clerics who seemed to dominate the Victorian natural history scene—produced regular monthly parts of his *Natural History of British Birds*, one of the most successful and most often reissued of all illustrated bird books. The 358 plates were all hand coloured and must have kept an army of colourists fully employed over the years. This was only one of three large, illustrated works which he brought out in parts during this period; he was simultaneously producing *A Natural History of the Nests and Eggs of British Birds* and *A Natural History of British Butterflies*. How he managed to get through so much writing while raising a large family and coping with an extensive parish is difficult to understand now, but such hyperactivity then was considered normal, especially among clerics.

Morris, Wood and a no less prolific writer of popular natural history books, the Revd C. A. Johns, typify the prevalent attitude to work in high Victorian times. To such men, idleness or even occasional relaxation was abhorrent; they felt a burning compulsion to fill every minute of their lives with honest, productive toil. Wood's appetite for sustained and concentrated work was amazing. 'He was always at his desk,' wrote his

Right: Squacco Heron and Water Rail. Hand-coloured wood engravings from the Revd F. O. Morris's *British Birds*, 1864.

Far right: 'Square-Browed Malthe and Double Fish'. Wood engraving from John Timbs's *Excentricities of the Animal Creation*, 1869. The 'Square-Browed Malthe' was found on the Labrador coast by an expedition led by Sir John Franklin. The pair of Catfish, joined like Siamese twins, were caught alive near Fort Johnston, North Carolina, in 1833.

biographer son, 'by half-past four or five o'clock in the morning at all seasons of the year, lighting his own fire in the winter, and then writing steadily until eight. Then, in all weathers, he would start off for a sharp run of three miles over a stretch of particularly hilly country, winding up with a tolerably steep ascent of nearly a quarter of a mile, and priding himself on completing the distance from start to finish without stopping, or even slackening his pace. Then came a cold bath, followed by break-fast.' They were all like that—Gosse, Kingsley, the entomologist Edward Newman, the polymath parliamentarian Sir John Lubbock, and dozens more. They drove themselves to inhuman limits for the benefit of the masses and the good of their own souls.

We now reject most of their pious, prolix texts as unreadable but have an increasingly high regard for the illustrations that accompany them. Had Victorian natural history books been unillustrated, most of them would now be considered as interesting and collectable as plastic

drinking straws. The current trade in prints torn from those books will cease only when there are no more Victorian books left to be ravaged. The fate of so much of that vast expenditure of energy at the hands of a later, less pious and less industrious generation is, in part at least, explained by the combination of charming pictures and turgid text. The high sales figures achieved by many popular Victorian natural history books were largely proportional to the quantity and quality of the pictures in them. Victorians, too, liked pretty pictures. Gosse achieved fame in spite of, not because of his writing; without A. F. Lydon's colour-printed plates, few would have been willing to discover what natural curiosities the Revd W. Houghton and his offspring encountered on their walks in the country and by the seaside. Almost alone among the popularisers, Kingsley owed his fame mainly to his mastery of the written word. But even *Glaucus*, his one outstanding contribution to popular natural history, derived its eventual success from the illustrations which were added to its later editions.

It is easy to say that the breaking up of so much of the literary legacy left to us by the Victorian popularisers is an unforgivable sacrilege and should be stopped. Indignation at this refined vandalism is understandable, but it could equally be said that the vandals are merely saving the only parts of the legacy that are worth saving. Perhaps the vandalism would have been less severe if bibliophiles' indignation over this practice had been matched by a greater willingness on their part to buy undefiled copies of the books. Meanwhile, thousands of Victorian books, denuded of their pretty pictures, are regularly laid to rest among other waste paper. Their sleep is unlikely to be disturbed by anyone looking for something stimulating to read.

Vignette showing the shells of *Nautilus* (centre)
and *Spirula* (upper corners), both Cephalopods.
Copper engraving from Ignaz Born's *Testacea
Musei Caesarei Vindobonensis*, 1780.

APPENDICES

Tasmanian Wolf or Thylacine. Wood engraving after Friedrich Specht, from Carl Vogt and Friedrich Specht's *Natural History of Animals (Mammalia)*, English translation by G. C. Chisholm, 1887.

Techniques

To obtain a print from a block of wood, it is not necessary to cut a design into it. Make a pattern on the smoothed side of a block with a greasy (i.e. oil-based) ink, press a piece of paper on it, and the ink pattern will be transferred to the paper. As exactly similar multiple copies cannot be taken from the block, the result, strictly speaking, is not a print, but it is close to being one. All that is needed to make the product truly a print is to cut into the wood surface so that the design stands out in relief. Apply the ink and the paper to the cut surface, as before, and you will obtain an impression again, but now it will tend to be sharper and the process can be repeated many times. The only significant differences between a nineteenth-century wood engraving and any of the crude woodcuts in Conrad von Megenberg's *Book of Nature* are those born of artistic and technical skill, not of basic materials.

A woodcut is obtained by cutting away the unwanted wood from the 'plank' side of a block of wood, usually pear, apple or sycamore. Wood engraving, a much later development, utilises the 'end grain' of certain very hard woods, in particular box and yew. A wood engraving allows much finer work to be executed than does a woodcut, and this usually allows the two to be distinguished. Broadly speaking, the term woodcut, in the present context, refers to a print produced before the beginning of the last quarter of the eighteenth century, the term wood engraving to one produced later.

Woodcuts and wood engravings have had a long life—they are with us still—but even as they maintained their supremacy in the field of printed illustrations, they were being challenged, and eventually they were almost eclipsed, by line engravings produced with lines incised in a metal plate. A line-engraved illustration is the result of a process exactly the opposite of that which produces a woodcut. Until the advent of photographic reproduction processes, late in the nineteenth century, line engraving in one or other of its numerous forms was easily the most popular method of reproducing illustrations. Potentially this kind of engraving is capable of giving a much finer line than is possible by woodcutting or wood engraving. This is because the paper is pressed into grooves rather than pressed on to raised ridges. A much thinner line results from an ink-filled groove than from an ink-covered ridge, and it is easier to gouge out a thin groove in a metal plate than it is to cut and pare away the surface of a block of wood to obtain a thin ridge.

The discovery of lithography by Alois Senefelder at the end of the eighteenth century was an epochal development for zoological artists. Previously an artist had made a drawing and then handed it over to an engraver whose expertise, acquired only after a long apprenticeship, was required to translate the original drawing into an engraving. The artist therefore had little control over what happened to his work after it left his hands. Lithography changed all that because the artist could, if he chose, be his own lithographer. All he had to do was draw his design directly on a thick slab of limestone with a greasy crayon, copying his original drawing in reverse. After he had completed his drawing, the worked surface of the stone would be wetted all over with water and a roller charged with a greasy ink would be passed over it. The lines of the drawing would retain the ink, but the dampened parts of the stone would reject it. An impression could then be taken on paper. That, in the simplest terms, is the technique of lithography. It proved to be a very suitable medium for drawing animals and was particularly favoured by bird artists. It is doubtful whether many of the finest biological illustrations of the nineteenth century would ever have come into being if limestone did not equally absorb two immiscible substances, greasy crayon and water.

There is also a group of what are called tonal processes. This group, which includes stipple, mezzotint, aquatint and some allied processes, was concerned with the reproduction of tone and texture in print. By pricking and piercing the surface of a woodblock or a plate of soft metal, a stippled ground effect, made up of different-sized dots, was produced. Variation in the sizes of the dots and their relative positions could be used to obtain delicate gradations of tone. The stipple effect was latterly obtained by etching the metal plate with acid. Sometimes stippling was limited to the outlines of an object, with the intention of merely indicating a shape so that a colourist could then work within the outline.

The mezzotint has never been excelled for its ability to express tone and texture in monochrome. Its development began around the middle of the seventeenth century, and it survived up to the early years of the nineteenth as a viable alternative to other forms of printing. It is regarded by many as the ultimate expression of pictorial printing. A copper plate is worked over with a rocker tool or emery cloth; out of the resulting roughened surface a design is scraped or burnished. The shading and half-tone effects obtainable by this method were often superb, and nothing comparable was achieved until photo-assisted methods of reproduction were developed. There are only a few examples of mezzotinted illustrations in zoological books as the process was used predominantly for elegant human portraits.

The aquatint, similar in its textural richness to the mezzotint and capable of passably imitating the transparently clear brushwork of a watercolour drawing, originated in France in the late 1760s but achieved its noblest effects in England a little later, when the process was taken up and improved by Paul Sandby. A copper plate was strewn with powdered resin and the plate heated. When it had cooled, the plate was treated with acid which bit into the metal through the cracks which had formed in the resinous covering. The longer the immersion, the more the acid would bite into the metal. Liquid varnish was applied to areas which were to be white on the print. After each immersion, other areas which had reached the required depth of tone were varnished. The resulting prints are noteworthy for their clarity and luminosity; they show no subtle blending of tones and would be less striking if they did. Audubon chose to have his *Birds of America* illustrated by aquatint, and a few other zoological books have aquatinted plates but, by and large, this whole group of tone processes was used very sparingly for zoological illustration. For the portrayal of the larger forms of animal life, lithography proved to be more popular than any of these processes.

The origins of mechanical colour printing go back to the mid-fifteenth century. In the sixteenth and seventeenth centuries, two-colour title pages, printed in red and black, became commonplace. Some books published before 1500, such as the *Hortus Sanitatis*, are seldom seen uncoloured, although the colouring of incunabula and other very early printed books is usually rather crudely applied. Perhaps the majority of printed illustrations with colour embellishment published before the twentieth century have been hand coloured. But true colour printing has been around for a surprisingly long time. Developed in late eighteenth-century France, it was utilised in the production of some fine books, but colour printing by wholly mechanical processes did not become commercially successful until the early nineteenth century. Until then, most colouring of prints was done by hand. For a long time, publishers favoured hand-coloured prints. Rudolf Ackermann was only one of the publishers who were employing dozens of colourists in the first two or three decades of the nineteenth century.

During the 1840s, the publication of colour prints for popular consumption really came into its own. Men like George Baxter, Charles Knight and the Le Blond brothers produced many prints using wood or metal blocks—the colouring of a single print with oil-based colours sometimes required as many as thirty separate blocks. Later on, the Vizetelly brothers, Edmund Evans, William Dickes and others produced many colour prints which were used as book illustrations. Chromolithography—colour printing from stone—was also perfected in the mid-nineteenth century and persisted, with many modifications, into the twentieth.

Nature printing, as might be expected, was a process developed for the purpose of illustrating natural objects. In effect, it was a way of allowing them to illustrate themselves. It required a natural object, usually a fern, a seaweed or some other flattened plant, to give an impression of itself on paper; in its crudest form, an object could be blackened with some substance such as lamp black and covered by a piece of paper, the upper side of which was then rubbed. In the mid-nineteenth century, impressions were taken from plants, the impressions electrotyped and prints taken from the electrotypes. The process is noted here because pictures of fossil fish—naturally flattened objects—and butterfly and moth wing-scales are known to have been nature printed.

The expression 'electrotype' requires explanation, if only because it has been used in the preceding paragraph. If an engraved wood block is subjected to a great deal of use, it will give progressively weaker impressions and may crack or buckle. In any case, where many impressions were required in a hurry, as in many forms of commercial printing, one block was inadequate. To overcome these problems and to make near-identical duplicates of rare prints the printer resorted to electrotyping. The process utilised the principle of electrolysis to build up a very thin deposit of copper over the engraved surface of the block. This not only strengthened the surface of the block and allowed more prints to be pulled from it, but it was also possible to take a cast from it; other electrotypes could be obtained from the cast. The printing process could be speeded up considerably if several identically 'engraved' blocks were available. This explains why so many copies of the Illustrated London News could be printed so quickly. The process was so effective that it is practically impossible to tell an electrotyped print from a print of the same subject obtained from the original engraved block.

These various processes were developed in answer to many needs. In the early years of the nineteenth century, most of them were being used at the same time. To a considerable extent, however, most of them were trying to achieve effects which were not within their reach. In particular, none gave a high-quality continuous tone effect. It was not until photo-assisted processes were developed that this effect was achieved.

Lion. Wood engraving from Thomas Bewick's *General History of Quadrupeds*, 1792.

References

The following short list is limited to titles which have been found most helpful in the writing of this book. Bibliographical details of illustrated zoological books are to be found in the works of Nissen, Wood and Lisney and in the British Museum (Natural History) Catalogue. Certain booksellers' catalogues, particularly those issued by Bernard Quaritch and by Wheldon and Wesley, have been found extremely useful as they often call attention to errors in the major bibliographies and add many useful snippets of their own.

ANKER, J. *Bird Books and Bird Art*. Copenhagen, 1938.

BRANDER, M. *Hunting & Shooting*. New York, 1971.

BRIDSON, G. D. R. 'The treatment of plates in bibliographical description.' *J. Soc. Biblphy Nat. Hist.* vol 7, pp. 469–88, 1976.

BRION, M. *Animals in Art*. London, 1959.

BRITISH MUSEUM (NATURAL HISTORY). *Catalogue of Books, Manuscripts, Maps and Drawings*. London, 1903–40.

CLARK, K. *Animals and Men. Their Relationship as Reflected in Western Art from Prehistory to the Present Day*. London, 1977.

CLARKE, T. H. 'The iconography of the rhinoceros from Dürer to Stubbs.' *Connoisseur* vol. 185, pp. 2–13 and 113–22. 1973, 1974.

COLE, F. J. *A History of Comparative Anatomy*. London, 1944.

DANCE, S. P. *Shell Collecting an Illustrated History*. London, 1966.

GOMBRICH, E. H. *The Story of Art*. London and New York, 1950.

GOSSE, E. *The Life of Philip Henry Gosse F.R.S.* London, 1890.

GRASSÉ, P. P. *Larousse Animal Portraits*. London, 1977.

HUGHES, T. *Prints for the Collector. British Prints from 1500 to 1900*. London, 1970.

JACKSON, C. E. *Bird Illustrators. Some Artists in Early Lithography*. London, 1975.

KLINGENDER, F. *Animals in Art and Thought to the End of the Middle Ages*. London, 1971.

LEE, S. E. *A History of Far Eastern Art*. London, 1964.

LISNEY, A. A. *A Bibliography of British Lepidoptera 1608–1799*. London, 1960.

LYSAGHT, A. M. *The Book of Birds. Five Centuries of Bird Illustration*. London, 1975.

NISSEN, C. *Die illustrierten Vogelbücher, ihre Geschichte und Bibliographie*. Stuttgart, 1953.

NISSEN, C. *Die zoologische Buchillustration, ihre Bibliographie und Geschichte*. Stuttgart. 1966–.

NORDENSKIÖLD, E. *The History of Biology*. New York, 1935.

PALMER, A. H. *The Life of Joseph Wolf, Animal Painter*. London and New York, 1895.

PEATTIE, D. C. *Singing in the Wilderness. A Salute to John James Audubon*. New York, 1935.

PEATTIE, D. C. *Green Laurels. The Lives and Achievements of the Great Naturalists*. New York, 1938.

RAWSON, J. (Ed.). *Animals in Art*. London, 1977.

SIMPSON, C. *Animal and Bird Painting. The Outlook and Technique of the Artist*. London, 1939.

SINGER, C. *A Short History of Biology*. Oxford, 1931.

TAYLOR, B. *Animal Painting in England*. London, 1955.

WAKEMAN, G. *Victorian Book Illustration. The Technical Revolution*. Newton Abbot, 1973.

WOOD, C. A. *An Introduction to the Literature of Vertebrate Zoology*. Oxford, 1931.

Biographical Notes

The purpose of this biographical appendix is to provide additional information on most of the authors, artists and engravers who are mentioned in the book, where such information has been obtainable. The entries give dates of birth and/or death (or the period during which the subject flourished), nationality and any personal details that may be of interest or documentary value. Early authors and illustrators are listed under their given names (e.g. Conrad von Megenberg, Leonardo da Vinci).

Abbot, John (1751–1840). English entomologist and artist. 17 volumes of his original water-colour drawings of the insects and plants of Georgia, formerly the property of J. Francillon, as well as other original drawings of insects and birds of Georgia are in the library of the British Museum (Natural History).

Adams, Arthur (1820–78). English naturalist, traveller and natural history draughtsman. Surgeon aboard HMS Samarang, 1843–46. Published many articles and books on conchology, mostly illustrated by himself.

Adanson, Michel (1727–1806). French botanist and conchologist. His *Histoire Naturelle du Sénégal* was to have been a monumental treatise, based on his own observations during a long stay in Senegal, but only one volume—on molluscs—was published. His *Familles des Plantes* (1763) is of fundamental importance in plant classification.

Albertus Magnus (1193–1280). Dominican monk of wide learning. Thomas Aquinas was one of his pupils. Wrote many of his books, including *De Animalibus*, at Cologne.

Albin, Eleazar (fl 1713–59). English author of books on insects and other animals. He was a teacher of water-colour drawing.

Aldrovandi, Ulisse (1522–1605). Italian encyclopedist and naturalist. Pupil of Conrad Gessner. Had a large museum of natural objects.

Audebert, Jean-Baptiste (1759–1800). French painter, water-colourist and engraver of animal subjects. Illustrated books by Vieillot and others besides his own *Histoire Naturelle des Singes et des Makis* (1799–1800).

Audubon, John James (1780–1851). American ornithologist. His father was French and his mother came from Santo Domingo. Studied painting under Jacques-Louis David in France. Taught dancing for a time.

Baldung, Hans (?1476–1545). German painter and engraver. Contemporary of Dürer.

Banks, Joseph (1744–1820). English naturalist who sailed with Captain Cook on his first circumnavigation. Became President of the Royal Society. Corresponded with most of the scientific men of his day.

Barlow, Francis (1626–1702). English painter and engraver of animal subjects. Illustrated *Aesop's Fables* (1666). Adept at bird studies and landscapes. Played an important part in the development of the sporting picture and contributed to the rise of landscape painting.

Barraband, Jacques (1768–1809). French artist who specialised in paintings of birds and flowers. Worked at the Gobelins tapestry factory and produced designs for the Sèvres porcelain factory. Illustrated bird books for Levaillant.

Bartholomew the Englishman or **Bartholomaeus Anglicus** or **Bartholomew de Glanville** (fl 1230–50). Was Professor of Theology at Paris. Wrote *De Proprietatibus Rerum (The Properties of Things)*, first printed, c1470 at Basle; first English version issued by Wynkyn de Worde, c1495.

Bell, Thomas (1792-1880). English dental surgeon and naturalist. Professor of Zoology at King's College, London. Published numerous works on British natural history as well as the most authoritative edition of Gilbert White's *Natural History of Selborne*.

Belon, Pierre (1517–64). French pioneer of comparative anatomy. Travelled widely in Europe and the Near East; studied fauna of the Mediterranean. Murdered by robbers while gathering herbs in the Bois de Boulogne. Wrote the earliest published treatise on fishes.

Besler, Michael Rupert (1607–61). German collector of natural curiosities. Author of *Gazophylacium Rerum Naturalium* (1642), illustrating his collection.

Bessa, Pancrace (1772–?1835). French painter, especially of flowers and fruit. Taught by Spaendonck and Redouté. Occasionally painted birds. Contributed to the collection of animal drawings on parchment—the 'vélins'—preserved in the National Museum of Natural History in Paris.

Bewick, Thomas (1753–1828). English wood engraver who revived and advanced the technique of wood engraving. Executed many engravings of animal subjects; wrote and illustrated his own books on birds and quadrupeds. His brother John worked in his style and collaborated with him.

Bloch, Marcus Elieser (1723–99). German author of several important books on fishes.

Bohn, Henry George (1796–1884). Second-hand bookseller and publisher born of German parents in London, where he carried on his business. Specialised in remainders, reissuing many classic works at remarkably low prices. In 1841, issued his 'Guinea Catalogue' of second-hand books, containing 23,208 items. Also translated some works published in his own 'Classical Library' series.

Bol, Hans (1534–93). Dutch artist who specialised in landscapes and village scenes in which animal subjects and flowers are often predominant. His *Venationes* (1582) contains domestic and hunting scenes with lively animals.

Born, Ignaz or Ignatius von (1742–91). Transylvanian by birth, Born trained as a Jesuit and lived for many years in Vienna. Became famous as a mineralogist; wrote books on mineralogy and conchology.

Bouchard, Maddalena or Magdalena (fl 1772–93). Illustrator of books on birds and plants. Seems to have worked in Rome.

Bree, Charles Robert (1811–86). British naturalist who wrote books on insects and birds of Britain and Europe.

Brehm, Alfred Edmund (1829–84). German naturalist who travelled widely in Europe, Siberia, Turkestan and Africa. His *Tierleben*, a popular survey of the animal kingdom, went through many editions and had several imitators.

Brisson, Mathurin-Jacques (1723–1806). French naturalist and author who collaborated in his youth with Réaumur and later became a physicist. His *Ornithologie* (1760) was important for its careful attention to classification and in this and other respects was better than the ornithological part of Linnaeus's *Systema Naturae*.

Brockes, Barthold Heinrich (1680–1747). German poet who was born and died at Hamburg. His *Betrachtung der Wilden Thiere (Contemplation of Wild Animals)* (1736) is noteworthy now only because of J. E. Ridinger's illustrations to it.

Buffon, George-Louis Leclerc, Comte de (1707–88). French polymath, son of a wealthy lawyer. Studied law at Dijon but devoted the greater part of his life to science and philosophy. An eloquent writer who tended to be over-confident in his speculations. His *Histoire Naturelle*, begun in 1749 and unfinished at the time of his death, brought him an immense reputation. His ideas on the mutability of species, which were examined by Erasmus Darwin and influenced later students of evolutionary theory, are perhaps his most important contributions to speculative science.

Buonanni or **Bonanni,** Filippo or Philippo (1638–1725). Italian Jesuit and author of the first illustrated encyclopedia of shells.

Burgkmair, Hans, The Elder (1473–1553 or 1559). German. Pupil, for a time, of Dürer. Besides painting scenes of everyday life and vigorous portraits, he was an engraver and miniaturist of rare talent. His style is often similar to Dürer's.

Carpenter, William Benjamin (1813–85). English naturalist who studied medicine and held numerous posts before becoming Registrar of the University of London. Published many books and articles and was closely involved with deep-sea research. His well-known book *The Microscope and its Revelations* had reached eight editions by 1901.

Catesby, Mark (1683–1749). English naturalist who collected plants and animals in North America, 1710–19 and 1722–26. Later wrote and illustrated *Natural History of Carolina* (1731–43). His original paintings for this book are in the Royal Library at Windsor.

Chemnitz, Johann Hieronymus (1730–1800). Danish clergyman and conchologist. Published numerous works on conchology the most important of which was his contribution to the *Neues Systematisches Conchylien-Cabinet* (1769–95), the last eight volumes of which were entirely by him (the first three having been the work of F. W. Martini).

Chenu, Jean-Charles (1808–79). French naturalist, prolific author of books on molluscs and other animals. Succeeded L.-C. Kiener as curator of Baron Delessert's collection of natural objects at Lyon.

Conrad or **Cunrat** or **Konrad von Megenberg** (c1309–74). German philosopher and theologian. The first man to write in the German language on scientific subjects. Very interested in the education of women and the 'man in the street'.

Cramer, Pieter (d 1777). Dutch entomologist and collector of natural objects. The British Museum (Natural History) Library has some 2,700 original water-colour drawings by him which were used to illustrate *De Uitlandische Kapellen* (1775–84).

Crouch, Edmund A. (fl 1800–30). English lithographer who illustrated conchological works.

Curtis, John (1791–1862). English entomologist, artist and engraver who executed many engravings for other naturalists; wrote and illustrated his own book on insects.

Cuvier, Léopold-Chrétien-Frédéric-Dagobert or Georges, Baron (1769–1832). French naturalist, one of the foremost comparative anatomists of all time and the leader of science in his day. *Le Règne Animal*, first published in 1817, embodied a lifetime of research on living and extinct animals but was only one of his many books which had enduring success. Cuvier believed in the fixity of species and propounded a series of catastrophes to account for the presence of fossilised remains of animal species which were no longer living.

Dapper, Olfert (d 1690). Dutch physician and author of several books of a geographical nature. The illustrations in his books are informative and well executed but his texts are usually prolix and unmethodical.

d'Argenville, Antoine-Joseph Dezallier (1680–1765). French connoisseur of the fine arts and dilettante in the sciences. Secretary to Louis XV.

de Blainville, Henri-Marie Ducrotay (1777–1850). French zoologist and author of books on many branches of zoology.

De Geer, Charles (1720–78). Swedish industrialist and naturalist. Continued the entomological investigations begun by Réaumur and published a sequel under the same title to Réaumur's *Mémoires pour servir à l'Histoire des Insectes* (1752–78).

Delessert, Jules-Paul-Benjamin, Baron (1773–1847). French businessman and collector of natural objects, especially shells, which he housed at Lyon. Gave financial support to the production of several exquisitely illustrated shell books by Kiener and Chenu, the successive curators of his collection.

della Straca, Giovanni or **van der Straet,** Jan or **Stradanus,** or **Stradano** (1523–1605). Flemish artist who painted courtly scenes and wrote and illustrated *Venationes* (1578) showing hunting episodes.

Demidoff, or **Demidov,** Anatole Nikolaevich (1812–70). Of Russian origin, born in Florence. Son of a wealthy philanthropist and also noted for his own generosity. In 1837, he organised a scientific expedition to study the southern parts of Russia and the Crimea.

Descourtilz, Jean-Théodore (d 1855). French naturalist and artist who worked for the National Museum at Rio de Janeiro. Produced two magnificent books on Brazilian birds, with hand-coloured lithographs based on his own drawings. Died when still a young man from the effects of poison while experimenting with a medicine for birds.

de Sève, Jacques (fl 1742–88). French engraver who specialised in depicting classical scenes and illustrated Buffon's *Histoire*.

des Murs, Marc-Athanase-Parfait-Oeillet (1804–1890?). French lawyer who deserted his profession for natural history studies about 1840. Made collections of insects and also took a keen interest in mammals and birds. Wrote several books on natural history and other subjects.

Desportes, Alexandre-François (1661–1743). French artist who was the first in France to specialise in painting hunting scenes and animals. Worked for the Gobelins and Compiègne tapestry factories for a time. A prolific artist especially fond of painting hunting dogs.

Donovan, Edward (1768–1837). English author, naturalist and traveller. Studied and wrote on most branches of zoology. Formed a large museum of natural objects. Most of his many books are illustrated with gaudy hand-coloured plates.

Drury, Dru (1725–1803). English silversmith and entomologist. Published books on natural history and precious metals. Corresponded with Linnaeus.

Dürer, Albrecht (1471–1528). Son of a Hungarian goldsmith, Dürer was born in Nuremberg and died there. His impressive woodcut designs began to appear in 1498. His 'Triumphal Arch' was made up of 92 blocks and is the largest known woodcut (it measures about 335 × 305 cms). Executed about 200 woodcuts altogether, in addition to about 100 copper plates, many pen and ink drawings, watercolours and oil paintings. Work is characterised by great fidelity, delicacy and finish.

Edwards, George (1694–1773). English naturalist, librarian of the Royal College of Physicians from 1733. Drew animals for Sir Hans Sloane and was taught by Mark Catesby how to etch the plates for his own books on natural history.

Ehrenberg, Christian Gottfried (1795–1876). German naturalist who travelled widely in the Near East and Central Asia. Devoted a lifetime to the study of microscopic organisms and published fundamental works on them.

Elliot, Daniel Giraud (1835–1915). American naturalist and author of sumptuous ornithological books. A wealthy man, he was Curator of Zoology at the Field Museum of Chicago.

Ellis, John (?1705–76). English naturalist, correspondent of Linnaeus. Agent for West Florida, 1764, and for Dominica, 1770. Proved that hydroids (then known as 'zoophytes') were animals rather than plants.

Eschscholtz, Johann Friedrich von (1793–1831). Russian physician and naturalist. Took part in the round-the-world voyages of the brig Rurik from 1815 to 1818 under the command of O. Kotzebue.

Forbes, Edward (1815–54). English naturalist born in the Isle of Man. Held posts in several learned institutions, becoming Professor of Natural History at Edinburgh University in 1853. Collected marine animals in the Aegean and made several natural history excursions in Europe. His numerous natural history books were largely illustrated by himself.

Gaimard, Joseph-Paul (1796–1858). French naturalist who accompanied the exploring vessels Uranie and Physicienne (1817–20) and Astrolabe (1826–29) and wrote up the natural history results of the voyages with fellow-naturalist J.-R.-C. Quoy.

Gervais, François-Louis-Paul (1816–79). French zoologist and prolific author of books and shorter articles on various animal groups, especially mammals, living and fossil.

Gessner or **Gesner,** Conrad (1516–65). Swiss naturalist and polymath. Published 72 miscellaneous works and left many others in manuscript. His *Historia Animalium* (1551–58) attempted to bring together all that was known about the animal kingdom in his day and was widely plagiarised for many years, his bold woodcuts re-appearing in the works of Aldrovandi and many lesser writers.

Giacomelli, Hector (1822–1904). French book illustrator who specialised in delicate and sentimental portrayals of animals and genre subjects. An industrious watercolourist, he began his career as a lithographer.

Goedart or **Godart,** Johannes or Joannes or Jan (1620–68). Dutch painter and miniaturist. Painted watercolours of birds and insects. Successfully reared many insects for study.

Goldsmith, Oliver (1728–74). Son of an Irish curate. Had a chequered career, including unsuccessful attempts to establish himself in the medical profession, a brief spell in prison, rather aimless wanderings in Europe and several years' work as a hack writer before *The Vicar of Wakefield* (1766) established his reputation as a novelist. Died deeply in debt.

Gosse, Philip Henry (1810–88). English naturalist whose numerous books on natural history, especially those illustrated from his own drawings, were immensely popular with the public. A pioneer in the development of the marine aquarium, his name is particularly associated with marine zoology and especially with sea anemones.

Gottwald or **Gottwaldt,** Christophorus (1636–1700). German physician and naturalist born at Danzig. His collection of natural objects was bought by Peter the Great of Russia.

Gould, John (1804–81). English ornithologist and publisher of sumptuously illustrated books on birds. Curator and taxidermist to the Zoological Society's museum. Visited Australia, 1838–40; described and illustrated many of the birds he found there. His large collection of humming birds was bought by the British Museum but his Australian bird skins were acquired by the Academy of Natural Sciences in Philadelphia. Drawings of birds by him or his wife Eliza are in the British Museum (Natural History), the Zoology Department of Cambridge University and in private hands.

Gray, George Robert (1808–72). English zoologist employed at the British Museum. Published ornithological works. Brother of J. E. Gray.

Gray, John Edward (1800–75). English naturalist who spent most of his working life at the British Museum where he made the zoological collections the most complete in the world at that time. His many works are mostly catalogues of museum specimens. Claimed—without justification—to have first suggested the idea of the Penny Post and became one of the world's first stamp collectors. Brother of G. R. Gray.

Gray, Thomas (fl 1813–90). British conchologist who wrote and illustrated two or three books on conchology, based on specimens in his own collection, but which remain unpublished.

Grew, Nehemiah (1641–1712). English comparative anatomist and London medical man. Secretary to the Royal Society, 1677–79.

Gronovius, Laurentius Theodorus or **Gronow,** Laurence Theodore (1730–77). A Senator of Leyden, though of German extraction. One of the best ichthyologists of his day and author of books about fishes and other animals. The British Museum (Natural History) has his collection and his manuscript description of it.

Gualtieri, Niccolò (1688–1744). Italian physician to Cosimo III, Grand Duke of Tuscany. Had a large shell collection and illustrated many of his own specimens in his *Index Testarum Conchyliorum* (1742).

Günther, Albert Carl Ludwig Gotthilf (1830–1914). German systematic zoologist and an authority on reptiles and fishes. Worked at the British Museum for many years. Wrote extensively about his specialities.

Haeckel, Ernst Heinrich (1834–1919). German naturalist who believed that the life history of an organism is a recapitulation of its historic evolution. An apostle of Darwinism, he was too prone to distort scientific truths to make them fit with his own hypotheses. The genealogical trees of animals he constructed demonstrate this unfortunate tendency only too well. His considerable artistic talent, assisted by his fertile imagination, produced many of the most beautiful representations of animal forms ever made. His monographs on the medusae and radiolarians are among the most outstanding and most exquisitely illustrated of the *Challenger* Reports.

Harris, Moses (1730–1788?). English entomologist and artist. Drew, engraved and coloured the illustrations published in his own entomological works. Some of his original drawings are in the library of the British Museum (Natural History).

Harting, James Edmund (b 1841). English author of popular natural history books including an authoritative edition of Gilbert White's *Selborne*.

Havell, Robert, The Younger (fl 1820–50). English artist and engraver. Aquatinted Audubon's *Birds of America* and engraved the plates for other natural history books.

Hawkins, Benjamin Waterhouse (b 1807). English painter and lithographer. Exhibited at the Royal Academy and subsequently executed many lithographs for natural history books.

Herbert, Thomas (1606–82). English traveller who visited Persia, 1628. Very friendly with Charles I of England. Created baronet, 1660.

Hills, Robert (1769–1844). English painter and etcher. Founder-member of the Society of Painters in Watercolours. Painted and etched many animal subjects.

Hoefnagel, George (*or* Joris) (1545–1600). Dutch painter, father of J. Hoefnagel.

Hoefnagel, Jacob (1575–1640). Dutch engraver and miniaturist. In addition to engraving various subjects from his own and other artists' drawings, he engraved the plates for the *Archetypa* (1592) of his father, G. Hoefnagel.

Hooke, Robert (1635–1703). English natural philosopher, inventor, architect, microscopist and prolific writer of books and shorter articles on a remarkably wide range of topics. He was the most brilliant and versatile scientist in the England of his day (though he lacked Newton's genius), an excellent administrator and helpful to other scientists, but had a deep hatred for Newton (which Newton reciprocated fully).

Horsfield, Thomas (1773–1859). American physician who became Keeper of the East India Company's museum after a stay in Java and Sumatra from 1799 to 1819.

Houghton, William (?1829–97). English rector and author of numerous popular natural history books.

Hudson, William Henry (1841–1922). The son of an Englishman who had emigrated to America and an Irishwoman, Hudson was born in Massachusetts. He became a naturalised British subject in 1900. Most of his many books deal with the British scene and British natural history, although *Green Mansions*, a novel set in South America, is his most widely known book. Soon after leaving Argentina for England in 1874, he met John Gould who treated him contemptuously. This helps explain the acid comments about Gould's portrayals of humming birds in Hudson's *Naturalist in La Plata*.

Huet, Nicolas (?1770–1830). French painter and engraver. The son of a distinguished animal painter he was one of the artists who contributed to the collection of animal drawings on parchment—the *vélins*—preserved in the National Museum of Natural History in Paris. Several of Huet's *vélins* were reproduced in natural history books of the early nineteenth century.

Hughes, Griffith (fl 1730–50). Rector of St Lucy's, Barbados.

Humphreys, Henry Noel (1810–79). English naturalist, artist and numismatist. Illustrated and published several popular books on natural history and treatises on coins and missal painting.

Johnston, George (1797–1856). British surgeon and naturalist. Published books on various branches of British natural history.

Jonston, Johann (1603–75). Born in Poland of Scottish ancestors. Visited England and Scotland, and studied at St Andrews, London and Cambridge. Also travelled in Germany and Holland. Not a profound or original thinker.

Keulemans, John Gerrard (1842–1912). Dutch bird artist who was persuaded by R. B. Sharpe to settle in England where he illustrated many bird books and innumerable lesser articles. An accurate but unimaginative artist, he seldom drew birds in flight. Many of his original watercolour drawings of birds are in the library of the British Museum (Natural History).

Kiener, Louis-Charles (1799–1881). French curator of Baron Delessert's natural history collection at Lyon. Author of conchological works.

Kingsley, Charles (1819–75). English naturalist, novelist, social reformer and poet. Curate and later Rector of Eversley, Hampshire. A friend of P. H. Gosse and Charles Darwin. In his natural history writings he attempted to turn young people towards the beauties of nature and away from idleness and dissipation.

Kircher, Athanasius (1602–80). German Jesuit who studied philology, physics and natural history, invented the magic lantern and wrote several books. His large collection of natural curiosities was described and well illustrated in P. Buonanni's *Musaeum Kircherianum* (1709).

Knorr, Georg Wolfgang (1705–61). German painter, engraver and art dealer. He engraved portraits, landscapes and animal studies after Dürer and the Kilian family and published scientific works distinguished for their beautiful hand-coloured plates.

L'Admiral *or* **Ladmiral**, Jacob, The Younger (1700–70). Dutch draughtsman and engraver of natural history subjects. Younger brother of Jan L'Admiral, artist, engraver and miniaturist, with whom he travelled and worked.

Leach, William Elford (1790–1836). English naturalist. Studied medicine before becoming an assistant librarian in the British Museum, 1813. Subsequently became Keeper of the Natural History Department. Published on various branches of zoology.

Lear, Edward (1812–88). English artist, traveller and author. Gave drawing lessons to Queen Victoria. Published books about his travels in addition to his folio iconography of the parrots. His *Book of Nonsense* (1846) was written to amuse the Earl of Derby's children, with whom he came into contact when drawing animals in the Earl's menageries at Knowsley.

Ledermüller, Martin Frobenius (1719–69). German physician who looked after the natural history collection of the Margrave of Brandenburg-Colmbach. Made many interesting discoveries with the microscope and wrote about microscopic organism.

Leeuwenhoek, Antony van (1632–1723). Dutch draper and amateur microscopist. Author of many works on microscopy most of which were published in the *Philosophical Transactions of the Royal Society*. Made his own microscopes.

Leonardo Da Vinci (1452–1519). Florentine artist, inventor, anatomist and scientist. Few of his paintings have survived but many of his drawings are in collections at Windsor, London, Milan, Paris, Venice, Vienna, Florence and elsewhere. He studied anatomy because he was convinced that such a training was indispensable to the work of an artist.

Lesson, René-Primevère (1794–1849). French naturalist who accompanied Captain Duperrey on his exploratory voyage into the Pacific on board the *Coquille*, 1822–25, and wrote an account of the zoology of the voyage. Also wrote several illustrated natural history books, mostly about birds.

Levaillant, François (1753–1824). French traveller and ornithologist. Explored South Africa, 1781–84, and was the first to describe and illustrate many African birds. Published sumptuously illustrated zoological books.

Lewin, William (d 1795). English painter, draughtsman, engraver and naturalist. Wrote books on the insects and birds of the British Isles.

Linnaeus, Carl *or* **Linné**, Carolus von (1707–78). Swedish naturalist, founder of the modern system of naming animals and plants. First to classify plants on sexual characters. Explored Swedish Lapland and Dalecarlia. Professor of Botany at Uppsala. Sent many pupils to various parts of the globe to collect animals and plants. The *Systema Naturae*, 10th edition (1758), is his most important contribution to systematic botany and zoology. His specimen collections, books and manuscripts are mostly housed in The Linnean Society of London. He was ennobled in 1757.

Lister, Martin (1639–1712). English physician, zoologist and author. One of Queen Anne's physicians. Contributed many articles to the *Philosophical Transactions of the Royal Society* and published several books. Correspondent of John Ray and Sir Hans Sloane.

Lizars, William Home (1788–1859). Scottish painter and engraver. Executed many book engravings including a series of large-sized plates for Audubon's book on American birds (but these were never published).

Low, David (1786–1859). Scottish agriculturist. Professor of Agriculture in Edinburgh University, 1831–54. Established *Quarterly Journal of Agriculture*, 1826. Published extensively on agricultural subjects.

Lucas van Leyden (1494–1538). Dutch painter and engraver. His paintings are extremely rare but his engravings, characterised by an extreme fineness of line, are relatively common. He is ranked only below Dürer as a master of wood engraving.

Lydekker, Richard (1848–1915). English authority on mammals of the world, especially game animals.

Lyonet, Pierre (*or* Pieter) (1706–89). Dutch entomologist, shell collector and connoisseur of the fine arts. His entomological studies are characterised by their meticulous attention to fine detail. His shell collection was one of the best in Europe in his day and his art collection contained masterpieces by Jan Steen, Frans Hals and Vermeer.

Malpighi, Marcello (1628–94). Italian comparative anatomist and pioneer in microscopy. His many publications were mostly concerned with anatomy, and his monograph on the silk moth (1669) was the first detailed treatise on the anatomy of an invertebrate.

Mandeville, John *or* Jehan de (fl 14th century). The assumed name of a French or English author of a famous book of travels, written between 1357 and 1371. His travels reputedly took in the best part of the then known world, and he tells of encounters with all kinds of monstrous beings. Undoubtedly, the book is a compilation from many sources.

Manetti, Xaverio (1723–84). Italian author of the most lavishly illustrated bird book of the 18th century. His text was in Italian and Latin.

Mangin, Arthur (1824–87). French writer and populariser of science subjects. Among his many publications are several on aspects of natural history.

Mansur, Ustad (fl 1600–30). Mogul artist who produced splendid naturalistic illuminations for manuscripts during the reign (1605–27) of Jahangir Akbar.

Marcgrave, Georg (1610–44). Dutch astronomer and naturalist. One of the men who worked in Brazil with Count Johann Moritz of Nassau-Siegen, the Governor-General of Northeastern Brazil appointed by the Dutch West India Company. Marcgrave contributed most of the botanical and zoological portions of the *Historia Naturalis Brasiliae* (1648), and possibly some of the woodcuts for the book were based on his drawings.

Martinet, François-Nicolas (fl 1760–1800). French engineer and engraver. Executed engravings for a large book about Paris and for several large ornithological books.

Martini, Friedrich Wilhelm (1729–78). German physician and naturalist. He wrote the first three volumes of the *Neues Systematisches Conchylien-Cabinet*, the first large-scale iconography of shells to be illustrated in colour (J. H. Chemnitz added eight further volumes after Martini's death).

Martyn, Thomas (fl 1760–1816). English publisher, artist and naturalist. Established an art academy in Great Marlborough Street, London, where his books, mostly on natural history, were produced. Bought natural history specimens from participants in Captain Cook's third voyage of discovery.

Mattioli *or* **Matthiolus,** Pierandrea (1501–77). Italian physician who studied botany, especially plants with medicinal properties. A friend provided him with two manuscript copies of the writings of Dioscorides and these inspired him to write his herbal, first published at Vienna in 1544.

Meidinger, Carl von (1750–1820). Austrian author of several illustrated works on the natural history of Austria.

Merian, Maria Sibylle (1647–1717). Born in Germany of a Swiss father and a Dutch mother, Merian was primarily an entomologist but, as an artist, she excelled equally in portraying insects and plants. Married Johann Graff of Nuremberg, a pupil of the Dutch flower painter Jacob Marrel (who, on the death of Maria's father, married her mother). Decided to go to Surinam, wanting to rival the accomplishments of Charles Plumier, the French naturalist who had visited the West Indies and had already published a work on the American flora, although he was no older than she. The fine lines of her drawings made it comparatively easy for the engraver to transfer them to his plates.

Merian, Matthaeus, The Younger (1621–87). Swiss-born painter, son of an engraver of the same name (the father of Maria Sibylle Merian). Travelled widely in Europe and worked in England under Van Dyck, to whom some of his painted portraits are often attributed.

Michelet, Jules (1798–1874). French historian and prolific author of books including the monumental but unfinished 21-volume *Histoire de France* (1833–75). His incursions into the sphere of natural history writing are more appreciated as literature than as serious contributions to science.

Mivart, St George Jackson (1827–1900). English barrister and biologist. Received Ph.D. degree from the Pope. A staunch catholic, he strongly opposed Darwin's views on evolution but, towards the end of his life, was excommunicated from the Catholic Church because he published several articles repudiating ecclesiastical authority. Published numerous biological and philosophical works.

Moffet, Mouffet, Moufet *or* **Muffet,** Thomas (1553–1604). English-born son of a haberdasher of Scottish descent. Studied medicine and travelled widely on the continent. Practised as a fashionable physician in London. Became member of Parliament for Wilton in 1597. Published various books and pamphlets, chiefly on medical subjects. The manuscript of his *Insectorum Theatrum*, now in the British Library, was not published in his lifetime.

Morland, George (1763–1804). English painter of animals and genre compositions. Lived a life of dissipation, was arrested for debt in 1799 and released in 1802. Died in a sponging house still in debt. Is said to have produced about four thousand pictures.

Morris, Francis Orpen (1810–93). English country vicar and author of many popular works on natural history. Anti-vivisectionist and anti-Darwinian. He lived close to Benjamin Fawcett the colour printer and worked with him to produce books such as his *British Birds*. Every plate for this book was engraved by Fawcett, whose wife coloured every specimen plate for the colourers.

Motonobu, Kano *or* Oinosuke *or* Gyokusen (1476–1559). Japanese artist whose most famous works, at the Reiun-in in Kyoto, show cranes, pines and other natural objects in a series of hanging scrolls.

Müller, Otto Frederik (1730–84). Danish biologist who was the first to give a systematic description and classification of the Infusoria. Having contracted a wealthy marriage, he was able to give all his attention to biology and published a large number of books, mostly about the Danish fauna.

Noseman *or* **Nozeman,** Cornelis (1721–85). Dutch clergyman who attempted to describe all the bird species that occurred in Holland in his *Nederlandsche Vogelen* but died long before the task could be completed.

Oudart, Paul-Louis (b 1796). French painter and lithographer. A pupil of G. Van Spaendonck. Specialised in animal subjects, particularly birds. Contributed to the collection of animal drawings on parchment—the *vélins*—at the National Museum of Natural History in Paris.

Oudry, Jean-Baptiste (1686–1755). French painter who was influenced by A.-F. Desportes, his only French rival in the portrayal of hunting scenes and still-life subjects. Court Painter to Louis XV. Worked for the Beauvais and Gobelins tapestry factories.

Peale, Titian Ramsay (1800–85). American artist and illustrator. The son of Charles Wilson Peale, the portrait painter. Specialised in animal subjects. Had a valuable collection of seashells.

Pennant, Thomas (1726–98). English traveller, naturalist, antiquary and writer. One of the most capable and respected writers on natural history during the second half of the 18th century but now known principally as one of the two correspondents whose letters Gilbert White published in his *Natural History of Selborne.*

Perrault, Claude (1613–88). French comparative anatomist, architect and naturalist. His architectural activities diminished as his interest in comparative anatomy grew, but his mechanistic attitude towards animal structure reflects the technical leanings of the architect.

Perry, George (fl 1800–20). English author known only from his two books, the very rare *Arcana* (1810) and the well known *Conchology* (1811).

Petiver, James (1663–1718). English apothecary, naturalist and author of numerous slender folios describing and illustrating many hundreds of new or little known animals and plants. His collection was bought by Sir Hans Sloane.

Pisanello, Antonio (1395–?1455). Italian painter, draughtsman and medallist. Portrayed animals objectively, realistically and accurately. Most of his medals have an animal motif on the verso.

Piso *or* **Pies,** Willem (1611–78). German physician whose father had settled his family in Leiden. One of the men who worked in Brazil with Count Johann Moritz of Nassau-Siegen, the Governor-General of Northeastern Brazil appointed by the Dutch West India Company. Piso contributed the medical portion of the *Historia Naturalis Brasiliae* (1648).

Pliny The Elder *or* **Gaius Plinius Secundus** (23–79). Roman soldier, traveller and author. Was appointed procurator in Spain. His *Historia Naturalis* was the only portion of his manuscripts to be transmitted to posterity. Died when too closely witnessing the great eruption of Vesuvius which buried Pompeii.

Pluche, Noel-Antoine (1688–1761). French ecclesiastic and author of a remarkably successful compendium of natural history, *Le Spectacle de la Nature* (1732–51) which was widely translated and went into many editions.

Pontoppidan, Erik Ludwigsen (1698–1764). Danish theologian who became Bishop of Bergen in 1747. Wrote on Danish and Norwegian matters.

Potter, Paul *or* Paulus (1625–54). Dutch painter specialising in animal subjects. His most celebrated picture, *The Bull*, now at The Hague, is life sized. Most of his high-quality animal pictures are rather small.

Prêtre, Jean-Gabriel (fl 1800–50). Swiss artist of great talent, about whom almost nothing seems to be known. Contributed to the collection of animal drawings on parchment—the *vélins*—at the National Museum of Natural History in Paris and illustrated many books and scientific reports dealing with birds and lesser animals.

Quoy, Jean-René-Constant (1790–1869). French naturalist who accompanied the exploring vessels Uranie and Physicienne (1817–20) and Astrolabe (1826–29) and wrote up the natural history results of the voyages with fellow-naturalist J.-P. Gaimard.

Ray, John (1627–1705). English naturalist and author of books on natural history, theology and proverbs. Between 1662 and 1666 travelled with F. Willughby over England and Wales and parts of Europe making observations on animals and plants.

Réaumur, René-Antoine Ferchault de (1683–1757). French physiologist, entomologist, metallurgist, mathematician, physicist and inventor. Invented a thermometer with 80 degrees between freezing and boiling points. An enemy of Buffon. Reputation suffered an unwarranted decline after his death. Among his unpublished manuscripts was a complete treatise on ants which was not published until 170 years after his death.

Reeve, Lovell Augustus (1814–65). English publisher and conchologist. Author of several conchological works. Also dealt in natural history objects, especially shells. The 20-volume *Conchologia Iconica* (1843–78), which was completed by G. B. Sowerby (2nd of the name), was his *magnum opus.*

Regenfuss Franz Michael (1713–80). German painter and engraver to Frederick V, King of Denmark and Norway. The original text to his enormous *Choix de Coquillages* (1758) was by F. C. Lesser, a German pastor, but this was greatly modified by other contributors before publication.

Richter, Henry Constantine (1821–1902). English artist who produced lithographs for many of J. Gould's bird plates.

Ridinger, Johann Elias (1698–1767). German painter and engraver. His paintings are very rare but his engravings are numerous and show him to have been a remarkably fine observer of living animals.

Rippon, Robert H. F. (fl 1880–1910). English entomologist whose speciality was the bird-wing butterflies. His collection of these insects is now in the National Museum of Wales, Cardiff. Very few copies of his sumptuous book on them were published and most of these are incomplete.

Robert, Nicolas (1614–85). French miniaturist and engraver. Produced many exquisite studies of animals contained in the Jardin des Plantes. His most celebrated work is a painting called *Julie's Garland.*

Roesel van Rosenhof, August (1705–59). German painter and naturalist. His published studies of insects include detailed observations of habits and development. He also made important observations on the development of frogs.

Rondelet, Guillaume (1507–66). French ichthyologist. Studied arts at Paris and medicine at Montpellier. As Professor of Medicine and Anatomy at Montpellier University he attracted students from all over Europe.

Rüppell, Wilhelm Peter Eduard Simon (1794–1884). German naturalist and author of many important zoological treatises.

Rumpf *or* **Rumphius,** Georg Eberhard (1627–1702). Dutch naturalist of German origin. Employed by the Dutch East India Company and spent most of his life on the island of Amboyna. His *Amboinsche Rariteitkamer* (1705) was seen through the press by others and includes illustrations of species not found in or near Amboyna. He was totally blind in later life.

Salviani, Hippolyte (1514–72). Italian ichthyologist, physician, poet and playwright. His great book on fishes was printed in his own house and was illustrated with copper engravings rather than woodcuts.

Say, Thomas (1787–1834). American pharmacist and naturalist. One of the founders of the Academy of Natural Sciences, Philadelphia. Moved to New Harmony, Indiana, in 1824 where he wrote, printed and published numerous natural history books on his own press.

Schlegel, Hermann (1804–84). Dutch ornithologist who became director of the Natural History Museum of Leiden. He helped J. Wolf, J. Smit and J. G. Keulemans to set themselves up as bird artists.

Schröter, Johann Samuel (1735–1808). German naturalist and prolific author of books on molluscs and other invertebrates. Edited the earliest conchological periodical, 1774–80 and 1782–87.

Sclater, Philip Lutley (1829–1913). English lawyer and naturalist. His special interest in birds resulted in the publication of almost 1,400 separate titles. His proposed classification of the zoogeographical regions of the world is still used by students of the subject.

Scopoli, Giovanni Antonio *or* Johann Anton (1723–88). Austrian (?) naturalist and author of books on botany, zoology, mineralogy and palaeontology.

Seba, Albert *or* Albertus (1665–1736). Dutch apothecary who amassed a large collection of natural curiosities which he sold to Peter the Great of Russia in 1717. Subsequently he made an even larger collection which was described in his *Locupletissimi* (or *Thesaurus* as it is often called) (1734–65). Owned the Hamburg 'Hydra' which was exposed as a composite fake by Linnaeus even before Seba had acquired it. His second collection was auctioned in 1752 for 24,440 guilders.

Selby, Prideaux John (1788–1867). English naturalist, High Sheriff of Northumberland, 1823. His *Illustrations of British Ornithology* (1821) was illustrated on the same grand scale as Audubon's later *Birds of America*.

Senefelder, Aloys *or* Alois (1771–1834). German, but born in Prague. Successively actor, unsuccessful playwright, and printer. Experimented with the Kelheim limestone and thus discovered (1796) the principle of lithography which he perfected subsequently. His process was patented, under the title 'Polyautography', in London in 1801. The process was renamed 'Lithography' in France in 1803.

Sepp, Christiaan (fl 1750–65), Jan Christiaan (1739–1811), and Jan (1778–1853). Dutch entomological family responsible for writing and illustrating the compendious entomological treatise *Beschouwing der Wonderen Gods* (1762–1860). The book was completed by other hands under the editorship of S. C. Snellen.

Sesshu, Go Bikeisai (1420–1506). Japanese painter who was much influenced by Chinese art. Painted landscapes and views of temples as well as animals and human figures.

Sharpe, Richard Bowdler (1847–1909). English ornithologist, first librarian to the Zoological Society, 1866–72; became Assistant Keeper of Vertebrates at the British Museum (Natural History) in 1895. Wrote many important ornithological books and completed several of J. Gould's works. Founded British Ornithologists' Club in 1892.

Shaw, George (1751–1813). English naturalist and author of several zoological books. Joint founder and vice-president of the Linnean Society, 1788. Became Keeper of the Natural History Department of the British Museum in 1807.

Smit, Joseph (1836–1929). Dutch artist and lithographer. Illustrated many natural history books and specialised in ornithological illustrations. He was particularly adept at drawing downy plumage and was considered to be the best animal painter in England after the death of J. Wolf.

Smith, Andrew (1797–1872). English naturalist and author of books on South African natural history.

Smith, James Edward (1759–1828). English botanist. Founded the Linnean Society of London, 1788. In 1784, purchased the collections and library of Carl Linnaeus. Published, among other things, several highly esteemed botanical works.

Solander, Daniel Charles (1736–82). Swedish botanist and favourite pupil of Linnaeus. Accompanied Joseph Banks on Captain Cook's first voyage of discovery in the *Endeavour*. Went to Iceland with Banks in 1772. Keeper of Botany at the British Museum, 1773. Classified the Duchess of Portland's collection of shells.

Sowerby, George Brettingham, The First (1788–1854) and The Second (1812–84). Father and son. English naturalists and publishers specialising in conchology. Two members of a talented family which played a significant part in the illustration of scientific and popular literature dealing with most aspects of natural history in Britain during the 19th century. Both mainly involved with zoology and botany. Both also dealt in books and specimens.

Sowerby, James (1757–1822). English botanical and zoological artist and author. Founded the Sowerby dynasty of natural history draughtsmen.

Sowerby, James de Carle (1787–1871). English naturalist and artist, the eldest son of James Sowerby. Executed many zoological and botanical plates and often worked in conjunction with other members of the Sowerby family. 65 watercolour drawings by him, the originals of subjects reproduced in T. Bell's *Monograph of the Testudinata* and E. Lear's *Tortoises*, are housed in the library of the British Museum (Natural History).

Specht, Friedrich (1839–1909). German animal painter and book illustrator. His principal work as an illustrator was produced for Brehm's *Tierleben*. He also illustrated children's books.

Stelluti, Francesco (1577–1646 or 1651). Italian naturalist and poet. The first to use Galileo's newly invented microscope for research. In 1630, described and illustrated the external morphology of the honey bee and the grain weevil with the help of his microscope.

Stubbs, George (1724–1806). English painter and anatomist, the son of a currier. His *Anatomy of the Horse* was published in 1766, probably the first artist fully to master the anatomy of horses. Painted many portraits of animals and rustic subjects for wealthy patrons and began executing pictures in enamel in 1771.

Sulzer, Johann Heinrich (1735–1813). Probably a member of the Swiss family Sulzer which produced many artists. Author of *Die Kennzeichen der Insekten* (1761).

Swainson, William (1789–1855). English naturalist and author. Visited Malta, Sicily, Italy and Greece and collected specimens in those countries. Spent a further two years collecting in Brazil, 1816–18. Learned art of lithography so that he could illustrate his own books cheaply. Subsequently wrote and illustrated many books on zoological subjects, including several in Lardner's Cabinet Cyclopedia series and Jardine's Naturalist's Library series. Failing to obtain a post at the British Museum, he emigrated to New Zealand in 1840. Lost most of his collections and manuscripts on the voyage. Had strange ideas about animal classification which lowered his reputation as a zoologist. Quarrelled with Audubon over a proposal that Swainson should help write Audubon's *Ornithological Biography*.

Swammerdam, Jan (1637–80). Dutch comparative anatomist. His most significant work is enshrined in the *Biblia Naturae* (1737–38), published a century after his birth. His last years were spent in religious exercises.

Temminck, Coenraad Jacob (1778–1858). Dutch naturalist, taxidermist and author of lavishly illustrated books on birds and mammals. First director of the Natural History Museum at Leiden. His house was almost entirely filled with stuffed birds.

Thomas, Michael Rogers Oldfield (1858–1929). English naturalist who spent most of his working life building up the collection of mammals in the British Museum (Natural History) and becoming an authority on antelopes.

Thomas of Cantimpré *or* **Thomas Cantimpratensis** (fl 13th century). Flemish Dominican friar who lived and worked in the monastery of Cantimpré in France. His *De Naturis Rerum*, a compilation of the nature theories of Aristotle and other classical authors, is full of moralising stories about real and imaginary animals.

Thorburn, Archibald (1860–1935). Scottish bird artist, son of Robert Thorburn, the miniaturist. Apart from illustrating his own books, was commissioned by other ornithologists to illustrate books for them. Contributed two-thirds of the plates contained in Lord Lilford's *Coloured Figures of the Birds of the British Islands* (1885–98). Considered by some to be un-rivalled in his portrayals of small birds and birds of prey, although tending to make most birds look more glamourous than they really are in life.

Timbs, John (1801–75). English author and editor of several periodicals. Published numerous works of an anecdotal nature.

Topsell, Edward (1572–1625). English curate and author of several religious works as well as his well known adaptations of Gessner's works. He had no first-hand knowledge of natural history and made many detrimental alterations to the text of Gessner's *Historia Animalium* when adapting it.

Trembley, Abraham (1700–84). Swiss naturalist who acted as a private tutor to certain distinguished families and became a librarian in his native town of Geneva. His reputation is based on his studies of the habits of the fresh-water Hydra, the animal nature of which he was the first to establish. His work on this creature opened up a wide field of research.

Tyson, Edward (1651–1708). English physician and compara-tive anatomist. Physician to Bridewell and Bethlehem hospitals. First Englishman to investigate animal structure extensively. The skeleton of the young chimpanzee (which he called an orang-outang and on which his most famous book is based) is still preserved in the British Museum.

Valentijn, François (1666–1727). Dutch priest, traveller and writer. Was sent to the East Indies in 1685. In Amboyna met Rumphius who inspired him to keep detailed records of his observations and to collect natural objects. Returned to Holland in 1795 and, ten years later, revisited the East Indies. Returned again to Holland in 1714 and wrote up his observations. A very industrious but uncritical writer.

Vieillot, Louis-Jean-Pierre (1748–1831). French naturalist and author of sumptuous bird books. Emigrated to Santo Domingo and subsequently to North America. He was a careful observer of the life histories of birds.

Vincent, Levin (*or* Levinus) (1658–1727). Dutch merchant whose large collection of natural curiosities is described in his *Wondertoonel der Nature* (1706).

Vogt, Carl (1817–95). German biologist whose involvement with revolutionary movements compelled him to quit Germany. Became a professor at Geneva and wrote several text books and popular scientific works. To support his ideas on the different origins of the human races he tried to prove that many species and varieties were constant, and thus was not a whole-hearted believer in Darwinism.

Vosmaer, Aernout (1720–99). Dutch naturalist and author. Director of the menageries and natural history cabinets founded by the widow of Prince Wilhelm IV in 1756. He published descriptions of many of the animals from the menageries. Edited the third and fourth volumes of Seba's *Thesaurus*.

Waterton, Charles (1782–1865). English traveller, naturalist and taxidermist. Travelled extensively in Guiana between 1804 and 1812. Published *Wanderings in South America* (1825) and a series of essays on natural history. His collection of stuffed animals is now in Wakefield City Museum.

Westwood, John Obadiah (1805–93). English entomologist and paleographer. First Hope Professor of Zoology at Oxford, 1861–93. Published many entomological books and edited reissues of books by other entomologists. Published various works on paleography.

Wilkes, Benjamin (fl 1700–50). English entomologist and artist. Published broadsheets illustrating British Lepidoptera, and a book, *English Moths and Butterflies* (c1749).

Willughby, Francis (1635–72). English naturalist. Accom-panied J. Ray on a botanical excursion through the northern midland counties in 1662. With Ray, he also travelled in Europe and brought back a great amount of natural history material. Willughby was to work up and publish the zoolgical, Ray the botanical material, but Willughby died prematurely and Ray saw the young man's works on birds and fishes through the press.

Wilson, Alexander (1766–1813). Scottish naturalist who emigrated to North America in 1794 where he conceived the idea of producing a book describing and illustrating the North American bird fauna. His nine-volume *American Ornithology* did not enjoy good sales. Wilson was a first-rate naturalist, and his descriptions of birds are better than Audubon's.

Wolf, Joseph *or* Josef (1820–99). German naturalist, animal artist and lithographer. Illustrated many natural history books and scientific treatises. His illustrations to *The Poets of the Woods* (1853) were the first published chromolithographs of birds. One of the first artists to make a full time career painting wild life.

Wood, John George (1827–89). English naturalist and prolific writer of popular works on natural history. Chaplain at St Bartholomew's Hospital, London. Lectured widely in England and North America, illustrating his talks with imaginative blackboard sketches. Although his many books lack originality, they were immensely popular and most went through several editions. All are well illustrated.

Worm, Olaus *or* Ole (1588–1654). Danish archaeologist and physicist who formed a museum of natural and artificial curiosi-ties in Copenhagen.

Index of Authors, Artists & Titles

The index concentrates on the book titles and proper names mentioned in the book. The names include all the authors, artists, engravers and publishers that are referred to in the text and captions together with the place names and other more general headings that are dealt with in Chapter I. The biographical appendix is not covered in the index.

Page numbers in italic indicate references in picture captions.